"Kara is inspiring all generations searching for their own passions to just go make it happen. Take risks. Stop being afraid of failure. And align what you are good at, what the world needs, and what makes you happy. Read this book!" —Sarah Friar,
CEO at Nextdoor, Member of the Board of Directors of Walmart and Slack, and Cofounder of Ladies Who Launch

"I've watched Kara grow Hint and show the world that it is possible to create something healthy that tastes great with love in each bottle. Kara's work as a female leader shows women that it is possible to challenge the status quo. *Undaunted* takes us through the journey and helps us understand that even when we think it can't be done, if you can believe it, you can achieve it!" —Ronnie Lott,
NFL Hall of Fame Legend from the San Francisco 49ers and Founder of All Stars Helping Kids

"Kara is a masterful entrepreneur who figures out *how* to make the impossible happen. When others quit, she proceeds and makes it look easy. The lessons in *Undaunted* will undoubtedly make you feel like you need to go build something too." —Roland Frasier,
Co-Founder of DigitalMarketer.com and *Business Lunch* Podcast

"Kara Goldin's story about building a company in the wellness industry is a terrific chronicle about how well-being is front and center in people's everyday lives. Kara is making an impact as a businesswoman, a leader, and a health activist. She is *Undaunted.*"
—Nancy Brown

"Kara's leadership is a shining example for women who are aspiring to be and do more. Whether in business, social impact, or women's empowerment, Kara is a trailblazer, and *Undaunted* provides a vulnerable, courageous, honest look at what it takes to build something that truly matters." —Shiza Shahid,
Cofounder of Our Place and the Malala Fund

"Grit and resourcefulness define the best founders I've known, and that's why I was the first investor in Hint and their biggest cheerleader throughout the company's amazing story. Read *Undaunted*, and you'll be inspired by Kara Goldin to discover within yourself the intensity and determination that are the primary requirements for success."
—Geoff Ralston,
President of Y Combinator

"*Undaunted* is a perfect read for anyone who is motivated by pushing boundaries and who dreams of one day disrupting an industry. Goldin shows us how it's done."
—Alison Levine,
Team Captain of the First American Women's Everest Expedition
and *New York Times* bestselling author of *On the Edge*

"If you are looking for lessons on how to get through tough times, or a pandemic, there is no better person from whom to learn. She inspires."
—Kerrie D MacPherson,
Board Director, Retired EY Partner,
and Executive Sponsor of EY Entrepreneurial Winning Women

undaunted.

OVERCOMING DOUBTS + DOUBTERS

kara goldin

Founder and CEO, Hint Water

with John Butman and Theo Goldin

HARPERCOLLINS
LEADERSHIP

AN IMPRINT OF HARPERCOLLINS

Published by HarperCollins Leadership.

Book design by Aubrey Khan, Neuwirth & Associates.

Any internet addresses, phone numbers, or company or product information printed in this book are offered as a resource and are not intended in any way to be or to imply an endorsement by HarperCollins, nor does HarperCollins vouch for the existence, content, or services of these sites, phone numbers, companies, or products beyond the life of this book.

ISBN 978-1-4002-2052-6 (eBook)
ISBN 978-1-4002-2028-1 (HC)

Library of Congress Control Number: 2020941186

Printed in the United States of America
20 21 22 23 LSC 10 9 8 7 6 5 4 3 2 1

To all who have helped me throughout my journey,

My family. My friends. My teachers and mentors.

My children, Emma, Kaitlin, Keenan, and Justin. Sadie and Buster too.
Each teach and inspire me in their own way.

And to the women on whose shoulders we stand, who give me hope.

And finally, to my Theo, who always believed in me. From Day 1.

CONTENTS

contents.

IF I CAN DO IT . . .

When you're the youngest of five kids, you can easily get lost in the family shuffle, which I did a lot. But you can also learn to fend for yourself, which I did eventually. And, ultimately, you can achieve more than anyone might have expected of you.

I never thought I would become a leader, run a company, or do anything particularly great for that matter. But when an executive at one of the world's largest beverage companies told me no one would want my unsweetened flavored water, something clicked. I decided to prove him wrong.

And I did.

This is the story of how I overcame a seemingly endless series of *no* and *you can't* and *it's impossible* to create a unique product, build a thriving company, compete with some of the biggest beverage companies on the planet, and live a life filled with rich experience and constant learning. Today, my product, Hint Water, is the number one flavored water in the United States, and Hint is an iconic brand loved by millions of customers.

In this book, I share the lessons I've learned about how to get things done instead of letting real or imagined obstacles stop me in my tracks. The story starts when I was a little kid, but don't worry, this book isn't an autobiography. It's part business, part life lessons, and it's all about the most important things you need to know to be a successful entrepreneur.

I call myself an *accidental entrepreneur* because I came to the world of start-ups on a different path than many other entrepreneurs. Founding a company was never my goal. I didn't go to business school. I was in my midthirties when I founded Hint. I had held a number of media and tech jobs, lived in New York and San Francisco, got married, and had kids.

Then, like many other people in the early 2000s, I discovered that kicking the diet soda habit and drinking more water helped me lose weight and get healthier. But I learned I could only drink so much plain water before I got bored, so I threw some slices of fruit into the pitcher to make it tastier.

That was the start, but I wasn't the first person to put fruit in water or try turning unsweetened flavored water into a product. I was, however, the first to create a successful product, while others made compromises that led them astray.

I let my passion and commitment to making a great product be my guide, and I stayed focused on what mattered most about the product—taste.

I started Hint in 2005 with my husband, Theo. At the time, enough consumers were making the move away from sugary and diet-sweetened drinks to bottled water that the large beverage companies, as well as a few entrepreneurial brands, started to include the word *water* in the name of their newest sweetened drinks. Brands like vitaminwater attempted to give consumers the feeling they were making a healthy choice, when actually they were getting more of the same.

Hint, by contrast, made water taste great without turning it into a sweet soft drink. No sugar. No diet sweeteners. No preservatives.

At first, I wasn't confident I could get the message across in this confusing, highly competitive marketplace, but I wanted to show people that drinks could taste great without having to taste sweet.

I didn't anticipate how technically difficult it would be to turn what I made in a kitchen into a product that went on the shelf in a store. Everyone in the business told us we would have to use preservatives or other chemicals to ensure the product had a reasonable shelf life. I refused to make that compromise. I asked Theo to research the issue and, after weeks of phone calls and visits to other bottlers, he told me, "There's no way to get the taste you want and still have enough shelf life to distribute this product around the country."

Theo assumed this was the end of our young project. I wasn't willing to quit so easily.

"Well, what *can* we do?" I asked.

"We can have a product with a very short shelf life that we deliver locally out of our Jeep in a limited area in San Francisco."

"Perfect, that's what we'll do. We'll find out what people think of the product and if it's worth trying to solve this problem."

We went ahead with confidence, but on the inside I was filled with doubts about whether we could pull this off. We started to distribute the product to local stores, achieving some positive responses from consumers and retailers. It gave me enough encouragement to begin networking with industry people to see if I could find someone who could advise us about the shelf-life issue.

When I'm facing problems I can't solve on my own, this approach—reaching out and asking questions, learning as much as I can, digging into the problem rather than running away from it—proved invaluable for getting Hint to where it is today.

Through one of those weird six-degrees connections, I was put in touch with a senior executive at Coca-Cola. Somehow, in the back of my mind, I figured this top leader of the most famous beverage maker in the world could solve our problem, just like that.

I called the exec at his office in Atlanta. He had no obligation to take my call, yet he was cordial and engaging. I told him about our unsweetened, fruit-infused water. About why I had started the company. How we had gotten good distribution in local natural foods markets like Whole Foods. But that we were up against an issue we couldn't solve: shelf life.

He launched into a long discourse on the technical issues involved—bottling and preservation, additives, transport, and warehousing—and he told me about some of the many past efforts related to the shelf-life issue that had failed. He seemed to know everything and everybody. He used technical jargon and business lingo that went way over my head. The longer he went on, the more I thought it was over. That my company could never succeed as anything but a nice little side business.

When the exec finished with his discourse, I felt defeated and more discouraged than ever. *I have no idea what I'm doing. I know nothing about this industry. This is all way beyond me. Why did I ever get involved in the first place?*

I was ready to throw in the towel. I even asked him: "Why don't you just take over my company? I don't care if you pay me anything. I just want to get this product category out there, and you seem to have the resources to take on the challenge."

"Listen, sweetie," he chuckled. "I've been in this business a long time. There's one thing I know. Americans want sweet drinks. Sure, you might sell your fruit drink in places like San Francisco, but outside of your friends in Marin County, no one really wants unsweetened drinks."

All I heard was "sweetie."

Did he really call me sweetie*!?*

It hit me then that people like him were so deeply invested in sugary and diet-sweetened drinks that they would never do what I was trying to do. Sweet was all they knew, and sweet drinks were all they wanted to sell. That was our big and very real advantage over them—we had the commitment, the understanding, and the passion for a new approach. If only we could solve the technical and business problems.

I realized the Coca-Cola executive did not have the answers I was looking for. I thanked him, genuinely, because he had given me valuable perspective and insight into not only what I *didn't* want to be, but also what we were up against.

Over the next two years, we built an early base of passionate fans of our product. As we expanded distribution, we incrementally improved the product's shelf life with a variety of expensive and proprietary methods. Then we had a breakthrough. We came up with our own solution in a way no one could have predicted, without help from any industry insiders. That enabled Hint to grow, widen distribution, win over more and more consumers, and confound industry heavyweights.

Today, Hint is a $150+ million company, our product is distributed in all fifty states, and we are the kind of brand known for products that make the healthy choice the most amazing choice.

Now I spend a good deal of time telling the Hint story at live events, in the media, on my own website, and in my podcast, *Unstoppable with Kara Goldin.* I am constantly amazed at how curious people are about how I started and built the company. Many want to create their own enterprises or further their careers within their companies. Everybody wants to find a way to live according to their values, both in their work lives and their personal lives.

In this book, I tell the Hint story. Not for its own sake, but as a way to offer insight and practical guidance on these issues. If I had to boil down the message to a single word, it would be the book's title: *Undaunted.*

That is the quality that, above all, is necessary to achieve success in creating an endeavor you can proudly call your own.

We all have doubts about our capabilities. I certainly did. My dad let his doubts derail his entrepreneurial ambitions. I refused to.

We all run into doubters who are too willing to tell us why we will never achieve what we envision. The sugar-soda exec dismissed me. Instead of giving up, I chose to take inspiration from that conversation.

We can't change the way of the world. What we *can* do is look our doubts and doubters in the eye and refuse to be stopped by them. It's not about high IQ, elite credentials, super skills, or any of those other traits we often convince ourselves we must have but are afraid we don't.

I wrote this book not because I want to hold myself up as the ideal model, but because everybody needs a little encouragement and advice to help them push away the doubts and doubters and achieve everything they believe they can.

If my story proves anything, it's that if I can do it, you can, too.

I submitted the manuscript for this book to Harper Leadership right before a novel coronavirus turned the world upside down. New York, second home to my company and family, quickly emerged as the epicenter of the pandemic. I considered making changes to incorporate this once-in-a-century event into Undaunted, *but decided to let it remain as is.*

No one at Hint knew this pandemic was coming, but we've been fortunate that the things we did to build a strong, adaptable business, along with selling through multiple channels of trade, are also allowing us to adapt quickly and successfully to consumers' needs. I hope that some of the stories I've shared in Undaunted *will help its readers find the courage and strength to chart their own course forward and upward as we emerge from these difficult times.*

undaunted.

open a lot of doors.

grew up in Scottsdale, Arizona, right next to Phoenix, in view of Camelback Mountain. My four siblings were always busy with school and sports and part-time jobs. My dad traveled a lot for business and, when he wasn't working, he was coaching baseball or football. When I was in kindergarten, my mom took a job working retail at a local department store and pursued arts and crafts projects on the side. So I was kind of on my own. Not neglected or ignored, just independent.

If I had a dominant trait as a kid, it was persistence. You have to be persistent when you're the youngest of five. If I wanted something, I had to figure out how to get it. Sometimes I had to argue, pester, or fight for it. Like those bright green pants with colored Life Savers printed on them I saw in a store window. My dad kept saying I didn't need them, and I kept pestering him to buy them for me until he finally came around.

"Kara," Dad would say, "you always think that 'no' means 'maybe' and 'maybe' means 'yes'!"

I drove him crazy sometimes, but he got a kick out of my unwillingness to give up. Mark Twain, who was also known as a feisty kid, said something similar about his mother: "My mother had a good deal of trouble with me, but I think she enjoyed it."

I did not give up easily on my interests, even when things got difficult. My best events in gymnastics were the vault and the uneven parallel bars. I wasn't great at them, but I kept at it. I broke every toe in both feet, some of them more than once, but that never stopped me. My friends and family got used to seeing me on crutches, and my mom and I spent a fair amount of time in the emergency room together.

"Maybe you could be a little more careful, Kara?" she would ask. But she never told me to stop.

I was curious and asked a lot of questions. I liked to hang out with my friends, and I always wanted to learn their stories. I would rain questions on them and their parents. *Where did you guys move from? What brought you to Scottsdale? What do you do?* I would get so engrossed that Mom would have to call and remind me to come home for dinner.

Throughout my life, especially when I haven't been certain about my next step, I have asked questions.

I was particularly curious about my dad. He worked for the Armour Food Company, which was later acquired by ConAgra, the big food conglomerate. He had dreamed of being an entrepreneur himself, but ended up taking the corporate job to support the family. I remember going with my mom to pick him up at the Phoenix Sky Harbor International Airport after he flew in from a business trip. There was only one terminal back then and no security, so I could run right up to the gate to meet him as he came off the plane. On the drive home, he'd vent his frustrations about working for a big company and not being recognized for his contributions.

It seemed to me that Dad had a legitimate complaint. He had invented a whole new line of frozen meals that was eventually marketed as the Healthy Choice brand, which became a big seller for

ConAgra and is still popular today. It all started when Mom went to work and Dad had to get dinner for us kids. He experimented with frozen TV dinners, but he thought they were awful—tasteless and unhealthy—and figured other people must feel the same way.

Armour let him engage Julia Child, who was famous for her pioneering cooking show on TV, *The French Chef,* and he worked with her to develop the new line of frozen meals. The Healthy Choice line he created made millions for the company, but my dad didn't benefit from it financially himself.

In the early 1980s, after the Armour acquisition, ConAgra decreed that all managers at a certain level had to have an MBA degree. Dad only had his bachelor's so, after a lifetime of service to the company, they told him it was time to take early retirement. His frustration, understandably, turned to resentment. Ultimately, the company offered him another job, but he would have to move to Omaha, Nebraska. He decided to take it. The plan was to work for four or five years and save up as much money as he could for retirement.

I wondered why he didn't go out on his own since he had been so successful with Healthy Choice and had a million ideas for other new products. I asked him why, and I'll never forget his response.

"Oh, Kara, it would be too hard."

I'm pretty sure my dad could have been successful if he had just gone for it. I could feel his frustration, but I couldn't figure out why he held himself back.

My mom, too, was frustrated. She had earned a degree in art from the University of Minnesota in the 1940s, a time when only a tiny minority of women went to college. She loved sewing and was a lover of arts and crafts, but apart from her own projects, she never pursued a career or followed her true passion.

My parents weren't unhappy, and we were comfortable as a family. But they both had personal dreams and had chosen not to fulfill them.

I had other models to look to, though. My oldest brother, Kevin, knew he wanted to be a lawyer. He needed money for law school tuition and didn't want to take on any debt, so he started a house painting business and got work all over Scottsdale. When he wasn't painting, he was running a second business reconditioning and re-selling old Volkswagens. His drive and ultimate success made a big impression on me.

My dad had been daunted by what he thought he couldn't do. Kevin had overcome obstacles to achieve what he could.

As for me, I didn't know exactly what I wanted to do for a career. Quite the opposite. I wanted to try a lot of different things and I ended up having a lot of different part-time jobs during high school. If one didn't work out, I'd try another. Most of my friends relied on babysitting to earn extra spending money, but I was looking for something different.

I landed my first job at age fourteen. It was totally opportunistic. My mom loved to go to a craft store in Old Town Scottsdale and would usually drag me along. She would spend hours studying yarn or fabric or patterns, so I'd wander out of the shop to the toy store next door. One day, there was a Help Wanted sign in the window. I had gotten to know the owner a bit, so I popped in and asked her for the job.

When I got home that day and told my dad that Nancy, the owner, had hired me, he couldn't believe it.

"She hired *you*?"

"Yes, she did."

"You don't know anything about running a shop!"

Nancy initially hired me to help out with the paperwork, but I ended up spending most of my time working the cash register. That was fine by me, because it meant I could talk with the customers. I got to know our inventory really well and, since I had played with most of the toys and read a lot of the books, I could advise parents on what to buy their children. I asked a steady stream of questions. *What kind of toys does your daughter like? What kind of books does your son read? How much do you want to spend?*

Nancy realized I understood what customers were looking for and had a good eye for toys, so she took me along on some of her buying trips to the big toy fairs.

That completely blew Dad's mind.

"That is super nuts! Now you're helping her buy the toys?"

"Yup."

From my first retail job experience, I learned how important it is to really understand what customers want.

In my sophomore year of high school, I was a little more deliberate about my choice of jobs. I had gotten seriously into beauty and was quite proud of my long red hair, so I decided it would be interesting to work at a hair salon. I wanted to make some money, but mostly I was eager to learn the fine points of hair styling and makeup. I did a year as a receptionist at a local salon called Butter. Not only did I pick up a lot of beauty knowledge, but I got to talk with a lot more customers and to learn about their jobs, their families, what they enjoyed, and the challenges they faced. The job I liked best was working as a waitress at a local Mexican restaurant called Tee Pee, just a couple blocks from my high school. I knew nothing about waitressing and I only got the job because I agreed to take the Sunday morning shift, which nobody else wanted. The place was a local institution, and the job brought me into contact with a lot of interesting people who came to Phoenix from all over the world. The restaurant is still there, all these years later, and some of the same people I knew are still there, too. I made a lot of connections at the restaurant, many of them businesspeople.

As a junior in high school, I heard that Arizona representative John McCain (later Senator McCain) sometimes hired high school students to work in his Tempe office, mainly answering phones and corresponding with voters who needed his help. After a quick screening interview, I found myself sitting across from John McCain. His first question: "Why do you want to work here?" I took a deep breath and told him the truth, that that my parents were both Republicans and that I wanted to figure out whether I was a Republican or not. He chuckled, then hired me. While I was one of many working in the office over the next six years, he never seemed to forget who I was or what my authentic answer had been. Occasionally, he would ask,

"Have you decided yet?" Once, I accidentally walked into a meeting where he happened to be sharing my response to his interview question. When I turned bright red with embarrassment, he quickly said, "Kara, never be afraid to tell the truth." When it was time for me to move on from that job, Senator McCain again asked, "So, have you decided?" I hesitated for a moment and then told him the truth. "No, not yet." I'll never forget his response: "I've always appreciated your honesty and I want you to know something else. It's okay to agree to disagree. Most of the people in both parties are deep down good people." This has stuck with me throughout my life. John McCain was a good person who believed that we make progress by advocating what we believe in and working toward a common goal. I use this philosophy to lead my company and my life every day.

> 66 I loved figuring out people, what would make them happy and what they would value and that I enjoyed their appreciation of what I had done for them. 99

The most important takeaway from those early jobs was not what I learned about toy stores, beauty salons, restaurants, or government.

It was what I learned about myself: that I loved figuring out people, what would make them happy and what they would value and that I enjoyed their appreciation of what I had done for them. That is what drove me to start Hint three decades later, and it's what still drives me today.

TWO

create your
own opportunities.

n 1985, following in the footsteps of some of my older siblings, I enrolled at Arizona State University. I wasn't entirely sure what I wanted to do for a career, but I chose to major in communications at the Walter Cronkite School of Journalism and Telecommunication.

I also thought it would be smart to learn more about the business side of things, so I signed up for some classes in finance, even though the subject didn't interest me and I don't have a natural inclination for numbers.

It was in my finance classes, oddly enough, that I began my life-long reading habit. One of my economics professors liked to illustrate his points by referencing articles in the *Wall Street Journal.* I had never even heard of the *Journal,* but I soon developed an obsession with the paper, and I still read it religiously every day. I was fascinated by its analysis of companies, products, and market trends. My roommates teased me about my *Journal* addiction. One day when I was at class, they ripped up a copy of the paper and taped the pages on my bedroom wall. They thought it was hysterical. I liked it and refused to take the pages down.

One of my classmates suggested that, if I liked the *Journal* so much, I should check out *Fortune* magazine. I loved its focus on people's stories—narratives of leaders and their companies, and of customers and their behavior. I read *Fortune* just as religiously as the *Journal*. I refused to throw out a single copy, and they stacked up in our dorm room, which also drove my roommates a little crazy.

That reading habit continues to this day. I make it a goal to read for at least thirty minutes every day. I scan, flip through, skim, check out all kinds of materials—magazines, news sites, blogs, and books. I want to stay current on market trends, and learn about how other entrepreneurs, especially in other industries, run their companies.

Most entrepreneurs and business leaders are avid readers. Bill Gates says he reads at least fifty books a year. Warren Buffett claims he read as much as a thousand pages a day at the beginning of his career. I have a long list of books that have made a difference to me. I've met or interviewed many entrepreneurs, and they can all point to a book that has inspired them, changed their lives, or positively affected their companies.

In college, those two publications gave me a picture of the business world that was very different from the theoretical stuff we learned in class. They pushed me to think more broadly about what kind of job I wanted to do when I graduated.

I had a general idea that I wanted to go into something that involved communications, such as journalism, publishing, advertising, or marketing. But I didn't have a clear idea of what that meant in terms of specific jobs or companies I might want to work for.

When senior year rolled around, a lot of my classmates were setting up interviews with corporate recruiters on campus. They mostly represented industries that did not appeal to me—big pharmaceuticals, accounting firms, financial service providers, and commercial real estate companies. I didn't want to do sales, and I was wary of big companies because of my father's experiences at ConAgra.

> 66 I've met or interviewed many entrepreneurs, and they can all point to a book that has inspired them, changed their lives, or positively affected their companies. 99

As time went along, it seemed to me that many of my classmates were taking any job they could. The economy was not in good shape then, and they just wanted to get a foot in the door somewhere, anywhere. Many were settling for unpaid internships.

I didn't want to do that, but I also didn't know enough about the job market to chart my own path. So, I did what I would do over and over again in my life to make an informed decision: I asked questions. Of anybody and everybody.

If the opportunities I want are not coming to me, I thought, *I'll have to create them for myself.*

Instead of meeting with the on-campus interviewers, I went out in search of interviews on my own. My favorite place for interrogating people was the Tee Pee restaurant, where I had continued to waitress throughout college. It was a natural place to dig for information because of the constant stream of people coming through from all over the country.

I started with a man who had been a regular customer over the years. We always chatted when I served him, but I never knew what he did. I decided it was time to find out.

He told me he lived in Los Angeles and came to Phoenix regularly for work. I told him I was job hunting.

"You should interview with my company," he suggested.

"Who do you work for?"

"Anheuser-Busch."

"What could I do for them?"

"Probably sales."

The idea of selling beer didn't interest me, but I figured there might be other things I could do.

"Is that what you do?"

He laughed. "No, I do product placement. The Hollywood studios shoot a lot of movies down here. I get them to place our products in their scenes."

That sounded interesting. "Could I get a job doing that?"

"Maybe. I could put in a word for you. You'd have to come to Los Angeles for the interview."

Until then, I hadn't thought about looking for a job outside the Phoenix area, but my customer opened up my field of view.

I kept pestering customers with questions in a somewhat normal way, and I was continuously amazed at how willing they were to give me information and advice. I talked with a couple from Chicago who owned a vacuum cleaner company. They invited me to move to Chicago and work for them.

"What would I do for a vacuum cleaner company?"

"Marketing!"

I didn't think that marketing vacuum cleaners would be my thing any more than selling beer would be, but I didn't want to rule anything out. Although my dad was a frequent flyer and I had spent plenty of time in the airport, I hadn't traveled to many places myself. If I was going to Los Angeles to interview with Anheuser-Busch, why not go to Chicago, too?

I put together a list of all the leads I got from customers and started sending out letters and making phone calls. I pitched myself hard. I said I was excited about the company, whatever it was, that I was a hard worker, that I'd consider any kind of job, and that I'd gladly fly at my own expense for an in-person interview.

Before I knew it, I had *ninety* potential interviews lined up. They were all entry-level positions in all kinds of companies, from consultancies to financial service providers.

But there was one place where I wanted to work above all the rest. It was a publishing company, based in New York, whose product I really admired.

Fortune magazine.

CHAPTER 3

show up.

U nlike most of the other companies I sent letters to, I didn't have a contact name at *Fortune*, but I didn't let that stop me. I figured it couldn't hurt to ask.

In fact, I've found that the most certain way to get what you want is to ask, directly and explicitly.

In all the letters I sent to prospective employers as a job-seeking college grad, I asked for an interview and a job, but I added a more personal touch to my *Fortune* letter. I wrote directly to Marshall Loeb, the managing editor of the magazine and a major figure on the New York and national publishing scene. I knew he was the person responsible for making *Fortune* the magazine I liked so much.

When he came on board as editor just a few years earlier, the magazine had been pretty stodgy, focused on finance and economics. Loeb livened it up with stories about businesspeople and their companies and introduced more photos and graphics. Those were the stories that had turned me on to business and the people who drove it.

In my letter to Mr. Loeb, I explained how much I liked the magazine and said that he had taught me more about business than my finance professors had. Even though I secretly imagined myself as a reporter or an editor, with my feature stories and byline on the *Fortune* cover, I made it clear that I would love to work for him in any position he had available.

I got a nice letter back, thanking me for writing and proposing that, if I was ever in New York, I should get in touch and they would see about arranging an interview. Signed, Marshall Loeb.

Wow.

That added New York City to my list of places to visit.

I called a travel agent and ran through my five-city itinerary with her: Los Angeles, San Francisco, Chicago, Boston, and New York. I was worried I couldn't afford to make the trip. But the travel agent told me the total cost would be $472. Still a lot, but much less than I expected. I figured it was an investment in my future.

What else am I going to spend money on that will be this important?

With the exception of Los Angeles, I'd never been to any of the cities where I had interviews, so that month of travel was eye-opening and inspiring in many ways.

I did the interview at Anheuser-Busch in Los Angeles, as my customer had promised. And although I was attracted to the Hollywood atmosphere and California lifestyle, I wasn't sure about working for such a big company.

In Chicago, I interviewed with McKinsey & Company, a management consultant firm, and I also met with the nice vacuum cleaner people. Given my educational background, I probably wouldn't have been on the partner track at McKinsey, and I didn't think marketing vacuums was for me. Plus, Chicago was awfully cold in the winter.

In Boston, I met with financial services companies. Even though I had minored in finance, I knew it was not really my thing.

Last stop: New York City.

show up.

I hadn't actually arranged for an interview as Mr. Loeb had suggested. I thought about calling ahead, but decided to just show up instead. My plan was to walk into the human resources office, show them the letter from Marshall Loeb, and ask for a job. That's how I had gotten jobs in high school. I had learned it's tough to ignore somebody who's standing right in front of you. So that was my plan: show up, do whatever it took to land an interview, get a job.

It was a cold January day in New York, 1989. I walked along Sixth Avenue to the famous Time & Life Building. I pushed through the revolving door into an almost overwhelmingly awesome lobby of glass, marble, and stainless steel, hung with enormous works of art.

> **I had learned it's tough to ignore somebody who's standing right in front of you. So that was my plan: show up, do whatever it took to land an interview, get a job.**

For the first time, I got a sense of the magnificence and prestige of the company. *Fortune* was part of the Time Inc. empire, which published more than a hundred magazines, including *Life, Time, Money, Sports Illustrated,* and *People.* In those days, it was the print media, not the internet, that shaped how people got their information and how they viewed the world.

I hesitated. Could I really go through with this? Suddenly, it felt like an impossible long shot. I took a deep breath. I got in the elevator, rode up several floors, found the human resources department, and went up to the receptionist.

"Hello. I'm interested in a job at *Fortune*."

She looked at me skeptically.

"Do you have an appointment?"

"No. I have a letter from Marshall Loeb."

I showed her the letter. She studied it briefly then looked at me as if uncertain what to do next. A woman standing nearby had heard our exchange. She came over and introduced herself as the head of human resources. She glanced at the letter. Obviously she had seen hundreds like it. The standard college student brush-off form letter. I had imagined Marshall Loeb read it and personally signed it. Now I realized he had probably never even seen it.

The head of HR looked at me with a mix of amusement and curiosity.

"What Mr. Loeb meant was that you should get in touch and make an appointment for an interview if you were planning to be in New York."

Although she was saying "No," what I heard was "Maybe."

"Well, here I am. I'm in New York now. I'm leaving tomorrow. I'd really appreciate an interview."

She again tried saying no. "I'm sorry, but there really aren't any openings at *Fortune* right now."

I didn't turn to go. I just stood there. Right in front of her. Hard to ignore. There was a pause. Then she remembered something.

"You know, I think there is a job available at *Time*. It's in the circulation department. Would you be interested in that?"

Now she was saying "maybe," but I was hearing "yes." I had only a vague idea of what circulation was. It wasn't *Fortune*. It wasn't Marshall Loeb. And it probably wouldn't involve reporting that resulted in cover stories. But if I could work in the building, I could meet the *Fortune* people and eventually get hired as a writer.

"Yes! I would!"

I am forever grateful to that kind woman. "Okay. Let me see if Brooke is available to see you now."

She disappeared for a minute, then came back and escorted me to an office on a different floor. There she introduced me to Brooke McMurray, who was head of third-party circulation and was looking for an executive assistant. I sat down and told Brooke my whole story—about how much I liked reading *Fortune*, my communications studies at ASU, my letter to Marshall Loeb, my seventy interviews, and my multiple job offers.

Brooke listened patiently. I can only imagine how I came across. I was twenty-one. My main work experience had been as a waitress at the Tee Pee restaurant. I had never lived in New York, had never even been to New York before this trip. Everything I knew about the publishing industry I had learned in class, and I knew absolutely nothing about circulation.

It must have been an okay story because Brooke didn't kick me out. She described the kind of assistant she was looking for. I had to be committed to supporting her. I had to be the kind of person who could help her get things done.

"Do you think you are that kind of person?"

I thought for a moment. *Executive assistant* wasn't exactly what I had in mind, but I would learn a lot about publishing, the corporate world, and about living in New York. I was in the right building, in the right city, with a person who looked like she could be the right boss. I could learn.

"Yes. Absolutely. I am that kind of person."

"Great," Brooke said. "I'll be in touch."

I flew back to Arizona. When I got home, I had a voice mail waiting. *Time* wanted to hire me as Brooke's assistant. I had landed a job.

Then I got cold feet. I called Dad, who was traveling at the time, to see what he thought.

"I'm not sure I should take this job with *Time*."

"Why not?"

"I have no idea what I'm doing. I know nothing about New York."

"Okay, but what's the risk?"

"What do you mean, 'what's the risk?'"

"Well, what's the worst that can happen?"

What was the worst that could happen? Total failure? Catastrophe? The end of the world?

"I don't know . . ."

"I'll tell you. The worst that can happen is that you sign a year's lease for an apartment. Maybe you have to buy a bed and a few pots and pans. You do the best you can. If it doesn't work out, you're out a few thousand bucks. You can find another job. You can come back home. It's not that big a risk."

He was right. I had already discovered there were plenty of doors out there. A lot of them had been opened for me on my trip. I had gotten many offers. If the *Time* door closed, there would be others.

I told *Time* I'd take the job.

I don't think I would have gotten the job at *Time* if I hadn't showed up and basically refused to leave. My good friend Alex Wallace, who is a very experienced media executive, did exactly the same thing when she started out. She got her degree from Columbia and started looking for jobs the traditional way—sending out tons of résumés and making phone calls. Finally, she marched in to the CBS offices and asked for an interview. She got a job with the evening news show and stayed at CBS for nine years before going to NBC. Ten years later, she was senior vice president of the news division.

> 66 What's the worst that can happen? I have asked myself that question many times as we were building Hint and considering one action or another. 99

And I probably wouldn't have taken the job if it hadn't been for my dad asking the turnaround question: What's the worst that can happen? I have asked myself that question many times as we were building Hint and considering one action or another.

What's the worst that can happen?

Usually, when you think it through, the worst is rarely as bad as you think. And even if something bad does happen, it's usually not what you had expected anyway.

Things work out.

Although I never got a job as a reporter at *Fortune*, I did eventually get a story in the magazine. In 2011, *Fortune* named me one of the "10 Most Powerful Women Entrepreneurs in America."

Thank you, Marshall Loeb.

CHAPTER 4

know where you stand.

C oming out of ASU, even though I didn't know what I wanted to do long term, I did know I was ready to take on my job and life in The Big City. While looking for a place to live, I stayed with my sister's friend in a not-so-great part of town known as Alphabet City.

On my first day of work, I put on my kelly-green business suit, opened the door to the street, and almost stepped right on the chalk outline marking where a body had previously laid on the sidewalk.

"What's going on?" I asked one of the officers milling about.

"Somebody got killed."

I didn't know what to say, so I just blurted out, "How do I get to the subway?" With my dad's voice echoing in my head, *What's the worst that can happen?*, I took a deep breath and set out for the office, vowing to accelerate my apartment search.

I made it to work a bit shaken but on time. After getting the usual new hire paperwork out of the way, I quickly began to develop the feeling that maybe, just maybe, I didn't fit into the world of Time. After staring at my bright-colored clothing from Arizona, the young people I met at work would typically ask, "So, where did you go to school?"

My answer, "Arizona State University," always seemed to provoke a raised eyebrow or a frown.

Their next question was often, "How did *you* land this job?" or "Who did your dad know?"

Turns out I was one of the few new hires in an entry-level position at Time who had not attended an Ivy League school. I learned that the magazine business had deep East Coast, Ivy League roots—and I certainly didn't.

Time magazine's founders were both Yale grads and had worked together on the school newspaper in their college days. Time Inc. regularly recruited from the Ivy League and ran most of its new hires through an elite training program that groomed them for a career at the company. Many of the trainees had business degrees from Harvard Business School (or "HBS," as they said). I was an anomaly, a "walk on," probably the first and only ASU grad ever to work in the hallowed halls of Time up to that point. I was given no formal training. I came in with the title of executive assistant, while the Ivy League trainees started out at as assistant managers. That bugged me at first, because our actual jobs were quite similar and the difference in title had nothing to do with skill or performance or potential. It was all about having gone to the "right school."

Still, knowing where I stood and how others viewed me helped me focus and set a plan in motion. There was absolutely nothing I could do about where I went to college, and I wasn't going to pretend I was something I wasn't, so I did the only thing I could do: I threw myself into the work and set out to be the best employee Time had hired that year.

Don't think about what you can't do. Figure out what you can do. Then do it to the best of your ability.

Not being in the training program, I found myself on my own, trying to figure out what to do. For a while, I felt like an outsider. It didn't help that, in the early days, Brooke spent most of the day in her office with the door closed. When she did come out or call me in, she seemed to keep her conversations to the bare minimum. I tried to be friendly and ask questions, but she just didn't appear to be interested. I wondered if the reason I got the job was simply that Brooke was a tough nut to crack.

 Don't think about what you can't do. Figure out what you can do. Then do it to the best of your ability.

Rather than take it personally or write Brooke off, I decided to figure out the job on my own. I quickly started building relationships with Brooke's team of ten women, who helped me better understand how things worked in the department.

We were responsible for finding and developing "cross-title" distribution opportunities for all the Time Inc. publications. That meant managing subscriptions for niche markets, like schools and the airlines. I learned that the most important part of our job was making sure that all the distribution of our magazines, whether sold as an individual subscription or sold to Publishers Clearing House for its sweepstakes mailings, had to be done in a way that the independent Audit Bureau of Control would count as "net paid circulation," meaning it would count when calculating the rates we charge advertisers. By talking with the rest of the team, I got up to speed on things I had never heard about and started to get a sense of how circulation fit into the Time Inc. business.

Meanwhile, I kept checking in with Brooke to see if there was more I could do to help her. Although she did start to give me more work, a couple weeks in, I still felt like we hadn't really connected.

One day, Michael Loeb, who ran ad sales at *Sports Illustrated* and was the son of Marshall Loeb, stopped by. After introducing himself, he said: "Will you please keep an eye on Brooke to make sure she's okay? Her husband passed away recently and she is still grieving and having a rough time. If she doesn't come out of her office at least once every couple hours, pick up the phone and let me know."

All of a sudden, Brooke made sense to me. I had assumed she was a difficult person when, in fact, she was just hurting badly and did not want to wear her heart on her sleeve. I decided to double my efforts to be a great employee and make sure nothing slipped through the cracks during this tough time for my boss. To best support her, I had to think about her job responsibilities *and* her personal concerns. I got to know what she expected and I always tried to over-deliver. I learned her hot buttons and how to avoid pushing them. I tried to see her as a whole person, not just my boss.

Years later, I still tell new recruits at Hint that the number one thing they need to do is make sure their boss and their team are successful. I run into so many people who make the mistake of worrying about how they look and concentrating on their own feelings to the extent that they don't appreciate what's going on around them. Focusing outward on those who depend on you and the rest of the team makes you a valuable person, gets you more responsibility, and ultimately gives you a chance to not just look like, but also to be, a superstar.

As I got familiar with our corner of the Time Inc. publishing business, Brooke gradually gave me more to do. One of my responsibilities was to call on the advertising staffers at the various Time know where you stand.

Inc. publications, all of which were headquartered in our building, to discuss placements with them. Through Brooke, I connected with more and more people at higher and higher levels at Time's other amazing magazines, including *Life, Money,* and *Sports Illustrated.* I got to know their businesses and the people themselves, which I loved. I may only have had the title of executive assistant, but I had much more responsibility than you would expect.

> 66 Focusing outward on those who depend on you and the rest of the team makes you a valuable person, gets you more responsibility, and ultimately gives you a chance to not just look like, but also to be, a superstar. 99

I learned that I had a great capacity for work. I got to the office before Brooke arrived in the morning and stayed late, leaving long after she had gone home. The effort paid off and Brooke included me on more details. The airlines were a critical customer for Time Inc., because each copy sold to them had a big impact on how much could be charged for advertisements in the magazines. Unfortunately, with a rough economy, the airlines were cutting back and were telling us they needed to cancel the magazine program. Rather than take *no* for an answer, Brooke pushed for a barter deal in which the airlines could give us flight credits for use by Time Inc. instead of paying cash. It was tricky getting the Audit Bureau of Control to sign off on the deal, but, with a lot of work, we convinced them, saving a key piece of distribution while cutting back on travel costs for Time employees. Even though the economy was in a slump, we actually expanded distribution of Time publications to airplanes flying to Canada and South America.

Over time, Brooke really opened up, we talked more, and she eventually became a mentor to me. I remember one heart-to-heart conversation we had. I had met a lot of people in Ad Sales and had learned a lot about what they did. I told Brooke that I wanted to get a better sense of how I could eventually get into the Ad Sales training program at one of the Time publications. She did not pull any punches.

"If you want to stay at Time and keep on moving up, you will absolutely have to get an MBA. Preferably, at an Ivy League school. People like you, Kara, and they'll talk to you all day long about opportunities, but nothing is going to happen without the right degree."

Ironically, I found myself in a situation similar to the one my dad experienced when ConAgra made him take early retirement because he didn't have an MBA. I thought long and hard about going back to school and getting the business degree. Many of my friends were doing exactly that, but I wasn't convinced the MBA was for me, and also I wasn't sure I wanted to work at Time indefinitely.

Although Brooke had made it clear what my long-term prospects were at Time, I did my best to network with the Ad Sales guys at all of the Time publications, hoping they would help me get into one of their training programs.

Over the next six months, I got to know a ton of people in the building who seemed to like how I thought about their business. No one was making any promises, but they did start to engage more in conversations and to turn to me as a resource to help work cross-title and unusual sales deals. Whether I would ever climb the ladder at Time was still in question, but I was starting to get the hang of living in New York. And even though I never seemed to have any money in my bank account, I was starting to meet people and go out a bit.

Shortly after starting work, I had found a tiny apartment on the Upper West Side, near Central Park. I could tell you it was a charming brownstone conveniently located near work, which it was, but it was also little more than a tiny, 150-square-foot box of a room with no closet, a stove and fridge in the corner, and a robust drug-dealing operation going on at the ground floor.

One day, I got home and found I could barely get the door open. When I managed to push inside, I discovered that the ceiling had collapsed. I called the landlord to ask him to fix it and got his voice mail. The next day, when I came home, there was superglue in my lock and I couldn't get in. I started crying and went back downstairs. Of all people, the drug dealer saw me crying and asked what happened. When I told him the situation, he offered to beat up the landlord, and he meant it. I asked him not to. He then said: "This landlord is a crazy, dangerous person. You should just pack your bags and get out of here."

I decided this was good advice, so I found a locksmith, got into the apartment, packed up my stuff, and went to stay with a friend.

A week later, I moved into a fourth-floor walk-up in the West Village. It was 450 square feet and looked out onto a brick wall, but it was in a great area. My commute had just gotten a lot longer, but I was now in a safe neighborhood, with a lot more people my age. The rent was a bit of a stretch, but a lot of meetings at Time were catered and there were always plenty of leftovers. Friends of mine throughout the company would tip me off every time a meeting with good food was about to end, and that's how I ate lunch and dinner most days. Eventually, Brooke gave me a decent raise, and I felt like I could almost make ends meet in New York.

During the early winter of 1991, I decided to go downstairs in Rockefeller Center and get some lunch. It was a snowy day and snow had blown into the underground shopping area. On my way back to the office, I slipped on a sheet of ice, slamming my knee into a marble step, shattering it into three pieces. It was a huge setback during a time of year when being on crutches in New York was not easy. After surgery, I decided to head back to Arizona for Christmas and a few weeks of recovery. Never fly across the country immediately after surgery. Trust me.

After a couple weeks back home, I was still on crutches but feeling a bit better. I headed out to a favorite bar with my lifelong friend Christy, who happened to be home on break. There, we ran into Bruce, a friend from high school who always used to laugh at how often I injured myself.

He saw the crutches and burst out laughing. "Kara! Did you break another toe? Is this ever going to stop?"

Turns out Bruce was studying for a law degree at New York University, and he lived just a few blocks from my new apartment. Bruce suggested we meet up with a bunch of his friends from NYU at a local bar called Down the Hatch, and he wrote down a date and time on a piece of paper (no smartphones or even cell phones back then).

Back in New York a few weeks later, I put on my jacket to go meet my friend Julie, and when I stuck my hand in my pocket, I found that scrap of paper. The date was that night, so I told Julie we had to go meet Bruce and his law school buddies. We got to the bar before Bruce arrived and, while we were waiting, I noticed a guy sitting at the counter. He was cute, had nice manners, and seemed to be genuinely listening to the person he was talking with. I pointed him out to my friend and said, "I wish I could meet a normal guy like that!"

A few minutes later, Julie told me that the guy I pointed to was waiting in line for the bathroom and I should go meet him. I decided to go for it. I made my way into the line right next to him.

If I drop my bag, I thought, *maybe he'll pick it up and we can have a conversation.*

Unfortunately, as my bag was in midair, the door to the men's room opened and he walked in, oblivious to my efforts. My bag spilled all over the ground and the next guy in line busted me for trying to meet that guy by dropping my bag. I was embarrassed as I got down on the floor to gather my stuff.

When I got out of the restroom and hobbled back to our table, I was shocked to see the guy I was trying to meet sitting in my seat, next to Julie and my friend Bruce. I reached my hand out and introduced myself, maybe a bit too loudly, but I got his attention. His name was Theo Goldin, and we hit it off right away. We spent a wonderful evening together and were soon dating seriously. We've now been married for twenty-five years.

How we came together shows that luck, coincidence, weird circumstances, and unexpected events play important roles in our lives, in our careers, and as entrepreneurs.

CHAPTER 5

know when to move on.

t was the fall of 1992 when I got the call, completely out of the blue, from CNN. They wanted me to come in to interview for a new position in Ad Sales. I went back to all the Ad Sales guys at Time and told them about it, hoping they would find a way to keep me at Time. I had developed good relationships throughout the building, and I genuinely loved working there, but they all encouraged me to take the position at CNN if I had the chance. As Brooke had said, I just didn't attend the right school, for some people, or have the right degree. When I told Theo about the phone call and the opportunity, he agreed that if I wanted to move my career along without going for an MBA, this could be a great next step.

CNN, the Cable News Network, was very hot. The network was founded in 1980 by Ted Turner, an aggressive entrepreneur who had turned his father's billboard company into a media empire. After a decade of broadcasting in the shadow of the Big Three networks (ABC, CBS, NBC), CNN burst into prominence in January of 1991 at the start of the Persian Gulf War. CNN was the only one with reporters in Baghdad who were able to broadcast live as the bombing began. None of the Big Three networks had that coverage, so all eyes were on CNN.

Arriving for my interview, my first impression of the CNN offices was closer to the Wild West than the Time Inc. environment. Television is a different animal from print. And this was cable, not broadcast. It was all about live breaking news. Everybody was young, moving a mile a minute. It felt like a start-up would feel today.

There was an aura of celebrity, too. Not only was Ted Turner a media legend, but he had just married Jane Fonda, an even bigger celebrity. She was a movie star and a highly successful business leader with a best-selling line of exercise videos. She was also a feminist and an outspoken activist against the Vietnam War. I admired her and, as ridiculous as it sounds now, I thought maybe I would get to meet her and even work with her if I took a job at CNN.

CNN was interested in me because Ted Turner had big plans for expanding the station's reach, and one of his ideas was to place TV monitors in airports, broadcasting CNN nonstop. The interviewer at CNN knew I had been running the airline circulation business for Time and figured I had good connections with the right people. Although the airport channel was a promising idea, they weren't exactly sure how it was going to work, and they wanted me to come on board to figure it out.

While I loved the people and business at Time Inc., this was the break I had been looking for. It would give me a chance to be creative, to take on a business challenge, and to come up with a solution. Plus, the salary was better than what I was making at Time.

I reported for work at CNN in January 1993, and it was nothing like I expected it would be. Every company and every work situation is different, but there is no question that young, fast-growing start-ups are full of uncertainties and play by a different set of rules than well-established companies.

know when to move on.

The first big lesson I got in this regard came very soon after I joined. I was just beginning to figure out a business plan for the CNN airport channel when Ted Turner put the project on hold. Instead, it was all hands on deck for advertising. I went into a CNN sales training program and spent the next two years selling advertising.

> 66 Every company and every work situation is different, but there is no question that young, fast-growing start-ups are full of uncertainties and play by a different set of rules than well-established companies. 99

It sounds similar to what I had been doing at Time, but it was actually very different. I saw my work at Time as building long-term relationships. At CNN, the sales were totally transactional. Make the sale, bring in the money, move on to the next one. The more, the bigger, the better. Money has never been a big motivator for me and still isn't. What's the point of making money doing something you don't love? I stuck with it, but I knew I wasn't going to stay at CNN for long. I started to think about my next step.

In retrospect, I did learn some valuable lessons during my time at CNN, but they were less about the work itself than about the work environment. I became aware of how different every business culture is and about the kind of culture in which I felt most comfortable and successful. At CNN, I enjoyed the energy and excitement, but I much preferred the people and the work environment at

Time. CNN was not particularly collegial or friendly. Even though it was a media business, it was not as creative as I had expected. I met some nice people, but it was hard to connect in the Wild West, cowboy-like environment.

It was, above all, not a very *kind* place. At least not for me. Don't get me wrong. I did meet some great people. In fact, one of those people, Joe Uva, is an investor in Hint. But as I look back, this is when I became aware of how important kindness can be in business, especially on the part of the leader. Certainly, I admired Ted Turner for what he had accomplished, and I was impressed with CNN, but I never developed a mentor relationship with anyone there as I had with Brooke at Time. I wondered, if I had smashed my kneecap at CNN, how would the company have dealt with it? Would somebody there have sent food to my apartment as Brooke had? Would they have let me take a month off to recuperate? Would anybody have given me the inside scoop on my chances for success at the company? I realized that I thrived on kindness—I still do—and I didn't find much of it at CNN. (That was then; I don't know what the work culture at CNN is like now.)

Those two very different New York work experiences would later be a big influence on me when I started Hint. I wanted to create a healthy, supportive company culture and learned firsthand that leaders have to set the right tone. This sounds obvious, I suppose, but a lot of entrepreneurs focus on funding, products, sales, profit, and fast growth. They don't talk nearly as much about self-awareness and kindness.

By the spring of 1994, after almost five years in New York, it was time to move on again. Theo graduated from NYU and asked me to marry him. I said yes. Theo wanted to get into technology law, specifically intellectual property work. Everybody was telling him he would have to be on the West Coast because that's where all the hot technology start-ups were and all the law firms that worked with the start-ups.

That spring we went out to San Francisco so Theo could look for a job. He was smart and knew a lot about tech, which was his passion, so he soon landed a job as an associate with Brobeck, Phleger & Harrison, a big law firm where he could focus on technology licensing and partnering deals.

We agreed to get married in Phoenix and set a date in March for the wedding. Theo passed the bar the summer we made the move to the West Coast. We found an apartment on Union Street in San Francisco with a great view of the Bay.

Now *I* had to decide what to do next. I felt like I was a senior in college again.

What do I really want to do? What am I good at? What jobs are available? Can I find the kind of work environment I thrive in?

I would have to figure it all out. I had found my first important job through my love of *Fortune* magazine. Ironically, I found my next opportunity in the pages of my other favorite publication, the *Wall Street Journal.*

> **What do I really want to do? What am I good at? What jobs are available? Can I find the kind of work environment I thrive in?**

CHAPTER 6

figure it out.

One day, I was flipping through the *Wall Street Journal* when I came across an article by Walt Mossberg, the technology writer. It was about the emerging business of online shopping. Mossberg profiled several companies in the San Francisco area that were getting involved in the business, including Apple, America Online, and PacBell.

The one that particularly intrigued me, though, was a start-up called 2Market. None other than Steve Jobs had conceived and incubated it at Apple, under the name En Passant.

At that time, internet access in homes was way too slow to provide a satisfying online shopping experience, so 2Market took a different approach. The company put product images and video content on a CD-ROM and mailed it to potential customers four times a year. Customers could load the CD into the computer and browse the entire catalog of products for an entertaining shopping experience.

When they wanted to make a purchase, they connected to the internet through the 2Market app and completed the transaction.

I was intrigued by the idea of online shopping, known today as e-commerce, and I thought there was plenty of room to improve the online experience. I had been spending lots of time on sites like LexisNexis, doing research on companies as I thought about my next job. The combination of slow connections, lots of text, and almost no images was giving me headaches. I also had plenty of experience with shopping and I felt I had a strong sense of design, so I was interested in learning more about the company.

Turns out that 2Market was headquartered in San Mateo, just south of San Francisco. In his *Journal* article, Mossberg had quoted Mike Minnegan, one of the executives, so I called the office and asked to speak with him. He was there and took my call.

"Hey! I was reading an article in the *Wall Street Journal* about your company. I would love to come down, buy you lunch, and talk about what you do. I'm not really looking for a job. We just moved to San Francisco, and I'm thinking about what I want to do next."

> " People often ask me how I have the nerve to make cold calls. First, I'm naturally curious, so I genuinely want to learn from other people. Second, people love to be asked about what they do and, generally, are eager to tell their stories. "

I told him a bit about myself and what I found so interesting about 2Market, and he invited me to visit.

People often ask me how I have the nerve to make cold calls. First, I'm naturally curious, so I genuinely want to learn from other people. Second, people love to be asked about what they do and, generally, are eager to tell their stories.

Besides, what's the worst that can happen?

I drove down to San Mateo a couple days later. 2Market consisted of one tiny office with maybe six people on staff. Mike and a few of his colleagues, including the CEO, Tom Burt, and VPs Greg Shove and Pete Baltaxe, joined me for lunch.

They told me the backstory of 2Market. Steve Jobs had originated the idea with a few people at Apple. In December 1993, En Passant entered the market by mailing thirty thousand CD-ROMs to potential customers. The digital catalog showcased products from about twenty high-end retailers, including Tiffany, Lands' End, Williams Sonoma, Pottery Barn, and Patagonia. The catalog had some advanced features for the time, including keyword search and a gift registry. It also had some magazine-style features about style and decorating. The release gained some attention in the media and the tech industry. In fact, a reviewer for *Wired* magazine, which was just two years old, wrote that the catalog was "beautiful."

But En Passant had plenty of competition, and many of the big players were trying to figure out how to build an online retail business. CompuServe, one of the oldest and biggest contenders, targeted geeks and gamers. Even my former employer Time Inc. was trying to find a way in with a shopping site called Pathfinder, which was advertised as "The World's Best Web Site."

Another important player was America Online, or AOL, which started out in 1985 as a messaging service and web portal. They were trying to figure out what kind of material they could offer beyond games, and they made a deal with Time Inc. to post content from their publications.

AOL had also taken an interest in En Passant and online shopping. They made a deal with Apple to take part ownership in the project, spin it out of Apple, and set it up independently. They renamed it 2Market. That's when Mike Minnegan and Tom Burt got involved.

Because there was so much to figure out about the industry, I got more and more excited about the potential of the company. The leaders didn't have a business strategy or a detailed business plan. They were basically signing up retailers for free, trying to build up the business before funding from AOL ran out.

I told them about my background, my experiences at Time and CNN, and my interest in online shopping. Toward the end of the lunch, Mike asked if I'd be interested in working with them. They urgently needed someone to call on retailers and convince them to offer their products on the 2Market shopping CD. It was nothing like what I had done at Time and CNN. They could offer a nice salary, more than I had made at CNN. More important, I would get equity in the company, a chunk of stock that would vest over a four-year period. That was a new thing in those days, and I didn't really know exactly how it worked but it sounded good.

I thanked them and said I'd think about it.

When I got home, I told Theo about the offer.

"That's fantastic, Kara. It's something you're genuinely interested in and it's a chance to build a whole new industry. You should take it. Besides, if you hate it, you can always quit."

That sounded like something my dad would say.

I accepted the offer on one condition: that I could take time off for my wedding and honeymoon in March. We planned to get married at the Wrigley Mansion in Phoenix, then spend a week in Tahiti. They agreed.

I plunged into the job. My responsibility was to build up the 2Market service by bringing on new retailers, but I started by getting up to speed about existing success stories at 2Market. Two brands that had signed up before I arrived were 1-800-Flowers and Omaha Steaks,

both of which were relatively small at the time, and had been selling
direct-to-consumer. I called Elaine Rubin of 1-800-Flowers and Jim
Simon at Omaha Steaks and learned more about the client perspective on our service. To this day, I consider the two of them among the
smartest people I met in the early days of online shopping.

I also asked the 2Market team to get me up to speed on our pricing model, but mostly got awkward smiles. It turned out they really
didn't have a pricing model; they were just doing one-off deals to
sign up as many good retailers as they could. They weren't particularly concerned about making money.

I knew that eventually we'd have to turn a profit, so I developed
an initial pricing model. With that in hand, I picked up the phone
to set up face-to-face meetings with customers.

It turned out to be harder than I expected. The problem was that
none of our potential customers had a staff person whose responsibility was online commerce, because that business didn't really exist
yet. So I had to figure out who I could speak with to get a deal done.
Some companies had media buyers for print or TV, but my gut feeling was that they would not be the best people to target, since their
instinct would probably be to protect their turf.

I decided to swing for the fences and go straight to the CEOs. Why
not? Since online shopping was getting coverage in the *Wall Street
Journal*, I figured plenty of CEOs were starting to hear about it and
might be interested in learning more. If I couldn't get to the CEO,
my fallback strategy was to get in touch with the head merchandiser.

One of my first calls was close to home—the Gap, headquartered
in downtown San Francisco. Mickey Drexler was the CEO, and he
was legendary as a clothing brand builder. He had rejuvenated Ann
Taylor before taking over the Gap, transforming the company into
a leader in sharp-looking casual clothing.

Given Mickey's innovative approach to retailing, I figured he
might be interested in putting the Gap brands, which included Ba-
nana Republic and the newly launched Old Navy, online. To get a
meeting with him, I used my tried-and-true method: I called him up.

People ask how I get appointments with interesting and powerful people. They're surprised when I tell them my super-secret method: a phone call. Today, in the world of email, a phone call may be more effective than ever. Don't get me wrong, I love email, but I don't rely on it as the only method of communication.

Getting ready for my first meetings, I knew I needed to have a way to explain what we were doing in terms that would make sense to a retail CEO. I thought about the brick-and-mortar shopping mall, a format that retailers like the GAP would understand. A typical mall was built around an anchor tenant, usually a department store like Nordstrom. Around the anchor, the mall tried to offer as wide a range of goods as possible, from home furnishings to clothing to electronics and food. Since physical space was finite, the number of stores and types of goods was limited and had to be carefully selected.

That model didn't apply to online shopping. We didn't need an anchor tenant at all and space was infinite, but the shopping experience would be just as important. I looked around at other physical models and was inspired by the Fourth Street Shops in Berkeley, just across the bridge from San Francisco. It got started in the early 1980s as a collection of unique shops devoted to home goods and gradually grew and diversified into a "neighborhood" of stores, including fashion and other categories, but all high-quality goods that you couldn't find just anywhere. It was one of the first retail venues to talk about the "shopping experience." That's what I thought 2Market could be, and that was the basis of my pitch to retailers.

I always brought a computer with me to client meetings so I could walk them through the 2Market shopping experience. Mickey was interested, but when I first set up the computer on his desk, I could tell he wasn't entirely sure what he was looking at.

"So, Kara, am I looking at TV or is this the internet?"

That was a telling and not uncommon question. It made sense because what I was showing him was closer to what you would see on TV shopping channels like QVC than it was to browsing the internet, which at the time was mostly text-based, non-graphical content.

Mickey is one of the smartest, savviest, most successful business executives you are likely to meet, so his uncertainty about online shopping shows just how new graphical interactive content was at the time.

I learned that I had to be careful not to make potential partners feel stupid when I made my pitch. I didn't know that much when I started, but soon I knew more than most of the people I was pitching to. You don't make a sale by showing people how smart you are compared to them. We ended up having a great meeting, and Mickey said he was interested in learning more.

I had several more meetings with retailers, and I came to the conclusion that the best way to sell a revolutionary concept like online shopping was to take a consultative approach. At the time, senior executives had limited knowledge about computers and the internet. My goal was to help them understand how online shopping could enable them to communicate about their brand, showcase their products, and create a great experience for customers in an exciting new way.

I found that Mickey and the other CEOs I met appreciated that I made this new world accessible to them in a friendly, nonthreatening manner, rather than try to hard-sell them. Word got around, and I was able to get a lot of time with the decision makers at the nation's top retailers.

I quickly established a network of major retailers who were eager to start experimenting with the 2Market shopping CD, but we soon learned that the brick-and-mortar retailers didn't have the infrastructure to fulfill and ship orders to individual consumers. Their warehouses were set up to deliver product to their stores in large trucks. In order to build any kind of online volume, they would need to make some significant changes in facilities and processes, which would take time.

2Market didn't have a pick-and-pack operation, and third-party delivery services wouldn't be available until many years later. Even Amazon didn't have warehousing and shipping set up yet. Jeff Bezos was working out of a home office and delivering packages to the post office in his station wagon.

It turned out that the best candidates for online retailing were companies that already did a lot of catalog and telephone sales, like Lands' End or The Sharper Image. They had the people and processes in place to take orders, pack up products, and ship them. Beyond the challenge of creating fulfillment infrastructure, retailers with national networks of stores and a presence in major malls also worried that internet sales would cannibalize their store or catalog sales. I understood that concern but thought it was short-sighted. I argued that online availability would increase awareness of their products and drive traffic to their stores. If their products *weren't* available online, customers would look at competitive products that were and that could hurt store sales. A few brick-and-mortar retailers saw the potential and made deals, but most of the retailers who signed up were catalog merchants and start-ups who were willing to build out fulfillment.

By early 1996, I had lined up a great roster of brands, including Starbucks, Eddie Bauer, Bare Essentials, Godiva Chocolates, Tower Records, Omaha Steaks, L.L. Bean, and Lands' End. Not only did we make the products available on the 2Market CD, we also began to feature them in a special 2Market area on AOL's online Shopping Channel. Access speeds had improved enough that the online shopping experience, even without the CD, was getting pretty good.

But it was ironic—some of the very best retailers in the country were in the 2Market area of the AOL Shopping Channel, while the remainder of the Shopping Channel was a random collection of lesser-known brands like the Hanes-Bally underwear outlet store. Our little site-within-a-site was the hottest spot on the Shopping Channel.

This got a little awkward, because the AOL execs started to ask their salespeople why all the best retailers were in the 2Market corner of the Shopping Channel. Soon, the AOL salespeople wanted to come along with me on sales calls, and it was hard to say no because AOL was our main financial backer. When we both showed up, our potential customers were sometimes confused. They couldn't tell if they were doing business with the little company called 2Market or the big online portal called AOL. Sometimes I got frustrated, because a potential account seemed more interested in AOL than 2Market. However, that awkwardness would not last long.

Later that year, 2Market needed more money to grow, but Apple was not interested in building its e-commerce business. AOL stepped in, made an offer to buy 100 percent of 2Market, and announced plans to fold the whole 2Market operation into the AOL Shopping Channel. I saw this as a great opportunity. I knew if I could take over sales at the AOL Shopping Channel I could really ramp things up. I figured it would be good financially, because my 2Market stock would roll into AOL stock, which was publicly traded and rising quickly.

During the first year after the purchase, the 2Market staff kept on working out of San Mateo, and AOL said it would keep the office open. Then we were informed that, no, the office would be closed. If we wanted to stay on with AOL, we would have to move to the company headquarters in Sterling, Virginia, a suburb west of Washington, DC. Good ol' company policy.

If we didn't want to move, we could take a severance package.

It was an absurd policy, if you asked me. At that time, I was on the road constantly. What difference did it make where I was based? Besides, I told them, this was no time to let me go. We were right in the middle of negotiating with our major clients to renew their annual contracts with the AOL Shopping Channel, and the deals were worth around $100 million. Most of them were companies with which I had built relationships. They knew me and wanted to negotiate with me. AOL was reorganizing its sales operation and didn't even have an executive in place yet to run the show. Who would oversee the negotiations?

The senior people at 2Market had all left or moved on to other parts of the AOL business, so I had no direct manager at AOL with whom to discuss the situation. I talked with one fairly unsympathetic lawyer at AOL who didn't seem to get the practical business implications. I guess he just assumed that I would move to Virginia because AOL was so great.

I talked it over with Theo. We had only been in San Francisco for a couple years, and we had come to love it. That's where we were building our life together. Besides, the exciting action in business was on the West Coast, with all the tech start-ups. The severance package was generous and would buy me a lot of time to figure out my next move.

I took the package and started exploring new possibilities.

CHAPTER 7

explore new possibilities.

Toward the end of 1996, happily without a job, I found myself idly wondering what AOL was going to do about Shopping Channel renewals when my cell phone buzzed. I wasn't expecting a call and debated whether to answer but finally did.

"Hi. It's Myer Berlow." Myer had just come on board as an executive at AOL and would have been my boss had I not taken the severance package. I had no idea why he was calling me.

"What are you doing?" he asked.

"I'm sitting on the beach."

"Really? Why are you doing that?"

"I'm enjoying not working."

"I didn't know you had the day off."

I realized then that Myer didn't know I had quit.

"No, I left the company."

"What?" He sounded a little panicked. "You can't leave. Who's going to handle renewals for next month?"

"Well, I did leave. We didn't want to move to Virginia. AOL offered me a very nice severance package and I took it."

"Look. I'm flying out to San Francisco tomorrow. Let's sit down and talk about this."

I couldn't really refuse. Maybe Myer would have a different view on the AOL relocation policy. After all, he was critical to the company's strategy. He had spent twenty-five years in the world of advertising in agencies in Mexico City and New York before joining the Griffin Bacal agency in Los Angeles. Myer had gone through his own buyout when Griffin Bacal was purchased by DDB Worldwide Communications Group, one of the world's biggest agencies.

Then Steve Case, the founder of AOL, approached Myer and asked him to help transform AOL from a web portal into a content provider, powered by advertising sales. The move to AOL marked a big change for Myer, from advertising to tech, and it was a big change for AOL, too, which had been founded almost altruistically to provide people with internet access. AOL had tried lots of ways to increase revenue. In addition to offering Time Inc. content, it had created a Hollywood studio project called Entertainment Asylum. None of those ideas had produced as much income as hoped, so now AOL was going to make money and do it by becoming an advertising medium.

Myer Berlow was the guy who was going to make it happen, but he obviously knew he needed as much help as he could get.

All of this background information was running through my mind when we met in San Francisco. Myer tried to hire me back. He offered a bigger salary and more stock options. He told me that he needed me on his team. He was excited about AOL's prospects. He said he would work it out with legal and HR. I said I would do it, but since I had done my best to avoid this situation and stay with the company, I had no intention of giving up the severance package. If he rehired me, it would be just like hiring someone new. Except, of course, I knew all the customers and how to handle the renewals.

Myer agreed. "Absolutely. I'll get back to you."

Myer set up a date to meet with an AOL lawyer and go over the paperwork. Unfortunately, it was the same lawyer who had been unsympathetic before.

He dug in his heels. "You can't be rehired without giving back the severance payment."

I wasn't going to give in. "Fine," I said. "I won't come back."

Myer almost had an aneurism and started haggling with the lawyer.

As the negotiations dragged on, I got worried. Even if Myer could work out a deal, I wasn't sure I'd have enough time to secure the renewals by the end of the year when they came due.

I discussed it with Theo, and he came up with a brilliant solution. He drafted a one-page agreement that I could take to my merchant customers. It said that they would renew their deals with AOL, but only if I could reach an agreement with AOL. At my own expense, I traveled around the country to meet with my contacts and, within a few weeks, every one of the Shopping Channel customers had re-upped.

I didn't tell Myer about what I was doing, and he was getting desperate, thinking he had a disaster on his hands. Once I had all the agreements, I suggested that he hire me back as a broker, rather than as a regular employee. For compensation, I would take 5 percent of AOL's fees for the merchants I signed up. We were getting down to the wire and there was a ton of money on the line—Myer could not be sure the retailers would stick with AOL if I left. Finally, AOL legal saw the light, and we reached an agreement.

The next day, I loaded a huge stack of renewal contracts into the fax machine, pushed SEND, and looked forward to what became the most profitable month of my life. Myer was thrilled because I had pulled off the impossible. The lawyer at AOL was livid because he felt he had been tricked. For some reason, he seemed to take it all personally. He couldn't understand the incredible disaster that I had averted for AOL. I had even increased revenue enough to more than cover my 5 percent commission.

Six months later, Myer told me that we couldn't continue the broker arrangement but he would hire me back full-time, with a raise from my previous salary, and more shares. The arrangement was fair for both sides, so I told him I would do it.

Since the time I "left" AOL several months earlier, the advertising group expanded from a handful of people to about seventy, most of whom were based in Virginia. Myer, I learned, was very different from the executives I had worked with so far in publishing, TV, and tech. He liked to call himself the "Darth Vader of AOL," because that is how he was seen by some of the original employees—the guy who was trying to kill the true AOL and turn it into a money machine, but I saw him as bringing a lot of discipline to the company so we could continue to grow.

With a bigger budget and a bigger mission, my travel schedule went nuts. I started flying all around the country to call on existing accounts or make sales pitches to potential new ones. I met with lots of the top retail and catalog merchants, including J.Crew, Bare Essentials, and a bunch of innovative newcomers. At least once a month, I had to jump on a United flight to DC to check in with Myer and other folks at headquarters. At the peak of my travels, I was logging two hundred thousand miles a year.

On the few days I was home in San Francisco, I needed a place to conduct business. All AOL employees were required to work out of an established AOL office, but there wasn't one in San Francisco. Theo and I had moved into a place on Clay Street and it had a spare room. We converted it to an office, and it became AOL's officially designated San Francisco office. When I wasn't traveling, I was constantly on the phone with accounts and staff members or handling email. I was often on a 6:00 a.m. conference call, in my pajamas, with the folks in Virginia, where it was 9:00 a.m.

After a few months, I discovered that running an "AOL office" had some odd side effects. For example, one day UPS arrived with a thousand AOL-branded umbrellas. It took a few phone calls to find out that every AOL office was receiving these promotional items, and one thousand was the minimum order. Soon after, AOL-branded notebooks arrived along with a variety of other promo items. Our garage started to look like a warehouse. I tried desperately to find someone at AOL who could stop the madness, but to no avail. One day, one of our vendors, Fossil watch, sent me a thousand watches. As part of their program to popularize the brand, they sent watches to every AOL office. When friends stopped by, I'd say, "Do you want an umbrella? Here, take a watch." But we still couldn't get rid of these things as fast as we received them.

All the travel, growth, and action were exhilarating and also exhausting. We were growing. Staff was ballooning. Online shopping was catching on. AOL was zooming. Things were moving so fast and we were growing so dramatically, I was constantly working, with all the stress and pressure that comes with that kind of job.

It was during that period that I increased my Diet Coke habit. To keep alert, to avoid getting bored, I'd pop open a can of Diet Coke. It was not unusual for me to drink ten or twelve cans a day. It was an addiction. Of course, I was hardly the only one who had a Diet Coke habit. I've met many people who always have a can at the ready. The good thing? There is no question that the addiction that took hold in those days is what would eventually lead to the creation of Hint Water years later.

On top of all that, there were other important things happening in my life that had nothing to do with my job. By 1997, Theo was feeling the urge to change up his career. He enjoyed the deals he was doing as a lawyer, but he didn't love life in a law firm. He was about to start looking for a job as general counsel at a tech start-up, figuring he could get in early with some equity in a company that might go public, but just as he was going to start his search, he got a phone call from Netscape, which had recently gone public. It wasn't exactly a start-up anymore, but it faced a huge threat from Microsoft, which was trying to crush its software business by giving away a competing product for free.

Netscape was about to launch a major online service called Netcenter and they asked Theo to be lead technology counsel for this new business, which was going to compete with AOL, Yahoo, and Microsoft. Even if he didn't make a huge amount of money on the stock, he felt that he would learn a lot being at a small company going up against massive competitors. It was a real David-versus-Goliath situation, and the company was filled with extremely young, smart, and hardworking people. I encouraged him to do it.

As soon as he gave notice to his law firm, the main partners he worked for took him into their office and let him know that they were leaving, too, and they wanted him to go with them to the new law firm. It would be a chance to be on a fast track to partner in a great firm. We talked it over and decided that Netscape was where he wanted to be, even if the law firm would be more lucrative, so in July 1997 he accepted the job at Netscape.

After a week, I knew for sure it was the right move for him. He was totally energized, working for Netscape's online portal and doing marketing deals with companies like Amazon.com and technology deals with a wide variety of companies ranging from giant IBM to tiny start-ups.

The new arrangement had a big impact on our family life. Between Theo's eighty-hour workweek and my crazy travel schedule, we didn't see much of each other. Two years flew by in a blur.

Because we were working so incredibly hard, we made sure to plan fun weekends. In 1998, I booked a room for Theo and me at the Ventana Inn in Big Sur for a long weekend. As we packed our convertible for the trip, Theo raised an eyebrow and scowled at me when he saw that I had loaded two huge whiteboards into the back seat. We were in the middle of a massive sales push to launch a new e-commerce business. I had two hundred salespeople on the case, but I still needed to coordinate with them by phone. I had laid it all out on the whiteboards and figured I could take the calls from the road and get it all done by the time we got to the hotel. Of course, the calls continued nonstop through the drive, the next day, and most of the day after that. Theo spent a lot of time hiking alone, but when it was all done, we had sold out all of our inventory, and Theo and I got to spend a whole day together in the beautiful woods along the coast.

In February 1999, I gave birth to our first child, Emma. We decided we needed more room, so we moved again, this time to a house on Scott and Jackson, a few blocks from the Clay Street place. We didn't need a home workspace, however, because by then AOL had opened an office on Montgomery Street downtown and I had a nice corner space there. (We had a yard sale to sell off all the umbrellas and watches and that paid for the move!)

Later that year, Netscape was acquired by AOL, which meant that Theo and I ended up working for the same company for a brief time. He worked on the merger transition team and was asked to interview for jobs in AOL's Business Affairs group, but I had some concerns about some of the people involved and I strongly recommended against it. Theo decided to take a severance package from Netscape after the merger closed, to work on the remodel of our new house and to enjoy some time with baby Emma. About a year later, we learned that I was pregnant with our second child.

Then, in 2000, came an event that dramatically changed the media landscape and ultimately changed my life forever—the merger of AOL and Time Warner. At the time, it was the largest merger in history, a $165 billion deal that created AOL Time Warner. The market value of the new company was estimated at $342 billion, making it the fourth-most-valuable company in the United States at the time. It seemed that AOL had taken over everything in my life, having bought three of my former employers: CNN, 2Market, and Time Inc.

I saw the merger as an opportunity, not to experience life inside an even bigger hierarchy, but to take my next step. At AOL, I'd learned I was happiest as a creator, not a manager. I felt most engaged when I was helping create something new. Some people are turned on by managing big organizations and reaching new growth goals. I am bored by those things. I like to come up with fresh ideas, to change things up, to surprise people. To figure new things out.

With the merger, because of some details Theo had negotiated, all my stock vested and I was able to cash out. I had had an amazing run—our revenue from e-commerce had reached about a billion dollars. I left the company in early 2001 to concentrate on Emma and our second daughter, Kaitlin, who was born in January. But it didn't take long for both of us to get the itch to get back to work.

> 66 Some people are turned on by managing big organizations and reaching new growth goals. I am bored by those things. I like to come up with fresh ideas, to change things up, to surprise people. 99

Not long after Kaitlin's birth, several of my old competitors sought me out to see if I was interested in a job. While it felt great to be in demand, I didn't want to do more of the same. I came to the same conclusion that so many entrepreneurs do: if you're not pursuing your passion, all that time on the airplane and on early morning conference calls is a waste of time, energy, and life itself.

I was just starting to consider what might come next when I discovered I was three months pregnant with our third child. This was something we were planning, but didn't expect to happen so soon. Still, we were excited about the future, until early one morning, the entire world changed.

I turned on the TV to an image of One World Trade Center, the "North Tower," belching smoke out of a huge gash in its side. Theo and I watched in disbelief and horror as a second plane hit Two World Trade Center, the "South Tower." With many of our friends and Theo's parents, sister, and extended family living in New York, we immediately picked up the phone, only to hear repeatedly, "All circuits are busy." Eventually, we learned our family and closest friends were safe. But we soon heard stories of friends of friends who had been swallowed up as the towers collapsed into an enormous pile of rubble. For weeks, all we saw on TV was footage of the disaster and its excruciating aftermath. We struggled to understand the insanity that had driven a group of men to such a cowardly, unthinkable act. And with our third baby on the way, we wondered what kind of world we were bringing our children into.

It made me resolve that, whatever I did next, I was committed to making a positive difference in the world.

After my son, Keenan, was born in March 2002, the sense lingered that the world had fundamentally changed following the World Trade Center attacks.

I kept thinking about what had happened, what it meant for the country and the world and, with three kids counting on me, what it meant for our family. Young men and young women were being sent overseas to serve. I worried for them.

How would I feel if my son or daughters were deployed one day?

I thought more and more about how the actions we take in our lives should contribute in a positive way—to our families, to our society, and to the world as a whole.

Theo, too, had similar feelings. In 2000, he had been drawn into the world of healthcare. His father, Howard Goldin, was a distinguished and well-known gastroenterologist and clinical professor of medicine at New York Hospital/Cornell Medical College. One of

Dr. Goldin's friends, Dr. David Zakim, was at the early stages of creating a start-up called ZMedix, based in San Francisco. Dr. Zakim envisioned using artificial intelligence to interview patients before they arrived at the doctor's office. The goal was to gather better, more complete information and enable doctors to address health problems before they became severe, debilitating illnesses. Early prototypes looked promising.

> 66 I thought more and more about how
> the actions we take in our lives should
> contribute in a positive way—to our
> families, to our society, and to the world
> as a whole. 99

Theo was intrigued by the idea, but had other opportunities as well. A former colleague at Netscape had joined a start-up called Google as head of sales, and they needed an in-house legal counsel. Theo was well qualified for the job. It was tempting to jump back in to a world he knew very well, but he really wanted to go beyond law and deal-making, so he accepted a job as CEO of ZMedix. He had some familiarity with the world of healthcare, because of his father's work and because he had worked with Dr. Zakim during high school and college doing molecular biology research.

Theo saw the opportunity at ZMedix as an exciting challenge, and one that wouldn't require him to work eighty hours a week as he had at Netscape. Although he had thrived on the excitement of fast-paced deal-making, he had seen the toll it could take on young families. He didn't want to put us in that situation just as we were figuring out how to be parents. He would have made an incredible amount of money at Google, but it was clearly one of the best decisions either of us has made. Family first.

Theo started at ZMedix in August 2000, and I found the work interesting and relevant to me personally. My first experience with childbirth, back in 1999, had been difficult and made me think more deeply about healthcare. Like a lot of first-time mothers, I learned as much as I could about pregnancy, but you can't know everything about what to expect when you're expecting.

For most of my pregnancy, there were no complications and I kept working and traveling nonstop. I was so committed to the job that I even made a trip to China when I was about seven and a half months pregnant with my first child, Emma. Myer, my boss, had been invited to speak about online shopping at a conference in Shanghai, hosted by Compaq, the computer company. At the last minute, Myer couldn't go and asked me to fill in for him. Dr. Goldin, my father-in-law, wasn't thrilled by the idea. As a specialist in gastroenterology, he knew the problems I could have with digestion and potentially disease when traveling in China. China was still considered by many to be very third world. He advised me to bring drinking water and fresh fruit, which I did. (An early hint of what was to come?)

It was my first trip to China, to Asia, or to any developing country, for that matter. I was one of the few Americans at the conference, the only female speaker, the only pregnant woman, and definitely the only redhead. After I spoke, I attended a fancy dinner with the senior executives of the company. I didn't want to eat anything that might upset my system, but I couldn't really say no.

I was doing fine until one of my tablemates, a Compaq exec who spoke excellent Mandarin, got into a long conversation with the waiter, obviously ordering some kind of special meal. It soon arrived in a big covered dish. When he took the top off, I almost lost it right there at the table. Eyeballs. The bowl was filled with eyeballs. I very politely excused myself, saying I was not feeling 100 percent, and of course my hosts graciously asked if they could help and wished me well.

That was one of the few times that I put my own health needs before the demands of work.

The rest of the pregnancy went fine until the very end. There were complications that put both my baby and me at serious risk. After my water broke, I sensed something was wrong. I went to the hospital and spent fifteen hours waiting to give birth. They gave me a drug to induce labor and tried to get me to push out the baby. But my heart rate dropped and so did the baby's. The nurses couldn't locate my ob-gyn, so the obstetrician who had opened the hospital, Dr. Laurie Green, rushed in to do an emergency C-section. Both doctors arrived at the same moment and got into an altercation about who would do the surgery. I was lying there doped up with morphine. I found out later that Theo was incredibly worried because he had been told that we might not make it.

Both Emma and I came through the surgery with no further problems. The next day, they got me up so I could take a walk along the corridor with Theo. After a few minutes, he suddenly went pale.

"Let's go back to the room; I think you should lie down."

"No, I'm fine, let's keep going."

He insisted. I got back to the room, looked down at my hospital gown, and saw blood everywhere. I had gotten an infection and my incision had opened up, putting me in danger again.

It was a close call. I was exhausted. I had to regain my strength and look after my new baby, Emma. Obviously, my recovery was going to take longer than two weeks. I told AOL I didn't know how long I would be out. They didn't have much choice but to say okay. The powers that be clearly weren't happy that their female exec and top salesperson would be out of commission for an extended period. There were very few women in tech at that time, and almost none were in senior positions. Most already had kids if they were planning to have them. Tech firms in general weren't known for their employee-friendly policies.

They wanted you to work long hours and have few other priorities. That does not fit well with new parenthood.

It took about three months for us to establish a good care routine for Emma and for me to feel well enough to go back to work. When I got there, I found somebody else sitting in my office. All my stuff had been moved into storage. Eventually, they managed to find me another space, minus the view and with less square footage.

This is what I get for being pregnant?

That episode at AOL was a turning point for me. From the summer of 1999 through the end of 2000, I showed up and did my job, but I didn't feel great about the way I was being treated. I had been with the company since the early days when the channel strategy was developed and had helped build the business from zero to a billion dollars. Now management looked at me like I was a problem.

In addition to the displacement from my office, I had some contract disagreements with AOL. My contract stipulated that I would receive a bonus for any new retailers I signed up for AOL's Shopping Channel. Now there were quibbles about how to calculate the bonus and which particular retailers I would get paid for. We finally reached an agreement, but the whole episode made me wonder.

Is this an acceptable way to treat the people who helped make the business what it was today? It was time to move on.

But it wasn't just a new job I wanted. I was wondering about how I could make that positive contribution to the world.

The answer was not at all what I expected.

CHAPTER 8

find the personal path.

The intense pace of work at AOL and the rigors of two pregnancies in quick succession had taken their toll.

Although there had been no problems with Keenan's birth, I didn't bounce back from the pregnancy as quickly or as well as I had from Kaitlin's a year earlier. I felt exhausted all the time. Although I had gained weight after each previous birth, I had been able to lose most of it. Now, I couldn't lose any of it. I was up fifty pounds from my normal weight. My skin didn't look as youthful as it used to. I started to break out and developed a serious case of adult acne.

I tried all kinds of remedies. Nothing worked.

I went to several doctors who came highly recommended and told them I was feeling drained, that I couldn't lose the birth weight, and my skin was breaking out. Their diagnosis was that my three pregnancies, one a year for three years, had thrown my system out of whack. My metabolism had slowed down. My hormones had been affected. I probably shouldn't have had three babies so close together.

I couldn't do anything about that.

I saw two other specialists who had basically the same advice to offer. They talked about the effects of the three births and the natural process of aging, about weight gain, and about hormonal changes. The final doctor I saw suggested I go on a course of drugs to "reset" my hormones, whatever that might mean.

Something didn't seem right about any of this advice. It struck me that none of the doctors had asked me about my lifestyle—diet, exercise, and work habits.

There's something going on with my body, I thought, *and I have to figure it out. I can't change the pregnancies but I can control a lot of things about my health, and I am not ready to go on meds.*

I started paying closer attention to my diet, shopping at Whole Foods and buying organic foods, but none of that seemed to help. I was working out almost every day with Theo, and while I did feel like I was getting in better shape, I wasn't losing weight and my skin wasn't clearing up. Worst of all, I just felt tired a lot of the time.

One day, I caught myself thinking about cookies as I put down my Diet Coke. I realized that after every Diet Coke I would grab something sweet. A small cookie here. A piece of a muffin there. It was adding up throughout the day. Maybe my Diet Coke was making me crave sweet things, even though it didn't have any calories itself. I took a look at the ingredients and, in addition to diet sweetener and preservatives, it had phosphoric acid, which I learned can reduce bone density, and caramel color, which is considered a carcinogen.

Maybe, I thought, *I should try giving up my diet soda addiction for a while.*

I decided to go cold turkey on diet soda and drink water instead.

When I told Theo, he was skeptical that I could do it. "That's not going to be easy for you. You've been drinking soda since you were a teenager. Why not just cut back? Drink a couple sodas a day, not ten."

"No. I'll still have the craving for more. If I drink one, I'll want another one. It's better to stop completely."

He shook his head. "Good luck."

I cut out diet soda completely and set an ambitious goal: eight glasses of water a day. I would fill the glasses and line them up on the kitchen counter.

You cannot go to bed until you have emptied all eight glasses, I told myself.

I drank water religiously for a couple weeks, but it was torture. I did not like the non-taste of water. It was *so* boring, and I kept opening the fridge as if I would find something better, but I had thrown out the soda, juice, and everything else that tasted sweet. Undaunted, I forced myself to keep going. I didn't touch a single Diet Coke. I drank my eight glasses of water a day. I stayed away from artificial ingredients and did my best to avoid sweets altogether.

> 66 I kept opening the fridge as if I would find something better, but I had thrown out the soda, juice, and everything else that tasted sweet. 99

Gradually, I noticed a little bounce of energy. I started to feel better in general. I felt like walking and exercising more. My acne started to clear up. My clothes felt a little looser. My energy level continued to improve.

I didn't know how well the water was working until I was out walking one day and ran into a friend I hadn't seen in a while.

"Gosh," she said. "Have you lost weight? You look good."

"What? Really?" I hadn't been thinking about losing weight so much as just feeling better.

Back home, I hopped on the scale. I was down twenty pounds in just two and a half weeks. If you have ever tried to lose weight, you know that's a lot in a short time.

I told Theo I had lost twenty pounds. "I can tell. Your skin looks better, too. How are you feeling?"

"I feel good!"

I told him I wanted to lose all the extra weight and get back to feeling like my old self. That I was resolved to keep going with my healthy food and water-only regimen.

"There's only one problem," I told him.

"What's that?"

"Water is so boring! I can barely stand it." If I was going to stick with it, I had to find a way to love drinking water.

One day, I looked at the bowl of fruit on the counter and found my answer. I grabbed a lemon, sliced it up, and put a few slices in a pitcher of water. Over the next week, I rotated through various fruits, putting a few slices in water or smashing up a berry and letting it sit in the fridge overnight. The infusion of fruit flavor made it much easier to drink my eight glasses of water a day.

I no longer stocked soda or juice boxes in the fridge, so eventually Theo, Emma, and Kaitlin had little choice but to try a glass of my fruit-infused water. They liked it.

The family members weighed in with their comments about the flavors they liked and didn't like. Emma was a fan of raspberry. Kaitlin preferred strawberry and kiwi. Theo and I liked them all.

I kept pitchers of our fruit-infused water in the fridge and offered it to any guests, adults or kids alike, who came by. They all said they liked the taste. I remember one mom in particular who called to ask where she could buy "the raspberry water her daughter had liked at our house." She told me she had looked in all the stores for it and had bought every raspberry-flavored water brand she could find. But with every one of them, her daughter would take a sip, wrinkle up her nose, and say, "Nope, that's not it."

I laughed and told her it wasn't from the store. "I make it at home."

"Oh. How much sugar do you add?"

"None."

She couldn't believe it. "That's weird. My daughter only likes sweet drinks."

One day when I was shopping at Whole Foods, I took a detour through the water aisle. There were lots of different types of water, from plain spring water to vitamin waters. There were some flavored seltzer waters, but they were made with artificial fruit flavors and most contained sodium. The vitamin waters also had preservatives and a lot of sugar. (No diet vitamin waters were available then.)

I approached a Whole Foods clerk who was stocking the aisle. "Do you sell a water with real fruit, no sugar, and no sweeteners of any kind?"

The guy hesitated, then pulled a vitamin water off the shelf. We looked at the label together. Water, vitamins, cane sugar, crystalline fructose. No real fruit. Lots of added sugar. We looked at a number of the carbonated seltzers with fruit flavoring. One popular orange-flavored brand had thirty-two grams of sugar and the flavor came from orange juice concentrate. The rest of the aisle was filled with many different brands of unflavored and sparkling water.

There was nothing like my homemade, sweetener-free, fruit-infused water. My question just popped out. "If I develop a water that's flavored with real fruit and has no sweeteners, would you stock it?"

The Whole Foods guy couldn't tell if I was serious. He had no idea who I was. He looked at me, thought about it for a couple seconds, and shrugged. "Sure. Why not? We could give it a try."

That struck me. I went home and kept thinking about my conversation in Whole Foods. My homemade drink, containing only water, fruit, and no sweeteners, had solved a health problem for me. Just by drinking plain, good-tasting water, I increased my energy, improved my mood, cleared up my skin, and lost fifty pounds. Plus, I liked the taste, which is more than I could say for plain water, and plenty of other people liked it, too.

> " My question just popped out. "If I develop a water that's flavored with real fruit and has no sweeteners, would you stock it?" "

It kept growing from there. I was working out at the local health club regularly and would fill my water bottle with my fruit-infused drink. One day, after my workout, a gym friend asked what I was drinking.

"Cucumber-infused water."

"Really? Where do you buy that?"

"I don't buy it." I laughed. "I make it."

My friend looked intrigued and that was another *aha* moment for me.

People should be able to buy something like this, I thought. *Could this be an idea for a product? Would people actually buy it?*

I knew nothing about producing a beverage for sale, but I did have a deep feeling I could develop something healthy and positive and that there was nothing else quite like it currently available.

find the personal path.

This might be the opportunity to make a difference in the world that I've been searching for. I could help make people healthier and feel better.

That kind of feeling doesn't come along very often.

When it does, I decided, you should not ignore it.

You may be looking at a new path forward.

CHAPTER 9

just get started.

wasn't thinking about founding a company or building a business. Nor did I picture myself as a national advocate for health or dream of being recognized as a leading entrepreneur. And I certainly had no vision of becoming a major player in the beverage industry.

I was just focused on one goal.

That's usually how a business gets off the ground successfully, even ones with a lot of capital behind them. The founders of *Time* magazine, for example, wanted to create a news magazine that a busy person could read in an hour or less. Amazon started as an online bookseller.

My goal was simple: show people that drinks can taste good without tasting sweet. Obviously, I couldn't do that by myself, slicing up tons of fruit and filling up my fridge with pitchers of water.

I had a lot to figure out, and it wasn't like I had nothing else to do. That spring of 2004, I was looking after our three kids—Emma, five; Kaitlin, three; and Keenan, two. Theo was busy navigating the world of medical care and insurance as CEO of ZMedix. I was serving on the board of our kids' preschool and volunteering at Sausalito's Bay Area Discovery Museum, geared to children from six months to ten years old.

I was also fielding requests from tech companies who wanted me to take a job with them and come back to work full-time. Because of my experience at AOL, I had a reputation as an innovator in online shopping and e-commerce. I got calls from people at Yahoo, Google, Microsoft, and other major industry players who basically wanted me to do for them what I had already done for AOL.

I was flattered and tempted by the offers, but ultimately I turned them all down for various reasons. I didn't want to travel a lot while the kids were young. I wanted to focus on my health. I had commitments to the community.

While those things were certainly true, there was another fundamental reason I didn't pick up on any of the tech offers. It would mean doing something I already knew how to do. I didn't want to repeat myself. I wanted to do something new and potentially life-changing. Something disruptive.

That's what I had loved about my previous jobs. When I landed the position at Time Inc., I knew next to nothing about publishing, sales, circulation, corporate empires, management, or New York City. When I started at CNN, I knew little about television, cable news, big-name entrepreneurs and movie-star activists, or fast-growing media companies. When I joined 2Market and eventually AOL, nobody—including me—knew much about the internet, online shopping, tech start-ups, or megamergers.

I had been attracted to each new position precisely because I *didn't* have all the answers about the business or the job. Each one presented me with an opportunity to gain experience and to learn. If I took another tech position related to online shopping, I would probably gain a little knowledge that I didn't have before, but I didn't think it would be life-changing. In fact, I thought it would be boring.

So, as I focused on my family, staying healthy, and volunteering, I took baby steps toward creating this thing that I felt really could be meaningful. Not just for me, but for lots of people. My fruit-infused water. I didn't tell any of my friends or family about my idea to turn it into a marketable product. I didn't even tell Theo the extent of my thinking. He thought I was just having fun "screwing around in the kitchen," as he put it. And that's pretty much what I was doing, because I definitely didn't have a product that was ready to go in a store. But I felt that there was something there, and I kept tinkering.

 Each one presented me with an opportunity to gain experience and to learn.

One of my first steps was to figure out how to make the water a little more attractive. Fresh fruit floating in water looks pretty nice, but to get the flavor into the water I had to let it sit for a day or two in the fridge, and with berries I had to muddle up the fruit. If I drank it too soon, it didn't have enough flavor, and if I waited too long, it ended up looking kind of smeggy, like the fruit was disintegrating or rotting. Not exactly appetizing. If I took the fruit out of the water after the flavor got to the right point, the water would stay good in the fridge a bit longer, but not very long.

The big question became how to get the right amount of flavor without letting the fruit sit in the water.

I did some research on the internet and learned that there were companies that made fruit essences used as flavorings for foods and beverages. I ordered samples and soon had a collection of little glass bottles. I would choose an essence, squeeze a few drops into a glass of cold water, take a sip, then make notes about the flavor. The notes turned out to be pretty much a waste of time, since almost all the flavors ranged from terrible to merely okay. They did not taste like real fresh fruit.

I also tried some essences from a small supplier that marketed its products directly to consumers as flavorings for water. When I got the samples, I was disappointed to see they had some artificial flavors along with the natural essences, but I tried them anyway. Although they didn't have the natural taste I was looking for, they were a bit closer than the natural essence samples I had received from the big flavor companies. I thought maybe the company could help me formulate a better natural essence flavor.

I called the company and was surprised to get the owner on the phone. Turns out the flavor business was a side project for him, and he bought the flavors from an independent consultant. I asked if he thought he could work with his flavor guy to make the type of flavor I was looking for.

"You know, I'm pretty sure he can help you, but this isn't really what I do." There was silence for a moment. "Why don't I just put you in touch with him directly?"

I thanked him, because it was a generous thing to do. I got in touch with the consultant. He couldn't help me right away but we had an incredibly helpful conversation, and he got me thinking about flavors in a totally different way. Ultimately, what I learned helped us come up with the recipes for our initial products.

Meanwhile, in July, I got a bad chest cold and by August I had started taking a course of antibiotics. I couldn't taste a thing, so I took a break from concocting recipes and focused on learning more about the industry. The biggest unknown for me was bottling. How would I make the leap from making up small batches of water in my kitchen to producing it in quantity and bottling it? I had no idea.

I had never been involved in the creation of a physical product before, so I started to research bottle designers and bottling companies to see if there were companies who would work with a start-up. I collared anybody with a connection to the food and beverage industry and peppered them with questions. I picked up industry jargon along the way. I learned, for example, that in beverage-industry-speak, a bottle cap is called a *closure*. Who knew? The most important term I learned was *co-packer*. I knew I would need some kind of bottling partner and had been calling bottling companies for information about their services. They all said they couldn't help me, but they didn't really explain why. Finally, a helpful guy at a bottling company enlightened me.

"You're not looking for a bottler."

"What do you mean?"

"The companies that call themselves bottlers or bottling companies are usually doing bottling and distribution. They work with big companies like Coke, Pepsi, and Dr Pepper and don't like to just make the product, especially if it's a small, unproven one. Co-packers just do bottling, and some of them are willing to work with small companies or new products."

> **❝** I was learning. Every day. That is how you stay fresh and motivated. Always be learning. An important lesson, for sure. **❞**

Co-packers, in other words, are for-hire manufacturers who work with all kinds of client companies to create branded products. You provide co-packers with your specs, and they do whatever needs to be done. Some can do everything, including sourcing ingredients, designing your label and packaging, formulating the product, filling the bottles, and shipping the cases. In addition, they have all the necessary certifications to ensure quality and safety.

This was another example of why I loved getting into this new project. At AOL, everybody was asking questions of me and expecting me to supply the answers. Now I was asking the questions. Which meant I was learning. Every day. That is how you stay fresh and motivated. Always be learning. An important lesson, for sure.

Not everybody I spoke with in the industry was as helpful or enlightening as the guy who gave me the co-packer heads-up. Just like the elite group of trainees at Time Inc., the beverage industry was a closed club that wasn't particularly interested in new ideas or different approaches.

The more questions I asked, the more convinced I became that the industry was ripe for a shake-up. The environment was so different from the tech industry that I was used to. At AOL, we knew perfectly well that we had no idea what we were doing, and we freely admitted it. We experimented all the time and learned from our mistakes as well as our successes. In the old-line beverage industry, there was none of that attitude. Time and again I heard: "That's how we always do it."

Another great thing about constant learning is that it builds confidence. Even the non-answers and rejections I got strengthened my resolve—perhaps they were the most motivating of all. Some of my favorite success stories are about people who are initially laughed at for their ideas or discouraged from pursuing their dreams. One famous example is Paul McCartney, whose grammar school music teacher told him to forget about becoming a professional musician, because he couldn't read music. (He still doesn't.) An example in my own family is a niece who was a talented soccer player. She loved the game, but one of her high school coaches told her she was too short to be a standout player and advised her to take up some other sport. That just made her more determined. She trained hard, became a star on the team, then had a growth spurt, played college soccer, and even played pro.

I'm the same way. Tell me I can't do something I want to do, and I want to do it even more. So, the "noes" and "you can't do thats" I got from beverage industry people just had an energizing effect on me.

One day in September 2004, I realized that I had learned enough and had confidence enough to make my vision a reality.

You can do this, I said to myself. *You're smart. You can figure it out. And you can help people by helping them enjoy water.*

> 66 You can do this, I said to myself. You're smart. You can figure it out. And you can help people by helping them enjoy water. 99

I sat down and wrote up a short business plan, a road map for what I wanted to do. I still had not told Theo I was doing this. I didn't want to present him with the idea until I felt it would work, and now I knew enough to believe it was possible.

Before I broke the news to him, there was something else I had to check out. I hadn't been feeling well for the past week, nauseous in the morning and draggy all day long. A quick trip to the drugstore confirmed my suspicion: I was pregnant, despite having been on the pill since our third child was born. I called my doctor, and after a few quick questions, she told me that the antibiotics I had been taking for my cold may have cancelled out the effect of the birth control pills. Evidently, that's a thing, but it was news to me.

I had always talked about having a lot of kids, so having a fourth seemed like a nice surprise, except that we were just getting past the diapers-and-stroller phase of life. While Theo loves being a father, he is not a huge fan of surprises. I got home before he did and sat down to think through how I was going to play this. He walked in a few minutes later, and before he could say hello, I said, "Theo, sit down." From the deeply concerned look on his face as he took a seat, I realized I must have put a lot of energy into that statement.

"Okay, listen. You know the flavored water I've been playing around with? I'm going to start a company, and I think I can launch the first products in about eight months, which is right around when we're going to have our fourth child, so I'm going to need your help."

> **66** I've figured out a lot of stuff in my life. I can figure this out. And if it turns out I can't, at least I can put this idea out there, that you can enjoy things that don't taste sweet. Someone has to do that. **99**

Silence. Blank look.

I kept rolling. "I've looked at all of the grocery stores from Whole Foods in San Francisco to King Kullen in New York, and there is no good-tasting, unsweetened flavored water. I've done enough research to know we can make water taste great without tasting sweet, and I think we can figure out the rest of the details in time to launch by April."

"Hold on," Theo said. "What did you say?"

"You know, the flavored water I've been playing around with . . ."

"No. The kid."

"Oh. Right. We're having a fourth child!" I explained about the antibiotics and birth control pills.

"Okay, you're telling me you're going to have a child and start a beverage company at the same time?"

"Right. Which is why I'm going to need help."

"But what do you know about the beverage industry?"

I described the research I had done and why I thought we could develop the right flavors.

"But what do you know about starting a beverage company?"

"Not that much. But I've figured out a lot of stuff in my life. I can figure this out. And if it turns out I can't, at least I can put this idea out there, that you can enjoy things that don't taste sweet. Someone has to do that."

Silence.

The next few days were a bit tense. I tend to take in information and make decisions extremely quickly, while Theo has a longer, more detailed decision-making process. I knew that he would ultimately be supportive and extremely helpful, but realized I needed to give him some space to sort things through. I just wasn't sure how long it would take, so I kept going on the research.

A week or so later, I was sitting at the kitchen table reading about beverages on my computer when Theo came in from playing with the kids in the backyard.

He said simply, "Okay. I'll help."

I tilted my head to the side of the computer so I could look him in the eye as he continued.

"What I've been working on with Dr. Zakim is meant to improve health in America, but if we could help even a small number of people fall in love with water, with no sugar or sweeteners, I think that will have a bigger impact than anything I can do with computers or AI." The main thing I heard was that word *we*. I jumped up and gave him a big hug.

"Oh, and the kid will be great. We're already playing zone defense with three kids, so what's one more?"

Theo and I had always brought work home and had always helped each other with our careers, but all of a sudden we found ourselves embarking on a mission together, to help America fall in love with water. It felt right to be doing this with my husband, my best friend, and now my business partner.

Over the next few years, the most common question I got about the business was, "What's it like working with your spouse?" For us, it just made sense and it worked great from day one, because in so many ways we had always worked together.

One of the first things we worked on was naming the product. I had initially planned to call it WaWa. Most likely because I had been living in a world of kids, parks, and play groups for the past few years, and *wawa* was how my kids had pronounced "water" when they were learning to talk. I liked the name, but I didn't want to give the impression that the product was meant exclusively for kids.

Then Theo, in his IP lawyer mode, realized that the name wasn't going to fly because of legal issues. There was a convenience-store chain, based in Pennsylvania, called WaWa. If we named our product WaWa and it took off, Theo said the company would come after us for infringing on their trademark.

The next idea I had was "hint." I liked it because it was a simple, four-letter English word that could be used a lot of ways. For example, you can give people a hint. They can take a hint. What I was trying to do was help people drink water instead of sugary drinks. Later, we launched with the trademark Hint: Drink Water, Not Sugar.

Initially, Theo shook his head and said "hint" was going to be a long shot. A few products already used the word *hint* as part of a trademark, although none of the ones he showed me seemed to be widely distributed. There were also some products using the word *hint* as a descriptive term. I recognized the risk, but it isn't easy finding a good trademark. I didn't want to settle for something safe. Sometimes you have to take a chance.

"We need a great name," I told Theo, "so unless you've got an-other winning idea, go ahead and file it and let's see what happens."

Theo applied for the trademark in late October, but we wouldn't know if we had secured the mark until after launching. He cautioned that using Hint as the product name meant we would have to be careful to avoid using it descriptively (as in "hint of flavor") because that would undermine its status as a trademark. To this day, I still find myself correcting new employees who make that mistake.

Now we were down to seven months before my due date, and I wanted to make sure we had product to launch in stores before the baby arrived.

I had settled on an initial source for natural essences, and Theo and I spent most of the rest of the year tinkering with flavors. The consultant helped me understand why essences don't taste like real fruit. There are many elements that make up the taste of a great piece of fruit. They are subtle and present in tiny quantities, which makes them hard to extract. We experimented with blending tiny amounts of essences from several fruits, vegetables, and other plants to get closer and closer to the natural taste we were going for.

Those early flavors were not even close to the ones we produce today, but they were way better than anything available on the market. We proclaimed a few of them to be "final" (at least for the time being) and turned our attention to designing the bottle and looking for a co-packer. I got in touch with several co-packers and told them I had developed a new line of unsweetened flavored water. I asked if they would be interested in doing a test bottling of a thousand cases. The only answers I got were "No," "No way," and "That's been tried before and it isn't going to work."

I had no leverage with them. I was an unknown in the industry, an individual, not a company, with no experience in beverages. The bottlers I spoke with didn't seem to believe it would be possible to make a beverage people would like without sugar or sweeteners. They implied that a thousand cases was way too small a run for them to bother with. One of them at least took the time to explain that it takes a lot of work to set up a production facility to handle a new product and that they needed to feel like it would be worth their while. Ideally, co-packers want to partner with big clients to produce well-known brand-name products that will ensure a steady stream of business for them over a period of years. That's how they maximize the efficiency of the plant and make the most profit. I understood, but I wasn't going to take no for an answer.

Many of my calls to co-packers weren't returned. Some of them hung up on me. Then, in November, I got lucky. I connected with a relatively small co-packing operation in Chicago that manufactured a range of food and beverage products. It was woman-owned, which I liked, and I went through my pitch with Lisa. Fruit extract. No preservatives. No diet sweeteners or sugar. She was interested. She said they used a "cold fill" bottling process, which would ensure that the fruit flavor wasn't altered by heating. She also agreed to accommodate a short run, at least for the test. Lisa was a great resource, putting us in touch with a company that could make bottles for us and providing contacts for a closure manufacturer, a box manufacturer, and a label company.

We scheduled an initial production run for early April 2005, since it was going to take a while to get everything lined up. The next four months flew by. We finalized our formulas. We designed a unique bottle, which looked a bit like an old-fashioned medicine bottle and worked well with the equipment at Lisa's plant. And we settled on a closure, a clear, twist-open sport-cap, custom made for Hint.

For the labels, I decided to work with a designer from outside the beverage industry, because I didn't want it to look like every other beverage package out there. My friend Sue Nahley Fleishman at Universal Studios connected me with Dominic Symons at Bluelounge, an amazing designer who had done everything from movie posters to Nike shoes, but hadn't done a beverage label. I loved his blend of creativity and practicality, and we quickly arrived at a label design with delicious fruit imagery. At last we could hold a mock-up of the actual product in our hands. It was starting to feel real.

I was committed and excited. I had newfound resolve and some funds in the bank to pay for the initial materials and run. In April, Theo and I flew to Chicago and watched as the first bottles of Hint came off the line. I have to say, seeing our physical product moving on the line was exhilarating, even though I was almost eight months pregnant and felt like I might give birth at any moment.

People ask me, "How did you create a whole new category of beverage while pregnant and with a budget of only $50,000?" The truth is, I did it pretty badly. It would take many, many millions of dollars and fifteen years to get from that point to where we are today, but I did accomplish my goal of making something that people could hold in their hand, that they could drink, and that could help them fall in love with water. That was the beginning, not the end, and I'm here to tell you that, sometimes, if you think too much about the end, you will never get past the beginning.

> **That was the beginning, not the end, and I'm here to tell you that, sometimes, if you think too much about the end, you will never get past the beginning.**

We had asked for and received a lot of help to get to the first run. As the plane took off to take us back to San Francisco, I knew we would need a lot more. As an entrepreneur, you can't be afraid to ask for help. I've found that when I let people know what I'm trying to do, why I'm doing it, and very specifically what I would like from them, they usually are more than happy to share what they can.

Often, what I needed was just information and advice. That's what we were looking for when we invited Josh Dorf to come over to our house one afternoon. He is the CEO of Stone-Buhr, an organic whole wheat flour company his family founded back in 1908. We had been introduced through a mutual AOL friend. We told Josh about our idea, what we wanted to do, and asked for his advice. He listened, but seemed baffled. "I don't really know how to help you guys," he said. "In the flour industry, we have only a few competitors. In the beverage industry, you're going to have a lot. I don't know why you guys would even want to get into that business."

"I understand," I told him. "But there is no product like this one on the market."

I proceeded to ask him a million questions about the food and beverage industry. The piece I hadn't really figured out was how to get the product into stores. Now that we were in production, we had to find places that would sell it. All we had was a vague commitment from one guy in one Whole Foods store in San Francisco.

Josh laughed. "Well, in the end, it's really just pick-and-shovel work."

"What do you mean?"

"You just keep picking away at it. You make your delivery to Whole Foods, and that will be great. Then you might get kicked out of Whole Foods. But by then you've gotten yourself into a few other stores in a region. That's why it's critical to constantly make new relationships with stores and other places that might be potential outlets for your product. You'll connect with a big distributor like UNFI and they'll broaden your reach and help you get into more stores. But some of those stores may eventually kick you off the shelf, which is why you always want to have others to work with. You take two steps forward and one step back. All the time. Then one day you're in lots of places, and you're hopefully not losing too much money, and you're on your way. It's waking up early every single day and fixing a bunch of problems you have fixed before."

"This is the craziest business."

"Yeah, and you guys are crazy to get into it."

I nodded. We probably were.

CHAPTER 10

test the market.

R ight before the Chicago test run, I made a great connection with the event planner at the arts and culture magazine *Black-book*. They were planning to host a major party at the Tribeca Film Festival, the biggest film industry event in New York, which ran for a couple weeks in late April. I knew that these industry parties attracted large and influential audiences and could be great platforms for introducing a new brand. You donate product, people try it, they see your logo, they talk it up, all of which can lead to great exposure, new connections, and sales. But it doesn't do much good to showcase a new product and get great buzz if people can't buy it anywhere.

When we lived in New York, we sometimes shopped at a cool natural grocery store called Gourmet Garage, located not far from where the *Blackbook* party would be. It was one of many tiny natural food stores in Manhattan before Whole Foods came to the city. (Gourmet Garage eventually tried to expand into a chain, but it was too late to

compete with Whole Foods.) As soon as we completed our test production run, I had our co-packer send samples directly to the store.

When we got back to San Francisco, I called the store and was
connected to Kara Rubin, the grocery buyer. I told her that my
name was Kara, too, and that my husband and I used to live in New
York and had enjoyed shopping at the Gourmet Garage. I explained
about Hint and what we wanted to do with it at the party. She asked
me to send some samples and I told her that I had already sent them
and they would be arriving that day. She called back later, said she
loved the product, and they would be happy to stock it. I don't know
if it was the product, the fact that we had the same name, or something else, but I've never had an easier time getting to "yes" before
or since then. I smiled ear to ear.

"Who's your distributor in the New York area?" she asked.

Of course, we didn't have a distributor in New York or anywhere
else, so I told her I'd FedEx some cases to her. She said okay, and
that if it all worked out and they needed a regular supply, she would
get us in touch with a local distributor. "It's crazy to ship cases of
water by FedEx."

I thanked her, and we said goodbye. When I told Theo about our
big win, he asked, "How much are they going to pay?"

I had neglected to bring up the issue of payment. I called Kara
back. We made a deal. Theo created our first invoice in Excel, since
we had no formal billing system in place. Or any systems, for that
matter.

Over the next month, Theo continued working with ZMedix
and had a lot to get done before the baby arrived. I was feeling
super-ready to deliver our fourth child. Everywhere I went, people
were asking me when the baby was due. "Not soon enough," I would
tell them. But I still had a few things I wanted to accomplish before
the birth.

We received a few cases from the Chicago bottler, so I decided to
give out some samples to retailers in the area. Of course, the first
place I stopped was our local Whole Foods. I found the manager I

had talked to in the fall and told him that we had produced our first run of product and the full shipment would be arriving in a couple weeks. He seemed surprised to hear that I had created the product, and then I pulled out a cold bottle for him to try. He seemed curious, but I wouldn't say he was exactly excited. He drank it and gave me a big smile, then asked a lot of questions. He wanted to know more about my industry experience, probably to see if I had any credibility or was just crazy.

"Have you worked at one of the big beverage companies?"

"Nope."

"What are the ingredients?"

"Water, natural flavor."

"Have you tested the shelf life?"

"Working on it."

"Are you distributing through UNFI?"

"Uh. No." (I didn't know who that was.)

"Then who is your distributor?"

"You're looking at her. And my husband, too."

He looked down at my gigantic baby bump and his eyes went wide. He seemed to decide it was time to level with me.

"Let me explain a bit about how we work. Normally we don't buy new products right in the store, but we try to support local companies. So it's possible we can get you set up that way, at least to sell a bit here in this store."

"Great!"

"But if the product takes off, you'll need to get a distributor and get set up with the regional grocery buyer."

"Okay!"

"Give me your email address. I'll send you some paperwork. I'll try to get you approved for this store and then it will be up to you."

Later that day, I drove out to Marin County to a store called Woodlands Market. The Whole Foods guy had mentioned that Woodlands was one of a few local stores that their regional buyers kept an eye on to make sure they didn't miss anything new and exciting. Woodlands was a wonderful natural specialty store in Kentfield, with some amazing produce and lots of unique specialty items.

I asked for the manager and soon found myself speaking with Glenn Dal Porto. I told him I was impressed with the store and that it would be a great place to sell my new, unsweetened flavored water, which would be available soon. I asked him about the store and how they worked with suppliers. I could tell he was extremely proud of his store and knew about everything in it. After talking for a bit, I pulled a cold sample out of my bag and offered him a drink. He loved the product and told me he'd be glad to give it a shot when we were ready. He didn't need a lot of information beyond the UPC codes and list of ingredients. On my way back to San Francisco, I called Theo to tell him we had lined up our third account (probably).

A few weeks later, a giant truck pulled up to our house and the guys started unloading four pallets of product. Theo wasn't home, so I waddled down the front stairs as fast as I could, afraid they were just going to leave it on the sidewalk. I must have been quite a sight, because the truck driver turned bright red and asked me if there was someone who could sign for the shipment.

"Just me."

He scratched his head. "Well, where are you going to put the pallets? And how are you going to put them there?"

After a brief conversation and a $20 tip, we came to an agreement. He gave me a couple minutes to move one of the cars out of the garage, and then they wheeled the product inside.

"You guys need to get a warehouse. I usually deliver to a loading dock. You're lucky I happen to have a liftgate on the truck. It's a miracle I could even deliver here."

He wished me good luck and drove off. I think he was just happy I didn't deliver the baby while he was delivering the pallets of water. A few minutes later, Theo arrived home, and we opened our first cases of Hint! We filled the garage fridge with as many bottles as we could fit.

That afternoon, the kids got back from school and asked why the car was in the driveway. I rolled up the garage door and showed them the pallets of Hint, and they started jumping up and down. Within minutes, they came up with a plan to sell Hint in front of the house. They found an old lemonade stand, crossed out the word *lemonade*, replaced it with the word *Hint*, and set up the stand just inside the garage door.

It was getting a bit late by the time they were ready and the fog was rolling in. Theo asked them how much they would charge.

Kaitlin thought for a second or two. "Two bucks a bottle." The other kids agreed right away.

"That sounds like a lot of money. It's late. It's getting foggy."

They were not into negotiation. "Two bucks!"

Theo shrugged. "Okay, let's see what happens."

We rolled up the garage door and two minutes later a car pulled up, and a couple got out, came over to the stand, and asked them what they were offering. The kids told them they were selling Hint Water, a new, unsweetened flavored water and that it was two bucks a bottle. The couple bought one, jumped in the car, and drove off. For reasons I cannot explain, a bunch of other cars stopped and within fifteen minutes the kids had sold twelve bottles! Mission accomplished, they decided it had gotten too cold to be standing in the garage selling Hint, and they all ran inside. When Theo asked them what they would do with the $24 they had collected, they huddled for a few minutes and then told us they would donate the money to the zoo. Theo told them that, because they were donating to a nonprofit, he would not charge them for the product. This led to a rather lengthy (mostly one-sided) discussion about pricing, the cost of goods, gross margin, and profit. The kids eventually lost interest and disappeared. Theo and I shared a Hint and celebrated our first sale.

That next week seemed to vaporize as I rushed to get the house ready for the new baby, who would be arriving by planned C-section on Friday, May 27, at 2:00 p.m. That morning, as we got out of bed,

Theo asked what I wanted to do before we headed for the hospital. "I would like to see if we can get Hint on the shelf at Whole Foods," I told him. Theo thought I was kidding. "Wouldn't you rather grab brunch or go for a walk?" I wasn't kidding. I had submitted the paperwork, but hadn't heard back. I had phoned the regional buyer but got a voice mail saying to please use email. I had emailed, but no response yet. I was out of time and wanted this to be done before I gave birth. That had been my goal all along.

> 66 That morning, as we got out of bed, Theo asked what I wanted to do before we headed for the hospital. "I would like to see if we can get Hint on the shelf at Whole Foods," I told him. 99

Theo knew that nothing was going to stop me, so off we went with a bunch of cases in the back of the Jeep. I would like to say I drove, but I was really nervous and honestly didn't fit behind the wheel all that well. I wasn't completely confident the direct approach was going to work, since I had no confirmation from the buyer, but I tried not to let that show. I remember thinking, hoping, that Whole Foods would actually take the cases. I was pretty certain the guy stocking the shelves wanted the product, and I was sure he would help clear up any delay in the paperwork. Maybe.

I realize this whole thing may sound implausible today—that a seemingly random employee could agree to take on a product from a seemingly random woman who had barely started her company. But Whole Foods was a different operation in 2005 than it is today. The chain was smaller and the company was independent, not owned by Amazon. People in the store still could make a difference, and they had a history of supporting local brands, as I had been told. So it wasn't as crazy as it might sound for me to think the guy would actually make good on his promise.

"I'm sure it'll be fine," I said as we pulled into the parking lot at Whole Foods. Theo didn't look convinced, but he loaded the cases into a shopping cart and we soon found our guy.

"Hi!" I said. "Remember me? I sent in the paperwork and here I am with your first ten cases!"

He looked me over. Remember that I was nine months pregnant and planning to give birth in a few hours. Theo tried to make himself look inconspicuous.

"Hmmm . . . You know, my manager talked to the buyer and I think it's going to work out but it can take a few weeks to get the products approved and in the system." He tried to scan a bottle using his handheld scanner, but it didn't work.

I launched into an almost frantic story.

"This is the day I've been working toward, getting Hint on the shelf before I have my fourth kid. I'm on my way to the hospital right now and I would feel so much better if you could promise me that we can get this sorted out."

He seemed confused, maybe about the fact that I knew I was having the baby that day, so I explained about the planned C-section.

"So, today's the day, and here I am on my way to the hospital."

I finally took a breath. I saw he still had a look of concern on his face, but maybe I had convinced him.

"Okay," he said. "I'm not making any promises, but you can leave the product with me. I'll see if I can sort it out while you guys sort out the baby and all that. By the way, what is a planned C-section?"

Never make decision makers feel stupid. Especially when they are making decisions about stocking your product. I gave him a quick explanation, we left the cases of Hint, gave him our cell phone number, and said goodbye. We drove to the hospital, not at all sure if Hint would end up on the Whole Foods shelves, but hoping for the best.

That afternoon, my son Justin was born without complications, and the three of us spent some time resting up in the hospital. The kids came in and met their new brother, and my mother-in-law arrived to help. We now had four kids under the age of six. What better time to start a company?

The next morning, my phone buzzed. I was still a bit wiped out, so Theo answered.

"Hello?"

Theo didn't recognize the voice. "Who's calling?" he asked.

I could faintly hear a guy's voice on the other end, but I didn't recognize it either. "Who is it?" I asked Theo.

"It's the guy from Whole Foods!" Theo whispered.

"What does he want?"

Theo looked at me. "He says all ten cases of the product are gone."

"Gone? What does that mean? Where did they go?" All kinds of possibilities raced through my mind. Maybe someone stole them? Maybe one of the big beverage companies was trying to take us down?

"Let me have the phone." I pushed myself up in bed, still sore from the operation.

"Hi, it's Kara," I said. "Who took the product?"

"The customers," the Whole Foods guy said. "We sold all ten cases yesterday and today. There's nothing left on the shelf."

"You're kidding!"

"I'm not kidding. When can you deliver some more?"

"Ahh . . ."

One delivery down. One to go.

ELEVEN

build the airplane while you're flying it.

When I speak with entrepreneurs and would-be entrepreneurs, they often ask me: "How do I know when to launch my product? How perfect does it have to be?"

The answer: perfect enough to deliver on the basic product promise.

Hint Water was far from perfect when we launched at Whole Foods. The flavors were good, but not as fresh and accurate as they would be. The labels were nice, but sometimes they came unglued and fell off. The shelf life was about three months (on a good day), nowhere as long as it needed to be to go national, but okay for local distribution.

But none of those things mattered very much, because we had the thing that really counts—a product that delivered what it promised. We said Hint was a delightfully refreshing, fruit-flavored, no-diet-sweetener, zero-calorie water unlike anything else on the market. And it was.

This is something I learned in my tech years: you have to have the basics right at launch, but you can fix everything else as you go along. You don't want your software to have any severe bugs or your hardware to catch fire. With beverages, you don't want your product to taste bad or make people sick. But if the product is basically right, you're good to go. Get out there.

Besides, there is no such thing as perfect. As soon as you launch your product, you're going to find five or ten things that need to be fixed or improved or added. With Hint, we knew we could make our flavors even better and add new ones. Obviously, the labels had to stick better. And the shelf life had to get to a year at least.

> 66 When I speak with entrepreneurs and would-be entrepreneurs, they often ask me: "How do I know when to launch my product? How perfect does it have to be?" The answer: perfect enough to deliver on the basic product promise. 99

Back in our days at AOL and Netscape, we often heard people say, "Don't be afraid to build your airplane while you're flying it." Now we were applying that mantra in a totally different setting.

To be honest, for at least the first couple years after our Whole Foods launch, it sometimes felt like we wouldn't get the airplane off the ground at all. With good reason. I learned later that the failure rate for start-ups in the beverage industry is ridiculously high. More than 90 percent fail in the first year of business. Around 99 percent fail before they reach $10 million in revenue.

But we didn't even think of ourselves as a start-up back in May 2005. And you could hardly call the test placement in Whole Foods a "launch"—at least, not the kind of launch that a major beverage manufacturer would do, with lots of advertising and promotion. But now the Whole Foods buyer was asking us for another shipment of product, as if we had a warehouse full of inventory and a local distributor who could throw it on a truck. It was nice he thought of us that way, but our warehouse was our garage and our distributor was us.

Even so, we didn't want to miss the opportunity. The Whole Foods guy made it clear that if we didn't get more product to the store, we could lose shelf space. So we checked out of the hospital a day ahead of schedule (in truth, they kicked us out because I was talking on the phone too much). The doctor had told me not to drive for two weeks while recovering from the C-section, so Theo agreed to handle deliveries, including the one to Whole Foods. He even hid the keys to the other car so I wouldn't be tempted to go out selling.

Theo loaded up the Jeep with cases from the Chicago shipment and drove them to Whole Foods. There he learned some of the basic rules of grocery retail. It was up to us, the supplier—not the store employees—to lug in the cases and stock the shelves. There is tremendous competition for shelf space, so if you don't keep a watchful eye on your real estate, you may lose it. And, most important, it's a relationship business. You need to get to know the store buyers and managers, spend time with them, learn how the store works.

While Theo stocked the shelves, he chatted with the manager. "You know," the guy said, "on the first day, several of our regular customers came in and bought one or two bottles. But one of them came back the next morning and bought a ton of it. She went on and on about how great Hint was. She said she liked how simple it tasted and that it wasn't sweet like all the other flavored drinks. You made a real fan right off the bat."

This wasn't surprising—we had seen the emotional connection people made to our homemade Hint—but it was super exciting.

While Theo was out making Hint deliveries and opening new accounts, I rested up from the delivery. I spent a lot of time with Justin and helped the older kids connect with him. By the end of the week, the kids were playing with their friends again, and I was feeling mostly back to normal. Then I started going a tiny bit stir crazy.

One day, I found myself thinking about a couple wonderful little stores that were just a few miles away and would be perfect for Hint. Theo was out for a couple hours. I wasn't supposed to drive for another week, but I felt fine. I found the car keys Theo had hidden, grabbed a few cold bottles of Hint, and headed out, leaving Justin with our babysitter.

I got a quick "yes" from one store and one "maybe" from another, which wasn't bad, and I thought I had just enough time to get home before Theo did. But as I pulled into the driveway, there was the Jeep. I knew the jig was up. I walked into the house and started talking before Theo had a chance to say a word. "I landed two new accounts!" (Remember, in my book, "maybe" means "yes.")

He started talking at the same time. "That's great! I'm not going to give you a hard time about driving, but please be careful."

Okay. I guess I didn't need to distract him. He seemed to have something urgent on his mind.

"Listen, Kara. I love Hint, and I think it might be turning into a full-time thing for me. But it's awkward."

"What do you mean? What's awkward?"

"I don't know what to say to people about what I do. What my role is. What do you think?"

build the airplane while you're flying it.

An important thing I learned while working in tech and watching start-ups grow: it's essential to have the right partners. You need people who complement your skills and fill in the gaps in your knowledge. That described Theo well. He had a strong science background, while my education was in communications and finance. He had expertise in intellectual property law, while I had experience in business development. We had both been executives in start-ups, but in different business areas. We were also alike in several ways: we both worked very hard, loved building businesses, and were committed to healthier living.

I didn't have to think too hard about having Theo as my business partner.

"How about chief operating officer?"

"COO. Sounds good."

Done. Hint officially had its first chief operating executive.

Later that month, our new COO grabbed some samples from the garage and was about to load them in the Jeep when he noticed a white cloud in the bottom of one of the bottles. He brought it in, showed me, and I got a terrible feeling in the pit of my stomach.

In a semi-panic, we called Lisa, our co-packer partner.

She had seen the same thing in one of the bottles and had sent it to a local lab for testing. The results were negative, which meant there was nothing dangerous in there, but who was going to drink from a bottle with a floating cloudlike mass sloshing around in the bottom?

Next we got on a call with Dale, Lisa's plant manager, to try to figure out the cause of the cloud. Dale said we might need to start using preservatives. That would probably solve the problem, but I was dead set against the idea. Preservatives are not natural and, for them to have the desired effect, you have to make the drink quite acidic. That would have a big, negative impact on the taste of the product.

When we got off the phone, I looked at Theo.

He knew what I was thinking. "I know. We need to solve this without using preservatives. But, to come up with a solution, first we need to really understand the problem."

Theo started by talking with the essence suppliers. They assured us their samples were clean and, besides, essences cannot support microorganisms, because they don't contain water. Next, Theo found a local lab in San Francisco that agreed to help us. They looked into the essence suppliers and the cleaning process at the bottling plant, and ruled out both as the source of the problem.

The lab concluded that the cloudy mass was caused by the presence of mold spores. They're present in the air and all around us and can easily grow in water. They told us they could be avoided by using a special bottling process that infuses ozone into the bottle right before the liquid goes in. That kills any organisms in the bottle but also affects the taste. So that wasn't an option for us. We learned about another process, used by makers of sports drinks and vitamin drinks, called *hot-fill*. The drink is pasteurized, then poured into special bottles at high temperature to sanitize the packaging. No preservatives necessary. It was expensive, but would not affect the taste. It sounded like it was worth investigating.

While Theo was making deliveries, I stopped by Whole Foods to see if I could find out about any hot-fill co-packers closer to home. I picked up a bottle of apple juice and noticed that it was produced nearby in Watsonville, California, by a company I had never heard of—H. A. Rider & Sons. The product and package looked good, so I picked up the phone and connected with Tom Rider, who ran the company. Tom said he would be happy to speak with us and give us a tour of his plant.

We drove down to Watsonville and turned into the farm driveway lined with apple trees.

Theo breathed deeply of the fragrant air. "I feel like we're traveling back in time. It reminds me of the orchard where I used to pick apples as a kid. I can almost smell the apple cider and donuts."

We walked into the office and, sure enough, there was a box of fresh donuts waiting for us. We both grinned. We spent at least an hour talking with Tom about Hint Water, our backgrounds, and about his family and the company, H. A. Rider & Sons. The Rider family had settled in the area in 1880 and had eventually planted apple trees on their land in Santa Cruz County. They pressed the apples into cider and the business grew. They got good at processing and made their services available to other companies, eventually expanding the bottling operation to multiple bottling lines. The shelves in his office were lined with bottles of every shape and size, many of them covered with dust, and occasionally he'd pull one down to support his story.

When we got down to the business of Hint, Tom told us that he had tried the hot-fill process to bottle flavored water before, without great success. The flavors were damaged by the heat and didn't taste great after bottling. Still, he was willing to give it another try.

Tom graciously took us on a tour of the entire operation. We met the plant manager, Alicia Heim, and others, many of whom had been working for Tom for years, some for as long as two decades. At last, we said our goodbyes and got back in the car for the drive home.

"Tom seems like a great guy."

Theo agreed. "Salt of the earth."

"He's got incredible experience. He knows his stuff. Treats his people well. I love that a woman manages the plant. She seems to run a tight ship, and the guys who work for her clearly respect and listen to her."

"Right. But we won't really know if hot-fill will work until we do some testing. I think I know enough now to simulate it at home and see how it affects our flavors."

It was a long quiet ride up the coast. I could tell Theo was going over the details in his mind.

As soon as we got home, Theo went into the kitchen and started tinkering with our espresso maker. I had no idea why. He explained that an espresso machine brews at about 195 degrees, which happens to be pretty close to hot-fill temperature.

This seemed like a strange idea to me. "What about the coffee taste?"

"I can redirect the water through the steam wand, so it won't be affected by any espresso residue."

Theo prepared some Hint Water with an essence we had on hand, ran it through the machine, cooled it down in an ice bath, and tasted it.

He didn't need to say a word. I could tell it was not right. I grabbed the glass anyway and took a sip. Definitely not good enough to put our name on.

But now Theo was motivated and got seriously on the case. A few days later, he flew to Los Angeles to explore some other possibilities. I got home late, and he was already home, sitting at the kitchen table with a serious look on his face.

"Kara, sit down."

I thought back to the last time I had said that to him and kind of laughed.

"This is serious."

I sat down. "Okay. What is it?"

"We've looked at all the options. We've talked with people all over the country."

"Right."

"We know what we want to do. Create a fresh-tasting, all-natural, fruit-infused water using no preservatives. With a reasonable shelf life that will enable us to distribute nationwide."

"Exactly."

"Well, I'm sorry, but, given the bottling processes available, it's impossible to do. There's just no way to do what you want."

For a lot of people, that might have been the end of the project. That's what Theo was thinking.

I smiled. "Okay, so what *can* we do?"

Theo burst out laughing and shook his head.

"What can we do? Well, we can do what we have been doing. We can sell a short shelf-life product. We can deliver it in our Jeep. We can sell to local accounts."

"Great! We'll do that."

Theo looked at me like I was crazy.

"Look, Theo, what's most important right now is to find out if the product matters to a lot of people. Maybe it doesn't. Maybe it's just a handful of us who care about it. But if we find it has mainstream potential, I have no doubt you'll figure out how to get a longer shelf life."

> 66 For a lot of people, that might have been the end of the project. That's what Theo was thinking. I smiled. "Okay, so what *can* we do?" 99

Theo agreed to the plan, such as it was, but I wouldn't say he was thrilled by it.

There was one thing we had to be sure of: safety. Although we couldn't stop the product from spoiling, we could make sure that our product didn't make anyone sick. Theo's law firm had advised the founders of Odwalla when they had a contamination issue with their juice. We didn't want to take any chances with our customers' health or with our company's future. Theo worked with the lab to set up a rigorous testing protocol to sample the heck out of every batch to ensure it contained no harmful organisms.

The testing protocol made us confident our product was safe, but we continued to have shelf-life issues. From time to time, we'd get a panicked phone call from a retailer who had found a bottle with the cloudy white stuff floating in it.

We always remained calm. "Don't panic. It's not anything that will get anybody sick. It's gross, I know. We'll be right over."

We would drive to the store, take a look at the water, and reassure the store manager or owner. "Look, this is a natural product, and any natural product can spoil. We test extensively and I can assure you there is nothing in the product that would get anyone sick."

Then came the dramatic part. Theo knew that even his verbal assurances probably wouldn't be enough to convince a skeptical manager who might be worried that his job was on the line.

"Look, I want you to feel comfortable that we would never take a chance with your customers' health."

Theo would twist the top off the bottle with the cloudy goo swimming at the bottom. "So I'm going to drink it. Right here. Right now."

That always made a big impression.

"Whoa, are you sure that's a good idea?"

"Well, it's not something I particularly enjoy doing, but it's important that you trust us."

Theo would then drink most of the water, mold and all, much to the amazement of the store manager.

"I'm not suggesting that you or your customers do this," Theo said. "Obviously you'll want to offer a refund to any customer who gets a moldy bottle. And, of course, we'll pay you back. But I hope I've demonstrated that the water is fine, and we stand behind it."

Theo probably drank a hundred bottles of moldy Hint that year. He insisted that this should remain a job for the COO, not the founder. But truthfully, if I didn't have a willing taster, I would have done the same. Well, maybe not a hundred.

Be willing to take one for the team.

CHAPTER 12

find partners you trust.

The plan worked.

We found that our little group of passionate customers was growing quickly. That summer and fall of 2005 and into 2006, we spent a lot of time in the Jeep, loaded up with cases of Hint. While one of us was at the wheel, the other would usually be at home looking after the kids, making phone calls, doing the books, and keeping the business rolling.

We talked and convinced our way into a number of stand-alone grocery stores and small chains in San Francisco, places you won't know if you live outside the area: Rainbow Grocery, Cal-Mart Supermarket, Mollie Stone's Market, and Bryan's Grocery. And we improved the production process to the point where we got to a shelf life of about six months. That meant we could start distributing nationally, if we managed inventory extremely carefully.

Even though we were getting traction with customers in San Francisco, we still had no idea if Hint could be a sustainable business. To me, it was just kind of a crazy game. It was a lot of fun, I was learning all the time, meeting new people, getting to understand the industry. We didn't have the kind of pressure I felt in the AOL days, because we didn't have any investors or a board of directors to answer to. We could develop the product and build the business on our own timetable, without having to meet monthly sales targets. We focused on learning the industry and making the product better and better.

The setup was also good for the family. Remember, we had four little kids, one of them a baby. With Hint, we could work from home, set our own schedules, manage the household, and look after the business, too. As we relentlessly refined our recipes and developed new flavor concepts, we often sat at the table with a meal on one end and essence samples at the other.

Our kids turned out to be not only successful salespeople but also great product testers. If they loved a new formula, the customers almost always loved it, too. If the recipe got even one thumb down, it was not going to make it in the store. Sometimes we'd bring one or two of them along on a delivery run, but we soon learned that only Keenan had a passion for getting "out in the trade." He loved putting bottles on the shelf and making sure they were nicely displayed.

When people ask how I was able to build a company and raise a family at the same time, I tell them that it was actually easier than if I had a job at a large company. I was in control.

That said, we knew from the beginning that we couldn't do it by ourselves. If we wanted Hint to become something more than a hobby, more than the two of us driving around town in our Jeep, we would need to attract and build a solid team. I started to think about the best timing for hiring and about how we would attract people in the San Francisco Bay Area. It's one of the most competitive talent markets in the world. We'd be up against Google and the other big tech companies.

I had found my job at 2Market because I had read about the company in the *Wall Street Journal*. I realized that to attract great employees, and also partners and suppliers, we needed to generate some buzz around the Hint brand.

> 66 When people ask how I was able to build a company and raise a family at the same time, I tell them that it was actually easier than if I had a job at a large company. I was in control. 99

I had learned from my customers about several big trade shows where new brands were often introduced. Even though we had been in business only a month and our sales were less than $1,000, I took a huge leap of faith and decided we should introduce Hint at the Fancy Food Show in New York City. The show, sponsored by the National Association of Specialty Food Trade, was one of the biggest events for food and beverage companies, held every summer at the Jacob Javits Center, the huge convention center in Midtown Manhattan. Everybody who is anybody in the food and beverage world shows up with their products, including high-end coffees, cookies, olive oils, vinegars, fruit spreads, and all kinds of beverages.

We made the decision to attend at the last minute, so the only display space we could get (and afford) was a tiny booth in a corner behind a concrete pillar. I enlisted two friends from my AOL days to help out. We had no time to create a fancy display, so we made do with the rickety folding table provided by the show managers. We dressed it up a little with a cheesy plastic tablecloth and hung a Hint banner we had made at a copy shop.

At first, nothing. Zero people stopped by. If you've ever attended a trade show, you know what that's like. At last, one person approached the booth. But it was not just any person. It was a buyer from Whole Foods. I told her that we already stocked their San Francisco store.

That piqued her interest to give the product a try. She loved it.

After the Whole Foods buyer left, word zipped around the show with amazing speed. Pretty soon people were lining up to try our flavors, stacking up six deep at times. We were stunned and delighted. The response was so overwhelming that we thought, *Wow! We'll be in all the big national chains in no time!* It turned out not to be quite so easy. It took several years before we were distributed throughout the Whole Foods chain.

I look at that show as the first lesson of our "Beverage Industry MBA," a self-taught, two-year crash course in this huge and complicated business. In particular, we learned about the many companies that had attempted to sell unsweetened flavored water over the years with no success. Tom First, one of the founders of Nantucket Nectars, had launched an unsweetened flavored water called OWater in Boston. It didn't taste very good, probably because of the high acidity required for preservatives, and it didn't sell much. The company that made vitaminwater had developed an unsweetened, flavored version of SmartWater in a couple Whole Foods regions. The product had done okay in early market tests, until they ran into a problem. Mold growth! They ditched the project. This was upsetting to some retailers and consumers, so they were excited when we came along with a similar, but much better tasting, product.

As we built the business, we heard over and over again from adventurous consumers that we were succeeding where our predecessors had failed. Our product just tasted better.

Then things took a turn for the worse in early 2007. As our distribution grew, we needed more and more product, but our co-packer at the time was reaching the limit of its capacity and failing to keep up with our orders. One day, out of the blue, they told us that to meet our growing demand, they needed $300,000 in new equipment and if we didn't buy it for them they were going to stop producing for us completely. Instead of explaining their challenges and asking if we could help them figure out how to finance their new equipment, they had chosen to make demands and hold our business hostage.

This was a serious problem, possibly an existential threat.

We had to make a difficult choice. We could invest in a partner who violated our trust. Or we could leave and look for another partner. If we couldn't find one fast, we might have to close the business. We didn't hold much inventory in those days and would quickly run out. Still, we chose the more risky alternative based on a simple principle: you can't build a strong business with an untrustworthy partner.

 You can't build a strong business with an

untrustworthy partner.

Our goal, above all, was to maintain good relationships with the distributors and stores carrying our product. First, we warned our local distributors and key customers that we might experience shortages for a month or two. We assured them we would solve the problem before summer when sales would rise dramatically. We promised to keep them fully informed and allocate available product among them fairly. In return, we asked for their support and understanding. They were surprised by our openness and promised to help, but we knew they couldn't hold their shelves open for us for long.

In search of advice, it was around this time that I made the famous (to us) call to a Coca-Cola executive. Now you can better understand my state of mind at the time. I was frustrated and discouraged after a couple years of driving around delivering product in the Jeep. That part of the work had become more of a grind than it was fun.

In addition to all the other problems, we always seemed to be starved for cash. The business required investment and the bills came in faster than revenue did.

What puzzles me now is why I assumed the Coca-Cola exec would have the answers to our challenges, and why he would offer them to me, if he did. I guess I had shifted into corporate mode when I made the call. I just wanted someone to tell me the solution so I could go do it. If there wasn't a solution, maybe it was time to give up and move on.

> **“** I just wanted someone to tell me the solution so I could go do it. If there wasn't a solution, maybe it was time to give up and move on. **”**

I went into the conversation assuming I would be treated with respect, as a colleague in the beverage industry. Instead, the executive clearly thought of me as a novice who was hoping to hear words of wisdom from the oracle. But as he went on and on about the technical issues, I just felt more and more defeated.

I guess that's why, in a down moment, I offered to give Coca-Cola the company. I still can't quite believe I did that. It didn't matter. That's when he called me "sweetie."

That was the turning point in the conversation. What was I thinking? Why would I give up on a company that had become my passion? I knew we were on to an important trend, and this guy just couldn't see it. He assumed that everybody wanted sweet drinks because that's what his company sold so successfully. The idea of a fruit-flavored water that tasted delicious without being sweet didn't compute for him. Besides, I didn't buy that all Americans fundamentally love sweet drinks. I believed they were drinking the sweetened stuff because that was what was most convenient and widely available. It had become an addiction. Now, at last, people were waking up to the problem, just as I had. They'd go for something different and better *if they had a choice.*

My attitude changed. I was no longer looking to the guy for information about how to fix our production process. Instead, I wanted to understand his thinking because I realized that he, and others in big companies, would *have* to wake up to the new reality someday. After all, Coca-Cola had branched out into plain water and fruit juice. When they did wake up to the idea of unsweetened flavored water, they would be a big, formidable competitor. I was right. In the next few years, Coca-Cola went on a buying spree, purchasing vitaminwater, Fuze, and Honest Tea.

There is a lesson to be had in that conversation. As an entrepreneur, you should take every opportunity to learn as much as you can from the experts in the big, established companies. They'll usually be glad to tell you what they know and to show off their knowledge, because they don't see you as competition. Connect with them whenever you can. Ask questions. Listen. You don't have to challenge them or prove them wrong. But you can learn and apply what you've learned—even if it's the exact opposite of what they advise—to build your business into a success. Eventually they'll take notice.

Of course, I didn't see it that way at the time. One evening, not long after that call, Theo and I had a difficult conversation. Maybe we *were* crazy to try to build a beverage company. Maybe it was just too hard to break into the industry. At that moment, we had no manufacturing partner. We were running out of inventory. We were burning through money. We had four kids at home in a house in the most expensive city in the country. What the hell were we doing? We'd both given up opportunities in executive roles at tech companies that would have meant great paychecks and fantastic stock positions.

Was it too late to go back? Should we give up on Hint?

It all seemed to come down to the shelf-life issue. We'd been working with the cold-fill process because we had assumed—and been told over and over—that it was the only way to get the taste we were after. Any hot-fill process, which reliably kills off impurities, also affects the taste profile. We all know that a cooked strawberry tastes very different than a fresh strawberry does. We had stuck with the cold-fill process to preserve flavor, but it still produced the occasional smeggy batch, had limited shelf life, and was getting in the way of expansion.

We didn't come to any final conclusions that night. I went to bed feeling frustrated, worried, and uncertain about the future. Around two in the morning, I was awakened by a clattering noise downstairs. I went down to see what was going on and found Theo in the kitchen peering intently at the espresso machine and a stream of what looked like hot water gurgling into a cup.

"What on earth are you up to?"

"I think I've solved the shelf-life issue," he said, his eyes fixed on the machine. "Through our work with the flavor team, we've improved the fruit essences a lot. They have greater purity and are better tasting. I figured they might be robust enough to be more heat tolerant. If so, maybe we can use the hot-fill technique without harming the fruit flavor."

He mixed up a batch of Hint and ran it through the espresso machine's steam wand. Then he plunged the bottle in ice water until it cooled. When he took a taste, the grin on his face told me everything I needed to know. Miraculously, his hunch proved to be right. The flavor came through as fresh and clear as it did with the cold-fill process.

Theo had solved the problem that had plagued us for so long, and he had done it in the middle of the night, using a home espresso machine and wearing pajamas.

It was a game changer in every way. Now we had a much wider range of potential partners to choose from. However, the hot-fill process also required a different kind of bottle, a different closure, and even different labels. We would need to line up a whole new supply chain, and we didn't have much time to do it before we ran out of inventory. Fortunately, we already knew where we could bottle it.

We dashed off an email to Tom Rider to see how quickly we could get a production run going. Then we started to email all the suppliers, but stopped.

"You know, we're asking for low prices, great quality, and speed. It's tough to get all three."

"We need what we need," I said.

We spent the rest of that night emailing suppliers, describing our needs, specs, and timeline.

We got a reply from Tom first thing in the morning. He could do a run within a week of receiving the bottles, caps, and other materials. What followed was a crazy month of reaching out to suppliers. One by one, they replied that they could deliver what we wanted, when we wanted it, at a good price. But they all said there was no way the suppliers of the other necessary materials could move that fast. Against all odds, we had product running at H. A. Rider & Sons four weeks after Theo's late-night experiment.

We were back in business and ready to grow.

From that episode—a time when we seriously considered throwing in the towel—we learned an important lesson: it's okay to admit that you have a problem or that you have no idea what you're doing. Just as Theo explained the mold issue to store managers, and in the same way we leveled with our accounts when we lost our manufacturing relationship, we realized that being honest and transparent is often the best way to connect with people who *do* know what they're doing. They can become allies and partners who can help you to the next stage of success.

> **We learned an important lesson: it's okay to admit that you have a problem or that you have no idea what you're doing.**

The Hint aircraft was gaining altitude. But, as it turned out, some of the roughest turbulence was still ahead.

CHAPTER 13

believe in
your product.

When can you be sure that your company is flying high and out of danger?

Never.

But, as 2007 went along, we did start to feel as if we had taken off and were gaining altitude. We had stabilized our production process, we were up and running with our new co-packer, and Hint Water had an extended shelf life of eighteen months.

And, at two years old, we had survived longer than most beverage start-ups, nine out of ten of which fail in the first year. Our revenue was on pace to reach $5 million by year's end. If we continued to grow at our current rate, we figured we could reach the $10 million mark in a year or two. Then we'd be the one-in-a-hundred beverage start-up that grows to that size.

We concentrated on the Holy Grail of start-ups: exponential growth. Up to that point, we had been relentlessly focused on getting the product right. Now we wanted to take the business we had built and scale it up. At AOL, I had successfully scaled our online shopping business from almost nothing to a huge business that led the industry for several years. But there I had access to a big team, and the company had deep resources. Even more important, AOL controlled distribution of its service, a digital connection right into the customer's home.

With Hint, by contrast, I was leading a tiny team. Hint was a heavy, physical product distributed through a system of independent companies we did not control. It was an exciting and intimidating challenge.

Just as I had done with everything else, I had to figure out the best growth path as we went along. That meant asking questions, learning, trying things, learning from mistakes, and leveraging successes—proceeding undaunted against incredibly unfavorable odds.

The first thing we had to attend to was the distribution system. This may sound pretty boring, but it's an essential element of building a successful, national brand. How do all those beverages find their way into the cases in your local grocery stores, vending machines, restaurants, and cafeterias? Before we began Hint, I had no idea. I assumed the brand owners delivered the product and store staff stocked the shelves.

That's not how it works.

The brand depends on distributors to take its product to the big retail outlets. Distributors warehouse and manage the inventory. They are responsible for stocking and shelving in the stores. They are one of the brand's key representatives in the marketplace. The brand counts on them to maintain a presence in existing accounts and find new opportunities to expand.

In Hint's two years of existence, we had gradually put together a network of small, local distributors in California and New York. Some of them were operations not much bigger than our own. If a guy had a truck, a heartbeat, and liked our brand, that was all we needed.

I had gotten my first inkling of how the big brands go about distribution in 2005 at the Fancy Food Show in New York. After the Whole Foods buyer came by our booth and tried the product, she said she was interested in stocking the product.

"Who's your distributor?"

It's hard to believe now, but I didn't know what she was talking about.

"What do you mean?"

"Who do you guys work with? UNFI? Sysco?"

I had never heard of UNFI or Sysco. "We just load up our cases in our Jeep and distribute them ourselves," I said.

This astonished the Whole Foods buyer. She made it clear that we would never get distribution in their chain, or any national chain for that matter, without going through a big distributor. UNFI, I learned, is one of the major distributors of natural foods in the United States and a key supplier to Whole Foods. Never afraid to show my lack of knowledge, I asked the Whole Foods buyer if she could give me UNFI's phone number, which she did.

We weren't ready for the big time yet, but we did make a connection with a local distributor in New York who agreed to take us on. They didn't do much to build the business, but at least we had established a toehold for Hint on the East Coast.

I'm almost embarrassed to reveal how we got our first distributor in San Francisco, but it's an important part of the story. I would go to Whole Foods and literally hang out, waiting for anybody who looked like a distributor to show up and start stocking the shelves. I got lucky when I approached one such guy and asked if he was a distributor. He said yes, and I told him about Hint. He said he was interested and to give him a call. His name was John Vanloo.

I called John later and he agreed to give Hint a try. He told me to bring a pallet of product to his warehouse and he'd give us space there to store it. He'd load it on his truck next time he went out and see what placements he could get.

A whole pallet of product? That may not sound like much, but it was actually a tall order for us to fill in those days. Most of our accounts were taking a few cases, each one containing twenty-four bottles, with each delivery. A pallet holds a total of seventy-two cases.

> 66 I would go to Whole Foods and literally hang out, waiting for anybody who looked like a distributor to show up and start stocking the shelves. 99

I asked Theo if we could deliver a pallet of product to John's warehouse. He groaned, but agreed. He had become an expert at packing cases into the Jeep and knew exactly how to load them in most efficiently. That day, Theo figured out how to cram seventy-two cases of Hint, one driver, and one passenger into the Jeep.

Wedged into the front seat, we drove to the warehouse. John greeted us and showed us the space where the Hint cases should go. We nodded and kind of waited, expecting a warehouse employee to unload the product. Nobody showed up and we got a little antsy.

"Can somebody help us unload?"

John looked at us. "Nope. This is a tiny operation. If you can't shift your own product, I guess we won't be able to work together."

"No, no. We're happy to do it!" We assured him. "But, um, are you going to pay us for the product?"

"Of course, I'll pay you. After you unload it."

Theo and I looked at each other and started laughing. Here we were, a tech exec and an intellectual property lawyer, lugging cases of fruit water from the back of a Jeep into a warehouse not much bigger than a garage. Later, we wished we had gotten some photos of the scene.

John became our first local distributor and, like so many other people we met in the early days, we are still good friends today.

From that base, we gradually added more distributors to our network. These were small guys with trucks who would pick up product from our location and drive it directly to the retail outlets—what's known as Direct Store Delivery, or DSD—rather than to a central warehouse, as the big outfits did.

Another promising sales channel was our website, drinkhint.com, and it was beginning to gain traction. After all, online shopping was something I did know a lot about, and we got the site up and running early on. At first, we did all the shipping ourselves. We'd print out the online order, pick the product, pack it up, and take it to the post office or FedEx for shipping. As the online business grew, order fulfillment took more time than we could devote to it.

I found a solution to that problem one day when I was getting my nails done at my favorite salon. My manicurist was upset that day and told me a long story about her husband, Jack, who was in a bad work situation at a local auto mechanic shop. Given our increasing online business, I figured we could use some help with fulfillment. We ended up hiring Jack to help out in the office and then take over as our "pick and pack" person—the one who fills the order, packs it for shipping, and takes it to the carrier. Jack is still with us today, our longest-serving employee.

To support our growing business, we had built up the organization. At first, we worked out of the house on Scott Street in San Francisco. Three or four of us—including me, Theo, a bookkeeper, and a marketing person—worked at the living room table. As we added more people, we eventually outgrew the house and moved into an empty classroom at The Bay School, a high school that was just starting up in the Presidio of San Francisco. When the school needed the classroom, we moved next door into a building that had been built during World War II as a temporary army barracks.

When we worked at home, we stored the product in the basement. As we grew, we took storage space in a warehouse on one of the piers in San Francisco. Unlike John, our distributor, the warehouse provided services. Each morning, we'd email them a list of product we needed for delivery. They'd pull the product and load it on a pallet so it was waiting for Theo or myself when we arrived in the Jeep.

Sales grew quickly. We took in about $50,000 in 2005, our first partial year of operation. By the middle of 2007, we were on track to hit several million in sales, and we thought we could continue to grow at a similar pace for the foreseeable future. Online sales were bringing in as much as $20,000 month. That doesn't sound like much today—compared to some days in 2019 when we were bringing in more than $1 million in a single day—but it seemed like a lot then.

And we kept building our base of impassioned customers, people who seemed to care about our products as much as we did.

We learned early on that the media seemed just as intrigued by our product as our customers were. In May 2006, we got a glowing review on a food website called Hungry Girl. It's the brainchild of Lisa Lillien, a *New York Times* best-selling author and self-described "foodologist." Lisa's many cookbooks have sold hundreds of thousands of copies, and her website has millions of subscribers who visit to download recipes, get the latest on food trends and events, and, most important to us, learn about new products.

"We LOOOOVE this stuff," Lisa wrote about Hint. "It tastes like crisp, fresh water, with a slight hint of flavor. It's extremely refreshing, not sweet at all, and the flavor is so subtle that it doesn't take over. Best served ice cold, we highly recommend Hint Water and think it's, without a doubt, the BEST flavored water out there . . . HINT WATER ROCKS!!!!"

After that review was posted, we got more than twenty thousand hits on our website, more than ever before, and saw a nice bump in online sales.

We thought that was great, but it was followed up in July with some exposure we assumed would be an even bigger deal. Things had gone so well at the Fancy Food Show in 2005 that we decided to attend again the following summer. A team from *Good Morning America* stopped by our booth and sampled the product. The next morning, Diane Sawyer, the host of the show, did a roundup of the most interesting products and trends. I will never forget watching her take a sip of Hint blackberry on air.

> 66 The next morning, Diane Sawyer, the host of the show, did a roundup of the most interesting products and trends. I will never forget watching her take a sip of Hint blackberry on air. 99

"Wow, that's really delicious!"

It doesn't get much better than that. A prominent mention by a major celebrity on a network television show watched by our core audience of women. It was especially gratifying to me because I learned that Diane was a Diet Coke fanatic, just as I had been.

As much as we loved that endorsement, we learned something important about the relative impact of different types of publicity. The reaction to the mention on the Hungry Girl site, which was only a couple years old at the time, way surpassed our expectations. The Hungry Girl site attracted young, health-conscious women who were actively looking for alternatives to the ordinary beverage fare.

The Hungry Girl visitors were also regular online shoppers who were just one click away from the Hint site.

TV viewers, by contrast, do not necessarily dash from their TV to their computer to make a purchase. They're more likely to look for Hint the next time they're at their local store, so the impact on sales is less immediate and harder to track. It further validates what I already knew well: online shopping had huge potential, which it was only beginning to realize.

Later that year, we got more attention, this time as a company and as a brand, not just as a product, when I did an interview with CNBC, the leading business news cable TV channel. One key question the interviewer asked me was, "How's business?"

"Business is good," I said. "In two years, we've grown from two employees, my husband and me, to twelve, and revenue has jumped."

What I didn't tell him is there was just one thing we didn't have if we wanted to go big: money.

persevere.

We never seemed to have enough money.

Even as sales grew, expenses grew faster. We brought on new accounts and sold more and more product, but sales volume is not the same as profit. To become profitable in the beverage industry, you need to get pretty big. To get big, you have to invest in inventory, people to sell it, marketing, and, ultimately, advertising. We worried that if we didn't invest and instead settled for staying small, a better-funded competitor would come along and grab the lead in this whole new beverage category we were building.

But where to get the money? In the earliest days, plenty of people had offered to invest in Hint, but we refused to take chances with their money until we fixed the shelf-life problem. Instead, we dipped into our savings, most of which had come from the sale of AOL stock, to fund product development, bottling, and shipping.

Toward the end of 2006, however, we knew we needed more money to keep going. We turned to a few of our friends and family members, described to them the challenges we faced in the starkest terms possible, and were incredibly gratified that they chose to invest anyway. It was humbling to see that the people closest to us had faith in what we were doing and were willing to risk their money. It was that investment that bought us enough time to solve the shelf-life problem.

By the start of 2007, we estimated that we needed a much bigger infusion of capital, at least $2 million, to drive the kind of growth we wanted to achieve. We were able to raise another $500,000 from our family and friend investors, but that was the limit.

> 66 Conventional wisdom says you shouldn't make more than one big change in your life at once, but I have never been a big follower of conventional wisdom. 99

It was time to consider working with an outside investor, and it seemed like this might be a good time to do so. Coca-Cola had just spent $4.2 billion to acquire the company that made vitaminwater, and a lot of new investors were suddenly interested in the beverage industry. Several local investment banks had been calling us wanting to help us raise money (for a fee, of course). We talked with a number of them and signed a deal with an investment bank that had a strong track record and assured us they could come up with the capital we needed fast.

Conventional wisdom says you shouldn't make more than one big change in your life at once, but I have never been a big follower of conventional wisdom. Sometimes you have to struggle through some chaos to get where you want to go. So, in addition to taking on new investors, we decided it was time to move out of San Francisco. Residents who want to get their kids into a decent public school in the city literally have to win a lottery, so we were paying for private elementary school for the two oldest kids, and day care and preschool fees for the younger two. Add to that the exorbitant real estate taxes and the high cost of living, and we were living proof that San Francisco is one of the nation's most expensive areas to live.

Thanks to a strong housing market, we sold the place on Scott Street quickly and for a good price. We found a beautiful house in the community of Ross, across the Golden Gate Bridge in Marin County, which had, and still has, an amazing public school system. We assumed it wouldn't be long before the investment capital rolled in, and we could stop putting our own cash on the line.

But the bankers were not able to raise the money as easily as they had predicted. While local technology investors had expressed a lot of interest because they had read about the vitaminwater deal, they were not prepared to make investments in an area where they had no experience. And the traditional beverage investors all felt we were too small or that our new category of unsweetened flavored water was too young and therefore risky.

Instead, we met with a number of private equity people to make our pitch. They spent time with us and gave us useful advice, but, when it came down to writing a check, they all declined. We didn't have much of a track record. We only had a few million dollars in sales, and most beverage companies tank before they hit $10 million. They preferred to hold off investing until the company hit at least $20 million in sales. Maybe later . . .

Theo and I discussed our options. We decided to put off buying the house in Ross and use the proceeds from Scott Street to make a loan to the company. But we had to live someplace, so we rented a place in Ross for a year. As a mother of four kids, I wasn't thrilled with the idea of not having a home we could call our own, but we had to protect the business.

Now we were under the gun. We couldn't continue self-funding forever. We returned our attention to individuals, angel investors who don't answer to a board of directors about their decisions. We sent cases of Hint to some of the people who had already invested and also to others who had expressed interest and who we thought had the capacity to write bigger checks. It worked. Many of them not only invested but also became our most active supporters. They turned their friends on to the product. They urged their local stores to stock Hint. It was like having an unpaid sales force and marketing team.

One of the first to invest in this round was Ken Sadowsky, who had served on the board of directors of vitaminwater for six years, so he knew all about its failed attempt to market a fruit-infused water like ours and was involved in the final stage of its acquisition. But he wasn't one of the entrenched industry figures I had run into, like the Coca-Cola executive who called me "sweetie." Ken well understood the challenges of growing a small company. His father had founded Atlas, one of our distributors in Massachusetts, so Ken appreciated the journey we were taking as founders. Ken had achieved a lot in his own right at Atlas, building up the nonalcoholic part of the business from around $50,000 in sales in 1988 to around $16 million in 2007.

Of most importance to me, Ken had been a pioneer in finding and championing interesting and alternative beverage brands, including SoBe, Honest Tea, and most recently, he had brought Hint to Atlas and a bunch of other related beverage distributors.

Not only did Ken himself invest; he introduced us to other potential investors. We were particularly interested in a firm called Verlinvest, because it was small, family-owned, and operated more like a family office than a traditional private equity firm. The firm was based in Belgium, having been formed by a group of shareholders involved with Inbev, the Belgian company with a portfolio of beer brands, including Stella Artois. They had provided financing for a number of food and beverage companies. We made an appointment to meet them in New York in a month's time.

Meanwhile, we were settling into our new hometown of Ross. Although our daughters, Emma and Kait, seemed to transition into school pretty smoothly, we wanted to make sure they were making friends, and we were getting to know their classmates' parents. As busy as we were with Hint, we made an extra effort to volunteer in the classroom and to engage with teachers and parents at school.

We also took every opportunity to become part of the community. Ross is a unique town with a lot of odd contrasts. Some of the most financially successful people in the country live there, but you would never know it by looking at the mostly modest homes. Ross doesn't have mail delivery, so residents have post office boxes. I'd stop by the post office regularly to pick up our mail, but mostly to meet people.

One day I opened our P.O. box, expecting to see the typical batch of catalogs, and was happy to find an envelope addressed to Kait from a classmate named Victoria Pekarovic. It was an invitation to the whole Goldin family to attend Victoria's birthday party.

We all went. It was one of the first such events we attended in Ross, and everyone was friendly and made us feel welcome. One person I talked with was Julio Pekarovic, Victoria's father. I learned he worked at Google, and he asked what I did.

"I was at AOL for several years, then left to follow my passion to start a company."

"What kind of company?"

"We make fruit-flavored, unsweetened water."

He seemed very interested. "What's the name of it?"

"It's called Hint."

Julio nearly leaped out of his chair.

"Hint?! That's my favorite drink at Google. I drink at least five a day. Everyone at Google drinks it."

I smiled.

I left the party thinking Julio was a good guy for us to know.

He called me the following Monday, all excited. Turns out that he had mentioned our conversation to Omid Kordestani, head of sales and operations at Google. Small world, for sure. Theo and Omid had worked at Netscape together, and Omid had tried to get me to work at Netscape and later at Google. He had even put me in touch with the people at Google's fantastic food service operation (although he says he doesn't remember that part), so he was at least partly responsible for our huge presence at Google. Now he was one of our biggest fans.

A few weeks later, we flew to New York to meet with the guys from Verlinvest. We felt comfortable with them because of their experience in the beverage industry, their track record, and, most of all, their values as patient investors. They agreed to make a $3 million investment and be our lead investor. By early January 2008, we had a signed term sheet setting out the specifics of the deal, including a deadline for completion: the end of January.

On our attorney's advice, to save money, we agreed to let Verlinvest's lawyers draw up the first draft of the legal documents. Terrible idea. Several weeks passed, and when we finally received the draft, it bore little resemblance to the term sheet we had signed. Now we were further away from closing a deal than we had been a month earlier and Hint was running out of cash. Verlinvest understood its lawyer had not delivered properly, but negotiations dragged on at a snail's pace, partly because of the nine-hour time difference between Belgium and San Francisco.

We took a huge gamble and loaned more of our own money to Hint, while the attorneys worked it out. By the time the deal closed in April, we had loaned Hint almost all the money from the sale of our home.

Hint made a partial repayment on the loan, enough for us to make a down payment on a wonderful house in Ross. With real estate values at an all-time high, it probably wasn't the best time to buy, but we wanted a place for the kids to grow up and to remember as their childhood home.

Under the agreement with Verlinvest, we expanded the board of directors from two members to five. Theo and I would continue to control the company, but we would pick one new director and Verlinvest would appoint its chairman, Frederic de Mevius, plus an additional board member to be named. All along, we had intended to appoint Ken Sadowsky as our board pick, but before we said anything, Verlinvest let us know that they were appointing him to their second spot. Ken officially became Verlinvest's advisor on US beverage investing. We were delighted to have him join the board. It felt like a fantastic gift because we got Ken, who would have been our choice anyway, and another pick, too.

Theo and I decided we needed a person with experience in finance, and Julio Pekarovic immediately came to mind. I called Julio and told him about our new investor partner and need for a board director. "I'd love to have you join me and Theo on the board. You built Google's sales finance group. You know e-commerce. You're a great fan of the brand. Would you consider it?"

He didn't hesitate. "Absolutely. But I don't know much about the beverage industry."

"Not necessary. We can get you up to speed."

He paused. "There is one condition, however."

Oh boy. "Okay. What's that?"

"I need to feel like I have skin in the game. Can I make an investment?"

"Deal!"

Summer, our busiest time, was just around the corner. Given how long it took to get the round of funding closed, we were behind on almost everything else. Most of all, we hadn't hired the additional sales and marketing people we needed to properly activate our new distributors and meet our very aggressive sales goals for the year.

Over the previous eight months, we had started working with a group of East Coast distributors that were part of the Northeast

Independent Distributors Association, a group of independent distributors who had helped build Snapple, vitaminwater, and several other recent success stories. We had negotiated our agreements with the NIDA distributors right after Coca-Cola purchased vitaminwater. They told us they owned all of the vitaminwater refrigerators that you see in small outlets, like delis and convenience stores, throughout New England and that they would be able to rebrand the fridges and use them for Hint. It seemed like a fantastic opportunity. Our product would have its own branded presence, separate from all the dozens of other drinks in the main cooler.

Didn't work out that way. During the transition of vitaminwater to Coca-Cola-owned trucks, our NIDA distributors agreed to sell all those refrigerators to Coca-Cola. Once again, big beverage paid big dollars to control a lot of shelf space. Gaining cold space in stores was suddenly looking like a much bigger challenge than we had anticipated.

In the wake of the $4.2 billion acquisition of vitaminwater, a record number of new beverage start-ups sprang up. They were often funded by clueless investors who hoped they, too, could build a company that would become a target of acquisition and strike gold, just as vitaminwater had. We found ourselves competing for shelf space with a bunch of vitaminwater wannabees, with names like Purple and Function Water, that were well funded and could hire big sales forces. The beverage market became a big mess. Everybody was competing for shelf space and consumer attention. We thought our new investment might not be enough to keep Hint in the game.

Then things got much, much worse.

In September 2008, Lehman Brothers, the fourth largest investment bank in the United States, collapsed. The failure is now seen as the beginning of one of the worst and longest recessions in American history.

There was widespread panic in the business world. Everywhere you looked, companies were cutting costs, hunkering down, reducing investment in innovation and expansion, scrapping programs, shrinking, and going bankrupt. Pre-crash, investors had pushed their companies. "Go faster! Spend more!" Now they hit the brakes. The new mantra was: "Cut costs. Slash budgets to the bone. Get profitable."

It was a scary time.

The food and beverage industry was hit as hard as any other. In 2008, Starbucks experienced its first decline in profit since 2000 and announced it would close hundreds of stores and lay off thousands of people. Even alcoholic beverages—a beverage industry sector that had long been considered recession-proof—saw declines in sales.

Hint felt the impact almost immediately.

First, we got kicked out of our office. We had been paying a reasonable rent to our landlord, Presidio Trust. Now they said we'd have to move, but could put us into a great, newly renovated space nearby, at $9,000 per month, a huge increase. Turns out one of the landlord's friends, a nonprofit organization, had been renting the fancy space but, with the recession, couldn't handle the cost. We couldn't afford the higher rent, either, and found a nice, cheaper space at 2124 Union Street, which is still the heart of our offices today.

That was a minor problem in comparison to the heat we felt from our partners and retailers, who were also under great stress to reduce costs. All at once, the retailers started demanding deep discounts and crazy deals. Even our oldest and most valued account, Whole Foods, got the jitters. They wanted us to do a buy-one, get-one-free deal, known in the trade as BOGO. Half price! We'd be losing money on every bottle we sold. The pressure was intense. We got the not-so-subtle message that if we didn't go along with the plan, Whole Foods would take Hint off the shelves. That might not necessarily have finished us off, but it surely would have put us in a tough spot.

We thought long and hard about how to respond. On the one hand, brands do promotions and special offers all the time, and we had done our share of them. The special offer is a treat, an act of generosity, a way to encourage people to try the brand. It also serves as a practical way to open up space for a new flavor coming in. But there's a difference between a limited, short-time offer and long-term, deep discounting, which this plan essentially was. That kind of discounting suggests that the brand has lost faith in itself, doesn't trust its customers to stick with it, and no longer believes in its value. Once you start discounting like that, it's very tough to stop.

> 66 The pressure was intense. We got the not-so-subtle message that if we didn't go along with the plan, Whole Foods would take Hint off the shelves. 99

In the end, we concluded that we had no choice. We could not go along with the BOGO deal. If we said no and lost the Whole Foods account, that would be painful. But it would be worse if we agreed because it would be a bad deal for everyone—for Whole Foods and for us. Whole Foods had built its brand on quality and innovation, service, and natural foods. Hint stood for innovation, healthy living, personal improvement, freshness, and great taste.

None of those values were consistent with discounting.

We said no. We can't do that. And you don't really want us to.

I explained our reasoning to the buyers. "People shop at Whole Foods because they want the best and are willing to pay extra for it. As soon as you fail to deliver on that promise, you will lose your identity. And so will we."

In a tense business situation like that one, when there is a lot at stake and the future is uncertain, it's easy to allow fear and emotions to get the best of you. I am proud to say we kept our cool, stayed the course with our original deal, and were able to preserve our Whole Foods relationship. Hint remained on the shelves without doing crazy deals and is still there today.

Two bullets dodged.

But there was another one coming. Our landlord and our retail accounts were not the only ones concerned about the future. Our investors also had to make hard decisions about how to deploy their money and what risks to take or avoid. Throughout the business world, investment money was getting tighter, fewer deals were being done, and the time between rounds of investment was growing longer.

I was more and more concerned that Verlinvest might decide to sit out a second round of financing. *That* would have meant trouble. With a late start on the summer and the financial collapse in the fall, we had burned through a lot of our capital. Sales were sluggish. We were unable to bring on many new accounts, because we wouldn't agree to bogus BOGO deals. We would need another round of financing by the end of the year to keep building the organization and, honestly, to avoid going under.

We had to get our investors to stick with us, so I called an emergency board meeting where Theo, Julio, and I presented our case.

"On the downside, we project that we will miss our sales target for 2008 and have a no-growth year in 2009. We're just too small to cut costs enough to be profitable."

On to the positive. "On the plus side, our analysis shows that our sales are actually growing in twenty-five of our most important Whole Foods outlets. Why is that? Precisely because we have been able to resist pressure to do deep discounting and have maintained our strong brand image. Consumers are willing to pay for Hint."

We couldn't tell how the Verlinvest guys were taking this. Nothing to do but keep going.

"Most of our competitors have taken the discounting route. They are desperate to show growth in sales, even if it isn't very profitable growth. How else can they prove to their investors they're okay? We believe they're betting the economy will recover quickly and they can go back to regular pricing. We think that's optimistic. The recovery will take at least a year. Time is going to run out on them. A lot of newbies will go bankrupt. We don't want to chase them down that rabbit hole."

Theo, Julio, and I then argued there was only one strategy that would get us through the downturn and give us a shot at a long-term future: we had to continue to protect the value of the brand. We believed the promise of Hint was every bit as bright as it had ever been. We just needed a little help to get through the worst economy in our history.

"You're crazy! Everybody else is hunkering down. But you want us to invest more money? Now?"

We held firm. "Yes. If we cut costs and lay people off, we won't be able to move fast when things turn around, which they will. Everyone else is destroying their brands. So when the time comes, we'll be in a great competitive position, and we'll be ready to grow like crazy."

The Verlinvest directors didn't agree to write a check that day, but in the end, they bought our analysis and agreed to a second round of funding. The catch? They wanted to dramatically reduce the valuation of the company, wiping out much of our friends and family investors' ownership and effectively taking control of Hint. We were in a terrible negotiating position, because we had no chance of surviving without a deal, but we couldn't let our individual investors down. Nor did we want anyone else to step in and make important decisions for the company.

We had a vision and were determined to see it through.

We solved the problem by agreeing that if we could maintain the same valuation of the company and retain control, Theo and I would guarantee it would work out well for Verlinvest. If things ended badly, we would give them our shares, and they would still make a lot of money. Theo and I were prepared to devote our careers to making Hint a huge success, but now we had to live with the possibility of a different outcome. If we didn't succeed, we could end up with nothing.

It was a huge bet, but I had no intention of giving up. As it turned out, the financing enabled us to weather the storm of the recession and maintain our sales growth in existing accounts, but it also kept us under a cloud of personal risk. We did not get out from under this obligation until 2016, when we negotiated yet another round of financing and the obligation was removed. For nearly a decade, we were literally at risk of personally losing all we owned if we didn't achieve, perform, and grow.

You get used to it.

> 66 For nearly a decade, we were literally at risk of personally losing all we owned if we didn't achieve, perform, and grow.
>
> You get used to it. 99

As fraught as that period was, it also taught us lessons and brought us benefits, as tough times usually do. We learned a lot about financing in those years and got more ambitious and innovative in how we raised capital.

People often ask if it was hard for me to raise money as a woman. My response is simple and a little cheeky. "I've never been a man, so I wouldn't know."

Honestly, that's just a wall that people put up for themselves. *No one will lend money to me, I'm a woman.* It's true that a lot of people we approached for money declined in the early days, but that's true for most start-ups. You just have to find your tribe and your fans. Let them advocate for you and make introductions to the right people. Eventually, we found people who believed in the product and in us, and that's how we got the financing done.

During this period, we also learned about an online investment platform called AngelList, which connects accredited investors interested in tech start-ups. The usual approach for a beverage company would be to work with a platform focused on food and beverage investment, not tech. But we believed the investors on AngelList were very likely to be our customers and brand believers, people who understood the value of our product. In 2010, as the economy started to recover, we raised several million dollars from AngelList investors.

We learned more about the nature and appeal of our brand. In difficult economic times, certain types of consumer goods continue to sell at their previous levels and even see a boost in demand— products like lipstick, food treats, small leather goods, and clothing items. That's because consumers may be tightening their belts in areas of major spending. They put off home renovations, buy a used car instead of a new one, delay a vacation, or spend less on groceries. They compensate by treating themselves to little indulgences, or "affordable luxuries." Hint Water was exactly the kind of small, affordable luxury brand that made people feel a little better about the world in uncertain times.

We also learned about the importance of perseverance. Through it all, I felt a tremendous obligation to carry on. I believed we could get through the crisis because I had no doubts about the long-term value of what we were doing. I had faith in the product, the business, and our worth to our customers and community. We had commitments to our co-packers and distributors and our own management team. Our retailers and customers were expecting us to deliver product. Our employees, friends, and professional investors were financially committed to our enterprise.

Personally, it had been a period of tremendous change. We had given up a house and lifestyle we loved in the city. My mom had passed away and my dad was in a care facility with Alzheimer's. As hard as those things were, we had also been able to create a different life in our new town with its own advantages and benefits. Our kids were thriving in the public schools. We could run a growing business and still have time with them. We had a nice house, a yard, and two dogs, Sadie and Buster. I wasn't going to give up on all that we had built and accomplished.

Nothing enabled me to persevere more than our customers. Throughout those difficult times, they wrote to me constantly and told me their stories.

I have never really enjoyed drinking water, but now I do!

I have more energy now. I feel much healthier.

My skin has cleared up, just like yours did.

I know Hint didn't change my life. I did. But you helped me take that one difficult first step and that means the world to me!

We heard from diabetics, cancer patients, and people who had had gastric bypass surgery. *Hint is a godsend for me.*

One day, Theo and I were walking near our office. Theo was wearing a backpack emblazoned with our *Drink Water, Not Sugar* logo. We passed a café where a woman was eating lunch at an outdoor table. When she saw the logo, she called out to Theo and asked him what it meant.

Theo stopped, told her about Hint, and she seemed seriously interested.

"You know, I'm a pretty big lady, and I think maybe that's exactly why I am. I drink sugar, not water." She spoke in what sounded to Theo like a southern accent.

"It sounds to me that you might be from Georgia. Is that right?"

The woman nodded. Theo got an idea. "Do you have a couple minutes?"

"What for?"

"Our office is right next door. I can run and get you a sample."

"Sure. Why not?"

Theo dashed into the office, all excited.

"I think I've found the perfect person to try the new peach flavor!"

He grabbed a bottle and dashed back to the café. The woman was waiting.

"I brought our newest flavor. Peach. We're just about to launch, and I would love to hear the opinion of a woman from the Peach State."

The woman looked at him skeptically. "Actually, no, you would not."

Theo laughed. "Why?"

"Because everybody tries to make peach drinks and none of them taste *anything* like a real Georgia peach."

Theo wasn't fazed. "That's *exactly* why I want your opinion."

She looked dubious but agreed to give it a try. Theo stood patiently while she opened the bottle and took a sip. She took another. Then a broad smile spread across her face. She stood up and threw her arms around Theo in a big hug.

"Son, now *that* is a peach!"

It had taken three years of hard, patient work, including a trip to Georgia, to get the peach flavor right. But no amount of our own belief in the product could compare to that small but triumphant moment of customer validation.

Theo strutted into the office. "It's a winner."

I smiled. I knew that already.

I love stories like that because they prove we are not only satisfying people, we are helping them. *Helping.* There is no better feeling. Helping consumers just enjoy drinking water.

Especially in tough times, the story behind the business—*your* story; who you are and why you started your company—is what gets you through and keeps your customers, employees, and partners with you. More and more, this is the key to building a successful brand. And sometimes, it's what keeps you afloat.

persevere.

That customer encouragement, combined with my unshakeable belief in our product, kept me and the company going through one of the most difficult periods of American business history and brought us to our biggest triumph yet.

> 66 I love stories like that because they prove we are not only satisfying people, we are helping them. *Helping*. There is no better feeling. 99

CHAPTER 15

celebrate the wins.

'm bad at remembering dates, but there's one I will never forget: March 9, 2010. The day Hint launched at Starbucks. The culmination of a multiyear effort.

During the recession, we had continued to grow same-store sales but had not been opening many new accounts because of the crazy discounting deals they were demanding. As we had predicted, many small beverage companies that had agreed to the deals went bankrupt. As the economy started to recover, we saw the benefit of sticking to our plan. We were still quite small, but we had everything in place. Product. Customers. Organization.

What we needed now was a breakthrough win. A prominent placement where Hint would be noticed. A big leap in exposure.

For several years, we had been working to get into some of the major, quick-serve chains like McDonald's, Dunkin', and Starbucks. They were attractive because of their huge presence in town centers, along highways, and in shopping malls across America. None of them offered many drink choices (apart from Starbucks' endless coffee drink varieties), so a deal with one of them would make Hint visible in a tremendous number of locations that Americans visit every week. Whole Foods, by contrast, had consumers who loved our brand and talked it up, but only had 299 locations (at that time).

I considered the chains a long shot for us, but that didn't keep me from pursuing them. I would send letters and make phone calls not just to the beverage buyers but also to the CEOs, making my pitch about helping America fall in love with water. I encouraged our team members to reach out to anyone and everyone they could find at these huge companies and make the pitch, too. (I often told them about the "dialogue" I was having with McDonald's or Starbucks, although Theo liked to say that it was really more of a monologue. Whatever it takes.) I always believed that eventually the big chains would have to start providing healthier options. If I talked to them early and often, maybe they would think of Hint when the time came.

In early 2009, to my surprise and delight, a Starbucks buyer called me. She had heard we had a product for kids and asked if we could bring it up to Seattle so they could take a look.

"One caution." She sounded quite stern. "We know all about the adult product. Don't bring any samples of that. Just bring the Hint Kids."

I said sure. Only one small concern. The Hint Kids product didn't exist yet. The Starbucks buyer was right that we were working on it. We had made beautiful mock-ups of the package, but had not produced the real thing.

Theo and I flew to Seattle that fall of 2009. I didn't mention that the buyer had told me not to bring samples. Of course, you can't bring water through security at the airport anyway. We got to Seattle and drove to the Starbucks office. Along the way, Theo suggested we stop at a Whole Foods. "We can pick up a few bottles of Hint to give the buyer."

"Ah, actually, no. She said not to bring any samples."

"What are you talking about?"

"I know. It's crazy, but she's only interested in the kids box."

Theo was not buying it. "That's the craziest thing I've ever heard. She has to try the water. That's what's going to be in the kids package!"

He had a point. It did seem ridiculous to meet with the Starbucks buyer without a sample of the product we were going to try and convince her to sell.

"Okay," I said. "We'll buy a few bottles at Whole Foods. I'll stick them in my bag."

We picked up several bottles at the store, including a couple of the apple flavor we had just introduced. Once we were in the meeting and the conversation was going along, I decided, what the hell. I pulled out a bottle of blackberry flavor and took a sip. The buyer stared at me as if I had violated the rules, which I sort of had.

"Oh." I looked at the bottle. "We were just checking stock at the Whole Foods nearby. And I always have a Hint handy to drink."

The buyer stared at me. "Hmm. I didn't know you had a blackberry flavor."

"Oh, really? I have a couple extra bottles here. Want to try it?"

"Sure." I think I noticed Theo trying to contain a chuckle.

The buyer took a sip and seemed to like it. I explained to her that it was the same product that would be in the juice-box-sized package. And I gave her my pitch about the harmful effects of too much sugar or diet sweeteners, particularly for kids. She listened but made no commitments. We flew home, not at all sure if we had a deal.

A couple days later, the buyer called. "We're not going to launch the kids boxes."

Okay. That was that.

"But . . . we are interested in testing your regular Hint product in our stores."

"You're kidding," I blurted out. I hadn't even thought that was a possibility.

"It's a good thing you brought those samples to the meeting. We're about to launch a small test of enhanced waters and juices in a few stores up here in Seattle. It would be a mistake not to include Hint."

I could only laugh. So much for abiding by ridiculous rules.

"We need a shipment in a couple days. There's a lot of paperwork you'll have to work through fast if you want to get paid first."

"If it's okay with you, we'll send whatever product you need. It's no big deal if we don't get paid."

Just before Thanksgiving, we heard from the Starbucks buyer.

"Hint turned out to be the most popular product in the test. We want to launch it in three hundred locations early next year."

We were very excited, but tried not to get *too* excited. Three hundred stores was great, but the ultimate goal was to get into all of Starbucks' 6,700 stores.

Right after Thanksgiving, we heard from the Starbucks buyer again.

"We'd like to expand your distribution even further. We'd like to put Hint in a thousand locations."

We got to know Starbucks' sourcing team very well in the following weeks. We went back and forth on the details, working through a mountain of paperwork, but a week or so before Christmas we had negotiated a deal that was a real win-win. Starbucks got an amazing price on Hint, and they agreed to pick up the product at our bottlers.

We were finalizing the details and getting ready to gear up for the May launch in a thousand stores, when we got another call the day after Christmas.

It was the buyer again. "I know this sounds crazy. Is there any way you could launch in a larger number of stores?"

"How many?"

"Six thousand seven hundred." That was our dream. Every one of the company-owned Starbucks in the United States.

It *was* crazy. Not two times or even five times, but *seven times* as many locations? We had never created that much volume before and we only had five months to work out all the details.

"Oh, and one more thing."

"What's that?"

"We want to launch on March 9. That means we'll need all the product ready to ship by the end of January."

What? Just one month to bottle our biggest order to our biggest customer ever. We might have said no or tried to push the date back, but it happens that March 9 is Theo's birthday. What better gift than a national launch for Hint in Starbucks?

> 66 We might have said no or tried to push the date back, but it happens that March 9 is Theo's birthday. What better gift than a national launch for Hint in Starbucks? 99

The quantity we had to produce was mind-boggling. Almost seven thousand stores. Each one would receive five or six cases of product. One case was reserved for the store employees, so they could be up to speed on Hint, and that case had to be marked with a special red sticker.

6 cases x 24 bottles each x 6,700 stores = 964,800 bottles.

Almost a million bottles of Hint! And we had to produce them in a matter of weeks while continuing to fill orders from our existing customers. A couple factors made it easier. We would launch with only one flavor: blackberry. And because Starbucks had agreed to pick up the product at our production facilities and manage the distribution, all we had to do was fill bottles. Still, we spent most of the holidays on the phone lining up production capacity.

We got it done.

So began a very successful relationship with Starbucks. The response was immediate and positive. For the first couple months, we were deluged with customer calls and emails from all over the country. Starbucks gave us a target of selling a couple bottles per store per week, and we were blowing it away. More people than ever were falling in love with Hint. Sales spiked. We got more and more distribution, until we were in about ten thousand Starbucks locations, expanding into independently owned shops. It was crazy and exciting.

It was the big win we thought it could be, but it was also just one of the successes we had as we left the recession behind.

One of the reasons for our increased popularity, I'm quite sure, is that we introduced a new label in early 2010, just in time for the Starbucks launch. We had been packaging Hint with a clear label since we first came on the market. Packaging and visuals are key to a brand's identity. To us, a clear label was right for Hint, because it connotes clarity, purity, and simplicity. The customer can see right into the bottle and be assured there is nothing but clear, pure water inside. (The days of smegginess were long gone.) No one had ever complained or even commented on the clear label. We thought of it as an important part of the Hint brand identity.

Then one day, we had a conversation with a well-known, very successful figure in the beverage industry, someone also known as a crusty and very direct person. He told us that we were "dumb" to be using a clear label, because it didn't show off the product properly on the store shelf.

At first, we were rather offended by the comment. We were doing just fine with a clear label. But when we really took a look at it, we could see the guy had a point. With a clear label, you can look right through the bottle and the water, to whatever is behind it—other products, or the shelf, or whatever. So, in a way, the look was confusing. At a dinner with our sales team in New York, Theo proposed the idea of swapping out the clear label for a white one. Nobody liked it. Theo grabbed a white napkin and wrapped it around the back of the bottle. Suddenly, the design popped out, the fruit was prominent, and all the visual background noise disappeared.

Done. Hint appeared in Starbucks with a striking, fresh, new white label.

Business continued to grow. We added more flavors and experimented with blends like pomegranate-tangerine, mango-grapefruit, strawberry-kiwi, and raspberry-lime.

We were also getting more and more recognition. We won the Retailer Choice Award from *CSP* magazine, an industry publication. *Men's Health* named Hint the "Best Flavored Water" on the market. The most exciting and dramatic coverage, however, was another feature by CNBC, this time on a show called *How I Made My Millions*.

Let me make it clear that we had *not* made even $1 million from Hint Water by that point, let alone "millions." In fact, we like to say that the show should have been called *How I* Spent *My Millions*. But that's okay. The company itself had taken in millions in revenue, even if we hadn't seen any profit. The fact that we were constantly starved for cash and were personally on the hook for the company is beside the point.

I was excited because I had never done this kind of television piece before, even though I had plenty of experience with TV from my CNN days. The show would be hosted by veteran reporter Tyler Mathisen, and they wanted to film us that summer on location.

At that time, we would spend some part of every summer on the East Coast, partly so we could be near the kids' camp and partly so we could check in with our accounts and co-packers in New England. That summer, we rented a beautiful house near the beach in Rowayton, Connecticut, so that ended up being the main shooting location.

The camera crew set up in the kitchen, and I told the story of founding Hint. As I talked about my health problems and dislike of plain water, about how I had cut up fruit and thrown it in pitchers of water, I actually cut up fruit and threw it in a pitcher of water as the cameras rolled. They got more shots of us driving around in our Honda Pilot that we had wrapped with graphics of fresh fruit and the Hint logo. What we found most amazing was that Tyler, the host, was nowhere to be seen during the filming. We never even met him. He was taped at a different studio and his questions and comments were intercut with the shots of me.

A five-minute segment aired in September 2010. Viewers loved it. CNBC showed it more than six hundred times. The producers told us it was the highest-rated segment in the history of the *How I Made My Millions* series. The response was incredible. For months afterward, people would come up to me and say hello, tell me they had seen the show, and let me know how much they enjoyed Hint.

I loved these conversations. That following spring, we took the whole family to stay at The Cloister at Sea Island, Georgia. We bought some Hint Water at a local store, and my daughter Kaitlin and I spent the afternoon lounging by the pool.

A woman noticed me drinking Hint and tentatively came up to me. "I'm so sorry to bother you, but I was just wondering where you got that drink." I told her I had gotten it at the local store.

"Oh, I've been wanting to try it. Ever since I saw this lady from Hint on CNBC on a show called *How I Made My Millions*."

"Really? Tell me about her. Who was she?" My daughter was not in the mood for Hint chatter. She got up and dove in the pool.

"It was the person who started the company," the woman said, getting into it. "She told all about how she had been drinking a lot of Diet Coke. She decided to start drinking water instead. She lost weight, but she really didn't like the taste of plain water. So she sliced up fruit and . . ."

She stopped in mid-sentence, looking somewhat cautiously at me, noticing the big smile on my face.

"That's my company," I said. "So I know the story."

"Get outta here! You work for her? What's she like?"

I burst out laughing. Kaitlin came out of the pool and grabbed a towel. "What are you guys talking about?"

"Your mom was just telling me that she works for Hint."

Kaitlin deadpanned, "Oh, yeah, she definitely does."

I don't usually tell people right away that I founded the company
and that I'm the CEO. It does kind of amaze me, though, that more
people don't recognize me from the TV show or publicity pictures.
I have long red hair and don't really look like an executive. So I
didn't tell the lady at the pool who I was during that conversation,
but later I bumped into her and her husband. She introduced us
and her husband asked me point-blank what I did for the company.
I finally had to come clean and confess my identity.

The woman was almost breathless. She told me how much the
CNBC show had meant to her. Not only did it make her think she
could start her own company one day based on her own personal
passion, but it also inspired her to take charge of her health.

That was just one of thousands of conversations I've had over the
years. A lot of them happen on airplanes. I have Hint logos on my
laptop and usually have a Hint luggage tag. People ask if I'm associated with the company. Sometimes I tell them who I am, usually I
don't. They almost always have a story they want to tell me.

On one flight, I met a guy who had recently started working for
Google. He said he loved Hint and asked why I had founded the
company. I told him the story and, as I did, I could see him really
connecting with it.

"That's so funny," he said. "Before I came to Google, I was drinking a ton of Diet Dr Pepper. It was like you and Diet Coke. When
I interviewed at Google, the hiring manager said, 'By the way, if
you take a job here, you need to start drinking Hint.' I thought he
was joking and he sort of was. But not really. Since Hint is all over
the place.

"They hired me and I tried Hint," the guy continued. "I just naturally started swapping out my Diet Dr Pepper for whatever Hint
flavor was on hand. After a few weeks, my wife said: 'You know,
you're looking pretty good. What's going on? Is it the new job? You
seem a lot happier.'"

The guy was thrilled his wife told him how good he looked. Then
he hopped on the scale and saw he had lost five pounds.

"When my wife's telling me I'm looking pretty good, that's something," he said. "And I have Hint to thank for that."

Conversations like that one and the one by the pool have convinced me that it's really important to bring your personal story into the brand identity. People associate the brand with a human being and that person's story. It adds tremendous meaning and value to them.

> ❝ It's really important to bring your personal story into the brand identity. People associate the brand with a human being and that person's story. It adds tremendous meaning and value to them. ❞

These conversations are tremendously meaningful and valuable to me. When people ask me what makes me happiest about my life with Hint, I always say, "Consumer stories."

Our sales doubled in 2010 and continued to grow the year after that. There's no question that getting into Starbucks was a turning point for us, but it was the way our team leveraged that win to get into more stores and gain more exposure that really made it pay off in the long run.

Lucky thing, as it turned out.

CHAPTER 16

transform setback into opportunity.

T hen, one day in 2012, we got *the* phone call from a Starbucks executive.

"I have bad news for you."

She explained that Howard Schultz himself had made a decision to add food to the Starbucks offerings. He wanted to try to build up the business in more of the "day parts," as retailers call them— lunchtime, in particular, when their business was slower than it was during the morning coffee rush. The sandwiches and yogurt and cheese sticks would be displayed in the cold case, which meant other items had to be removed to make room. Retail real estate, as we knew very well, is limited and precious. The exec told us they had decided to remove two Starbucks brand items and one Hint item.

"There is only one Hint item in the case. Blackberry."

"I know," she said. "That has to go. You have two weeks."

Just like that. We had been given two months to deliver a million bottles of Hint in March of 2010. Now, in 2012, we were getting our two weeks' notice.

There was nothing we could do about it.

That was a bad day and a very serious blow. Not only was Starbucks a major account, but we had built up about six months' worth of blackberry inventory, just to be sure we could fulfill Starbucks' demand.

I was polite and appreciative. I quietly hung up the phone and then started to scream. We pouted for a few days. But gradually I began to put the loss in perspective. That was just Starbucks' way of doing business. They do not have loyalty to third-party brands. They want to keep a steady stream of new products coming through because that's what attracts and keeps customers.

And Starbucks had done a lot for us. Millions of customers all around the country had discovered Hint. The recognition and success had enabled us to build our business elsewhere. As a result, Starbucks was actually a smaller part of our business than it had been when we started the relationship. We were strong enough now to take the hit. We had a lot of blackberry on hand but, fortunately, it was one of our top-selling flavors.

Still, it seemed like a disaster at the time.

I felt like I was back in my postcollege days, looking for a job. We needed more opportunities. The Starbucks door had closed, so we just had to find another door to open.

Lesson learned. Never put all your eggs in one basket. Or even most of your eggs. Minimize risk. Always.

Theo and I knew that Starbucks had helped us build sales and enhance Hint's brand, but we also came to another rather counterintuitive conclusion. In those first few months that Hint was stocked at Starbucks, we received all those emails from new customers who had just learned about us, loved the product, and were excited to hear about our mission to make people healthier. But over time, the communications dropped off, even though sales at Starbucks remained steady. We realized we were selling tons of product to the same people over and over again. Which was great, but the downside was that Starbucks wasn't bringing us a steady stream of *new* business. The upside was that we had formed a relationship with millions of Starbucks customers. Now that Hint was no longer available there, wouldn't they be looking for it elsewhere?

> **"** Lesson learned. Never put all your eggs in one basket. Or even most of your eggs. Minimize risk. Always. **"**

While still mourning the loss of our Starbucks relationship, we received a call from a buyer at Amazon. He was a fan of Hint and was interested in making it available in Amazon's new grocery business. They offered only a few grocery items at the time, but were getting ready to expand.

"Do you have inventory available?" he asked.

"Yes. We have as much of the blackberry flavor as you need." I didn't mention getting kicked out of Starbucks, of course.

"Okay. Sounds good. Let's do it."

Almost immediately, Hint became one of the top grocery products on Amazon.

Online sales seemed promising. Obviously, I knew a good deal about online shopping from my AOL days. And our own site, drinkhint.com, had been successful almost from day one, even though it was still pretty bare bones. Now, e-commerce was taking off for all kinds of products, but no one was really scaling it in food and beverage. Maybe Amazon could pull it off? So we set our sights on Amazon as our replacement for Starbucks.

After the launch, we flew to Amazon to meet with the buyer. He shared with us some data about the online sales. The profile of the Hint consumer was very different from that of the online purchasers of other beverages, like Coke or Diet Coke. The Hint consumer bought a whole range of health-related products, such as Kind bars, fitness books, and diabetes test strips. His analysis was that Hint customers genuinely cared about their health and some percentage of them were trying to permanently change their health habits or manage a health issue of some kind.

I asked if I could reach out to some of the Amazon consumers so I could learn more.

"No," he said. "The data belongs to Amazon. It's proprietary."

"What?"

"We buy your product. We own the data."

No discussion.

> 66 That would be the best way for us to truly understand our consumers. Why should Amazon know more about our consumers than we did? 99

As we flew back to San Francisco that evening, it became clear. As much potential as Amazon had for us, we needed to put more resources into building out our own e-commerce site. That would be the best way for us to truly understand our consumers. Why should Amazon know more about our consumers than we did?

Not everyone in our leadership was on board with increasing the investment in the website. Remember, no one had yet proved that online grocery shopping could be successful. There had been huge failures, including a service called Webvan in our area. And, if we increased our online presence, would we be in competition with Amazon? They could almost certainly beat us on price.

We decided to move ahead and enhance the site—not a complete overhaul, but appreciable and strategic, nonetheless. Our biggest advantages were our promise and our values. Yes, we could offer a wide selection. No, we could not match Amazon's prices. So, going hard for direct-to-consumer sales was a risk for us. But we believed Hint was the kind of brand our consumers would want to support. They would rather buy direct from us than from a big retailer.

We looked at the research, and it demonstrated that more and more millennials—people born in the 1980s or 1990s—were spending their money online, rather than in grocery stores or other physical retail outlets. They were an important customer group for us, and we were betting on them to buy Hint direct from our site.

Not everybody was convinced that a big move to direct sales was such a good idea. Our board of directors, for example, saw mostly danger ahead. "Amazon will treat you just the way Starbucks treated you. Sooner or later, they'll crush you."

Maybe. But it was worth the risk. We had no worries that Amazon would try to create a competing product. We knew our product was unique, very hard to replicate, and that our customers wanted to associate with a brand with a distinct identity.

While we were in some retailers, most notably Whole Foods, and lots of tech offices, what was most important was to be readily available to consumers. If they wanted to buy food and beverage online, we were more than happy to accommodate them.

Ultimately, we were proven right, I'm glad to say. Today, direct sales account for almost 50 percent of our business. That is very high for a beverage maker. And, here's the thing: we probably would not have gone after the online business as early or as vigorously if we hadn't had that shock ending to our Starbucks relationship.

We learned a lot from our Starbucks journey.

First, we learned the wisdom of staying on good terms with partners whenever possible, even when a relationship is souring and tempers could easily flare. When Starbucks called with the bad news that we were being kicked out of the cold case, I expressed disappointment but quickly let the exec know that we loved Starbucks and hoped to work with them again in the future. And they kept Hint in Starbucks branches inside Target stores as well as on military bases for years. While the volume was considerably smaller than we'd had in thousands of Starbucks locations all over the country, it was better than nothing and allowed us to grow our business with Target directly.

Second, we learned not to take business reversals like that personally. Howard Shultz had a business purpose—to improve performance at a certain time of day and to increase profit by selling food, which has much fatter margins than beverage products. Starbucks dropped us for a business reason. There was nothing dramatic, emotional, or spiteful about the decision. My only problem with the decision was how abrupt it was. Starbucks gave us two weeks' notice. That was not a lot of time to figure out how to make up for the lost revenue or decide what to do with the inventory that had been earmarked for Starbucks.

A third lesson, perhaps the most important one of all: never, ever put all your eggs in one basket. To be successful, you have to have options and alternatives, so that if one door closes, you can open another one quickly. That was one of the reasons we invested in our online presence. If a large retailer were to cut us off today, we can always reach customers in the affected areas online.

The lesson holds true for your advertising channels, too. When I hear from e-commerce companies that Facebook is their only way of acquiring customers, it makes me nervous. Figure out what other avenues are available *before* it's figured out for you.

And employees. While we all want to say that our favorite employees will never leave us, it happens. Always be on the lookout for current employees that could fill another person's shoes if someone leaves. Always be on the lookout for good candidates, and keep interviewing people even when you don't have an immediate job opening.

If you don't create a network of options, opportunities, potential partners, and employees, you're putting your company at risk.

When you have a setback like we had with Starbucks, it's important to take time to recognize what the journey did bring you, rather than just moan about what you lost. Starbucks introduced us to many places that we would not have been able to enter at such an early stage in our start-up life. They gave us the ability to connect with consumers, and those consumers stuck with us by finding another retailer or going online.

> 66 To be successful, you have to have options and alternatives, so that if one door closes, you can open another one quickly. 99

The final, crucial lesson we learned from the Starbucks experience was that, without the consumer, all you have is a good idea. Customer feedback isn't just interesting. It's everything.

Find out who your customers are and why. Discover what sets you apart from your competition in their eyes. This information is critical for researching marketing options, brand collaborations, packaging—you name it. The internet makes interaction convenient and abundant. It helps you keep all portals of communication open, and it allows you to maintain an ongoing conversation with your clientele. You keep them at the forefront, and they'll keep you in business.

Most gratifying of all, customers will bring you wonderful stories about how you have enriched their lives, which will enrich your life as well.

CHAPTER 17

define the meaning of your brand.

There comes a moment when a product becomes more than a product—it transforms into a brand.

It's not about reaching a sales or profit target or about getting a lot of media exposure, although those things are part of it. It's not a specific moment, either. It happens over time until, one day, you wake up and realize the product you created and know so intimately no longer completely belongs to you. Customers feel they are part of it. Its value goes beyond the immediate solution it provides. It has become part of the culture, with a meaning greater than what's in the package.

That is gradually what happened with Hint, starting around 2012 and continuing today. Hint became more than a selection of fruit-infused water products. Hint stood for the idea that healthy products should be the most enjoyable products. And the company—the entire organization—was part of the brand identity. We were not a member of the Big Sugar beverage establishment. We were more in the tradition of Silicon Valley, the land of technology and entrepreneurialism. We were disrupting the idea that your favorite drink has to taste sweet by delivering products that proved that assumption wrong.

How does the transformation happen?

Most important, customers become more than customers. They become fans and product advocates, believers, and participants. This transformation is hard to predict or control. For example, we knew that the tech companies might be a good fit for Hint, but had no idea how the brand would take off. At Google, Hint drinking reached the point of obsession. When the display cases were stocked with a new Hint flavor, Google employees would grab as many bottles as they could carry and stash them away. The practice got so prevalent that it became known as "Hint hoarding."

When something trends at Google, it can have a ripple effect throughout the tech community. When we saw how popular Hint had become there, we started reaching out to other tech companies, appearing at industry conferences, and generally working to build on that special customer base, but word of mouth outran our marketing efforts throughout Silicon Valley. Eventually, Hint was stocked in the cafeterias and break rooms at Uber, Facebook, Yelp, Spotify, Snap, Instagram, and Hulu. We heard about other fascinating Hint practices. At LinkedIn, for example, people experienced the "Hint Effect"—they drank so much, they were peeing more often than usual.

Why did Hint catch on with members of the tech community? One reason is that the values associated with the brand appealed to them. Not everyone in tech fits the media stereotype of the over-caffeinated, pizza-eating, sugar-craving coder. Lots of them— millennials, in particular—want to eat and drink in a healthy way, and Hint was there to help them do it. Although Hint wasn't available in many stores, the millennials discovered it. It was disruptive.

Another reason is that Silicon Valley folks identify with the Hint story and the company itself. As one industry journalist put it, "Hint, like many start-ups in Silicon Valley, started out as an idea in a kitchen—or a garage, if you prefer. The story resonates with the community, of building something—whether it be a product or an app—from the ground up. This is a familiar tale and endears Hint to the tech world and those within it who are building something of their own."

> **"** Hint, like many start-ups in Silicon Valley, started out as an idea in a kitchen—or a garage, if you prefer. The story resonates with the community, of building something—whether it be a product or an app—from the ground up. **"**

When people embrace a product like that, they begin to incorporate it in their lives in ways that transcend consumption. The Google game designers incorporated Hint into Ingress, their augmented reality game. One of the key characters is Klue, a "Niantic Investigator," who first appeared in 2012 and can be seen strutting down the street with a bottle of Hint in hand. (I think her favorite is blackberry.) That placement led to a special promotion in which we printed in-game codes in Hint bottle caps. (I couldn't help but think of the guy I had met years earlier at the Tee Pee restaurant who did product placement for Anheuser-Busch.) A couple years later, Hint showed up in the HBO TV series *Silicon Valley*, prominently displayed on a coffee table at the tech incubator where much of the action takes place.

Another reason that Hint became so popular in Silicon Valley is the founder story. I never intended to be the public face of the brand in the way that I did, and I'm not a natural attention-seeker, but Theo and I personally became a part of the story. That's because people love to connect a brand with a real human being, especially if the person has an interesting and authentic personal narrative that directly relates to the product.

As Hint gained popularity, the Hint story gradually came out in bits and pieces, in interviews and feature stories, and in speeches and conferences. People picked up on different elements of the narrative and played them up. Some focused on my background as the youngest of five kids and how that experience fed into my relentless nature. There was the story of my father, the guy who created the Healthy Choice products, but did not achieve his dream of becoming an entrepreneur, and how that affected me. Others highlighted our Silicon Valley credentials—me as an executive at AOL and Theo's work at Netscape.

The most essential part of the story was always how my health struggles led to the invention of Hint in our kitchen. People respond to that because it's so relatable—many of us are longing to take charge of our own lives, whether that be our health, our careers, our relationships, or all three.

And, of course, there's the start-up tale. How Theo and I built a company from scratch, pooh-poohed by the big players in the beverage industry, and succeeded against very long odds. It was not the story of a well-funded, MBA-holding, well-connected, master-of-the-tech-universe entrepreneur looking to make a ton of money fast. It was a business success story with a lot of simple, human touchpoints.

I spent more and more time telling our story, because it also created opportunities for me to learn what our customers liked and why they cared about Hint. I learned that "healthy" meant different things to different people—super-fit techies who watched every ingredient they consumed, diabetics looking to cut back on sugar, parents who wanted to teach their kids good consumption habits, cancer patients who found that Hint hid the metallic taste of chemo treatments, millennials who didn't want to support big corporations, and anybody and everybody who enjoyed fresh flavors and refreshing water. And again, these were other people's stories. How Hint helped them. Very different from Hint making health claims that we've all seen other food and beverage companies make. Real-life stories from customers are much more powerful.

As attention built around the product and the company, the greater business community took notice, and we started to win awards and gain recognition. In 2011, *Fortune* named me one of the "10 Most Powerful Women Entrepreneurs" and one of the "Most Innovative Women in Food and Drink." That award took me to a *Fortune* conference in Laguna Niguel, California, where I was honored alongside nine other female entrepreneurs. We got to meet and hang out with some of the members of the even more impressive list, *Fortune*'s "Most Powerful Women in Business," the leaders of major companies, including Arianna Huffington, Tyra Banks, Tory Burch, Chelsea Handler, and, interestingly enough, Indra Nooyi of PepsiCo, one of the grand poobahs of Big Sugar. (Warren Buffett was the honorary male guest.)

That kind of attention added yet another dimension to the brand. It said that not only did customers like us, but successful people in a variety of disciplines and industries recognized we were doing something notable. That made it easier to bring in new retail accounts, create new business partnerships, and attract people to work for us. It validated our mission, and it made us feel good.

And it helped us grow. In the years following the recession, we kept ticking past one revenue milestone after another—past $10 million, then $20 million, in some years doubling the revenue. The growth enabled us to continue to secure financing, and we raised a total of $72 million along the way.

The organization grew, too. Starting with just Theo and me in the Jeep, to five people around the dining room table on Scott Street, to twenty, then sixty-five, and now closing in on two hundred people contributing to all levels of the organization at our San Francisco and New York offices and in towns and cities around the country.

It's funny to think of that number of employees—two hundred. It was at about that phase in the growth of AOL when I started to get bored by the administrative duties and tedious tasks of day-to-day management.

But, at Hint, I feel energized and challenged by our growth, because the nature of the organization itself is an important part of the brand. Every employee at Hint has an ownership stake in the company. Each person has a personal commitment to help the company grow and succeed.

> 66 Every employee at Hint has an ownership stake in the company. Each person has a personal commitment to help the company grow and succeed. 99

We also have a distinct approach to hiring. The right person for Hint is someone who loves the product and believes in the mission. We want people who align with the values of the company, who are eager to learn how we do things, and who are motivated to help us innovate and improve.

For me, the key to hiring is to look for people who are better than I am at what they do, people who bring something important to the table that I don't. To think that way takes confidence in yourself and your abilities, along with a genuine desire to make the company better. It starts with self-awareness—you have to have a good sense of your own strongest skills and also be willing to acknowledge where you fall a little short. If you have the confidence (and the evidence) that you're good in particular areas, then it's easy to value skills others have that you don't.

> 66 You have to have a good sense of your own strongest skills and also be willing to acknowledge where you fall a little short. 99

Still, it's important not to get hung up on specific skills or on finding the perfect person for the job. You want people who bring more to the table than a single skill. You want them to think about how best to further the mission of the company in their area—whether it's marketing, sales, technology, or whatever—and it may not be in the way that you have planned or imagined. People need to have room to roam in their job description, to rethink processes and challenge standard ways of doing things, to come up with solutions and ideas that you might not have thought of. Having that kind of freedom will inspire their loyalty, and it will help keep the company fresh and exciting and more able to adapt to changing business conditions.

Once we bring people on board, we constantly push them to grow and to keep moving beyond their current level—often before they think about it themselves. People have a natural tendency to get into a work routine where they can be successful, but the comfortable groove can quickly become a rut.

Often, the best time to push people to move on is when they are most successful and happy. That's what I did with one of our most capable people.

"Do you like what you're doing?" I asked him one day.

"I love what I'm doing," he responded, a little surprised by my question.

"I think it's time for you to hire someone to replace you."

He looked worried. "What are you talking about?"

"I know you enjoy your job right now. You've been doing it well for the past couple years. But we're growing so fast, things are going to change in ways you can't predict."

I could see he was trying to understand where I was heading.

"I think you've reached the top of this particular mountain. Given the kind of person you are, that means you could get a little bored, without even realizing it. Your performance might suffer. Or you might start looking for opportunities outside the company. I don't want that to happen. So now's the time, when you've mastered this role, to move on to something more challenging. You have all the knowledge to train your replacement and enough ambition to want to succeed at the next level, whatever that is."

"Wow. I hadn't been thinking that way. But, you're right. I have been feeling just a tiny bit bored. I know the job too well. I hadn't thought about the next step at all."

I encourage everyone to be on the lookout for signs of complacency. We should always be asking ourselves, "What can I be doing better?" If you can't come up with an answer on your own, look for some outside perspective and guidance. Don't wait for a formal performance review. Talk to your boss. It can be as simple as saying: "I love my job. I feel like I'm performing really well. What else could I be doing?" At Hint, we try to promote from within as much as possible, and the people who get promoted are the ones who have already started doing the job they want next. Showing your boss that you're ready to step up is a lot more likely to get you the position you want than expecting to be promoted because you've been doing your current job well.

I never want people in the Hint organization to think their work requires nothing more than showing up at the office on time and doing what they have always done. That's how people stagnate, brands get out of touch with their customers, and companies lose the ability to innovate.

The same applies to the company founders: it's up to you to create an environment that encourages innovation.

CHAPTER 18

expand the mission.

For years, I had a tiny patch of dry skin on my nose, but I didn't think it was anything to worry about. It had been there so long, I just ignored it. In 2015, it got a little bigger and looked a bit red, so I finally forced myself to see my dermatologist, Dr. Kathleen Welsh. She didn't like the look of it, so she scraped off a bit and sent it to the lab to be tested. It turned out to be a precancerous basal cell tumor. I wasn't in any great danger, because basal cell skin cancers rarely spread to other parts of the body. Still, they can grow and be problematic, and in rare cases they can become malignant and metastasize.

Kathleen was taking no chances. She removed the dry spot and took a little extra bit of my nose with it, just to be sure she had gotten all the cancerous cells. When she was done, she said: "From now on, Kara, you absolutely have to wear sunscreen at all times. Once you've had one of these melanomas, you could certainly have another."

I had been using a foundation with sunscreen, but I probably hadn't been wearing it regularly, especially at the beach or pool. So, just as I had done when I was examining my soda addiction back in 2005, I started scrutinizing my sunscreen habit. As a kid, I hated putting on sunscreen because it felt oily or sticky or made my skin itch. I felt like taking a shower fifteen seconds after application. As an adult, I tried the new and improved unscented sunscreens, which felt better on the skin, but I still wasn't diligent about applying it and almost never reapplied as recommended. Like many things you know are good for you, you still don't use them if you don't love them.

Could I find a way to fall in love with sunscreen as I had found a way to fall in love with water? I didn't think adding fragrance was the solution, because I had never liked scented sunscreens. Then I realized that I had hated the flavored waters that were available on the market before I invented Hint. I solved that problem.

What if we could enhance the experience of applying sunscreen with a fantastic fruit essence, without leaving so much scent on the skin that people walk around smelling like fruit?

The idea was exciting but I had no clue how to make sunscreen. I did some research and learned that sunscreens have many ingredients, two of which are pretty scary. One of them, oxybenzone, is a naturally occurring chemical found in flowering plants. It absorbs sunlight, which is what makes it effective as a sunscreen. It was approved for use by the Food and Drug Administration in the late 1970s, but in the years since, questions have been raised about its safety. The substance is absorbed into the skin and some evidence suggests it might cause precancer cells to form and grow. Another ingredient commonly used in sunscreens, parabens, has been linked to hormone disruption and breast cancer.

I did not like the sound of any of these ingredients. I did not need any more precancerous cells, and I wasn't interested in trading skin cancer for breast cancer. I grabbed the sunscreens we had in the house, checked the ingredients, and found they all contained oxybenzone or parabens or both. My foundation makeup, with SPF, did, too.

I went back to my dermatologist and asked her what she knew about oxybenzone.

"Not a lot. Once a substance is approved by the FDA, that's pretty much it. Doctors are not researchers. We rely on the FDA to tell us what's safe for our patients."

Now I had a bigger challenge than just getting myself to wear sunscreen. I wanted to find one that did not contain these potentially harmful ingredients.

I checked out dozens of sunscreen brands and learned there are two basic types. There are "natural," mineral-based products that physically block out the sun, and there are products whose ingredients absorb the sun's rays before they reach your skin. I tried one of the popular mineral sunscreens, but it smelled kind of like dirt going on, and after an hour my skin itched and I had developed a rash. So much for being "natural." Next, I tried an oxybenzone-free and paraben-free active sunscreen. It didn't smell bad or irritate my skin, but it was super-expensive and totally bland. Why would I actually want to put it on?

After trying a number of other products, I thought we could do better. I asked Theo if he thought we could use fruit essences to make a spray-on sunscreen that would smell great as you applied it but not too strong afterward. It seemed like it was worth a try.

We worked on the project off and on for the next two years and came up with a number of prototypes. Some were too fruity and the scent persisted too long after application. Some barely had any scent at all.

Then one day, Theo asked me to try the latest version. "It's pineapple."

That sounded dubious. "Really?" I wasn't sure I wanted to try it, but I sprayed some on my arm. It smelled great going on. After a moment, the scent dissipated. My face lit up.

"You nailed it! It's perfect."

We got more proof a few days later. The whole family flew to Hawaii for the spring school break, and we took the prototype sunscreen with us. We used it for a couple days at the beach and liked it. It felt good on the skin and protected us from burning.

Then Justin, our youngest kid, gave it a try before going in for a swim.

"What do you think?" I asked.

"It's good." That could mean anything from "I love it" to "I'm humoring you."

An hour later, Justin ran back to me. "Mom, I need more of that pineapple sunscreen!" He loved the experience of spraying it on. After another hour, he was back again for an application.

I turned to Theo. "We've got a winner!"

We launched Hint sunscreen in the summer of 2017. Some of our customers and partners were surprised at our new product direction. Industry insiders didn't always see the connection.

"Is it, like, a water thing?" they wanted to know. "Fruit water and seawater at the beach?"

No. For us, Hint sunscreen made perfect sense, because it fulfilled the mission of the brand—helping people fall in love with healthy choices—in a whole new way. It was a good business initiative, too. It showed that our mission was bigger than water and that we had the ability to innovate beyond our original product.

One thing that Theo and I love to do is develop new offerings. Even today, when we have a talented flavor team and an organization to support us, we manage the innovation process. Over the years, we have developed a constantly changing lineup of flavors, as well as a number of new product forms. In 2012, we introduced Hint Fizz, the carbonated version, and Hint Kick, with added caffeine, in 2015.

Developing a sunscreen demonstrated we were willing to take big leaps, try things we had never done before, and act as a disruptor, shaking up another industry that had been complacent for decades. But most important, it *helped* people.

Soon enough, Hint sunscreen was getting the same kind of customer response our water had. We got emails from people all over the country. "Now I never have to fight with my kids to get them to wear sunscreen," one mom wrote. "It's a game now. I don't say, 'You have to put on sunscreen.' I ask them, 'Which scent do you want? Pear? Grapefruit? Pineapple?' They love it. It's a totally different experience for them and for me. Thank you so much!"

> 66 For us, Hint sunscreen made perfect sense, because it fulfilled the mission of the brand—helping people fall in love with healthy choices—in a whole new way. 99

Our move into a whole new category—combined with the success of our products, the growth of our sales, the devotion of our customers, and the growing reputation of the company—has helped us transform Hint into what I believe is becoming an iconic brand. I would love to think that Hint will someday be seen in the same league as great brands like Apple, Patagonia, Google, Whole Foods, Zegna, Toms, and The Body Shop. These companies have many things in common. They have a strong founder influence and presence. They are fanatical about their product. They maintain high standards of quality and innovation. They're committed to a cause greater than just financial success and growth.

What's fascinating to me is that the brand, the story, and the customer involvement all have an effect on the product itself. Hint

Water has a special and distinctive taste, not just because of the formula itself, but because of all the associations people have with the brand. The taste of the product is as much in your mind as it is on your tongue.

Not only is that great for the customer, it's great for the company, because the product differentiation makes it hard for competitors to replicate the experience or compete with the brand. Many business analysts still don't get that. Hint seems to just be a flavored water. One water industry analyst, for example, doubted our prospects, because he thought our idea was "relatively replicable. Adding not much to water is easy to do, and the proof will be in whether Hint can buck that when others start to encroach."

Well, here's the thing. Other companies have been trying for many years now to "replicate" our "easy" idea, and none have succeeded. There are many reasons for that.

> 66 Hint Water has a special and distinctive taste, not just because of the formula itself, but because of all the associations people have with the brand. The taste of the product is as much in your mind as it is on your tongue. 99

The first is that a fresh fruit flavor is not so easy to create as one might think. As proof, guess what the hardest flavor is to get right.

It's not mango-grapefruit or honeydew-hibiscus or peppermint or strawberry-kiwi.

It's lemon.

You would think lemon would be the simplest flavor of all to make. People have been squeezing lemon juice into their water for centuries. But sometimes the simplest things are the hardest. Turns out lemon is a highly unstable complex of flavor molecules. If you drop a lemon slice into water and let it sit for a few days, it's not going to taste great. Over the years, we tried lemon flavors from dozens of different flavor houses, from big guys to little guys, and our own flavor team. Every time we said, "It's not quite right." It took us almost twelve years, but we finally nailed it.

Other flavors we nailed on the first try—peppermint, for example. There was a competing product in the market already, but it tasted like dental rinse to a lot of consumers. We told our flavor team we were looking for something totally different—a peppermint reminiscent of candy canes, but not sweet. We weren't even exactly sure what we meant by that, so we had pretty low expectations, but the very first concept we tested tasted perfect.

Some companies have flavor panels and public taste tests and various consultants and outsourced partners who help them develop their flavors. Honestly, our taste panel is the Goldin family. Our test facility is our kitchen. Theo and I mess around with flavors and essences and get to a formula we like. We drink a lot of it ourselves, then we see if the kids like it. In our experience, if the whole family gives a new flavor the thumbs-up, it has a good chance of being successful with customers.

Our approach to product development is another reason Hint is hard to compete with. We keep the intellectual property close. Many of the flavor companies who want to work with us start by asking how we approach flavor development. We never discuss it, because we have no interest in training potential competitors.

That's why it's no wonder so many other companies have tried to create a product like ours and failed. Even before we launched in

2005, there were a number of flavored water products on the market from the big companies. But they all had preservatives and sweeteners, so they couldn't make the same promise we could when we hit the market.

At the end of 2008, just as we were negotiating our investment deal and the recession was closing in, Coca-Cola made a big play for the unsweetened market. They launched Dasani Essence in three flavors: Lime Essence, Strawberry Kiwi Essence, and Black Cherry Essence. "Water drinkers will find Dasani essence has a much lighter and more natural taste than other flavored products," a Coca-Cola exec said in a public statement. "Unlike highly sweetened and more intensely flavored beverages, Dasani essence offers the healthful purity of water with a splash of all-natural fruit flavor excitement."

Soon after Dasani Essence launched, we attended an industry show, the National Association of Convenience Stores, where Coca-Cola was offering samples of the new product. We tried the cherry flavor and almost gagged. "Oh, my God," Theo said, "they're using the cherry flavor from Cherry Coke! They think people are going to like this?"

Coca-Cola spent a lot of money on the launch of Dasani Essence. Pretty soon, it had significant shelf space in stores and outlets where Hint also had a presence. That made me nervous at first, but then we realized it was actually having a positive effect for us. Coke was doing so much promotion and advertising, and because its product was so visible in stores, it boosted awareness of the entire category. More and more retailers were open to the idea of stocking unsweetened flavored water—that's the power of a big brand name. Dasani Essence ultimately failed, but by that time customers were much more aware of the flavored water category in general. Now we could say to retailers, "You did the right thing by stocking an essence water, but you didn't pick the category leader. Now it's time to bring in Hint."

Other companies besides Coca-Cola tried to enter the category. Pepsi had at least five different teams working on knockoffs, but when they tested the prototypes against Hint, everybody preferred us. Same thing happened to Nestlé. They invested in developing a new water product, even going so far as to set up a production facility. But when they tested their version against other brands, consumers gave the same verdict. "Hint is way better." Nestlé mothballed the project.

As we developed new flavors and varieties and tasted the products of other companies, we have learned a lot about the relationship between the product taste and the brand. Taste is a complex perception that occurs in your brain. It synthesizes the signals coming from your tongue, the scent that's coming in through your nose, the visual impressions you're getting from the packaging, along with the memories and thoughts and stories you have stored in your mind related to the company and the brand. All those things mesh and complement one another and actually become part of the taste.

The point is, the experience of taste is complex. When you drink Hint, you're tasting elements of our story, your idea of the company, your view of business, and your commitment to health. That individualistic taste is not easy to understand or replicate, which is another reason that it will be a long time (if ever) before a Big Sugar company will come up with a worthy competitor to Hint.

CHAPTER 19

align with a cause.

Over the years, I have met many people who feel stuck at a certain point in their lives. They may know the mission they want to pursue, but they're so worried about obstacles and objections they can't move forward. Or they may not be entirely clear on what their mission is. Or they may find that their mission has changed over time and needs to be rethought.

Wherever you are in your journey, it can take some doing to figure out what your mission is, but you will never define it, let alone achieve it, if you don't open doors and try different possibilities. When you do that, your mission gradually comes into focus based on what you learn about yourself, your product, your company, and the world as you go along.

I wouldn't say that I had a clearly defined mission when we started out. At first, I was just trying to figure out what could help me fall in love with water. Then, once I solved that problem, I wanted to see if my product could help other people, too. I wasn't sure if anybody would even care. I did not expect the amount of passion our early fans expressed for Hint Water.

It was their support and appreciation that made it clear we were onto something bigger than a product—we were in service of a larger mission to make it easy and enjoyable for people to make healthy choices.

Having fans and hearing that your products make them happy is almost addictive, but it can also make you complacent in thinking your product is good enough and all you have to do is make more of it. So, as much as we loved hearing from our customers, we had to set our own standards and continue to improve in ways we believed would be beneficial to all.

After we had successfully launched locally, we had to find a way to achieve a reasonable shelf life, but we never stopped working to make our fruit flavors taste better and better. That relentless focus on great taste actually solved our shelf-life problem, because the improved recipes not only tasted better, but could hold up well to the heat of the hot-fill bottling process.

In early 2007, with our new process running smoothly, we knew for the first time since starting the company two years earlier that we could build this business nationally. Theo and I grabbed a beer to celebrate, but after enjoying a cold one, I saw a concerned look come over his face.

"What's eating at you now?" I asked.

"Well, we drink a lot of Hint, and our customers here in San Francisco drink a lot of Hint, and I think we can really build this into a billion-dollar national business."

"And that's bad?"

He laughed at himself. "We found a way to help people fall in love with water instead of sugary drinks, which is amazing. We're replacing drinks that make people sick with drinks that are good for them. But if we're going to make packaged goods that are better for people, we also need to find packages that are better for the planet."

align with a cause.

He had a point. We needed to work on reducing the amount of plastic we used in our business. This had been a concern for us from the very beginning, but, putting first things first, Theo had devoted his energies to getting the process right.

> 66 We're replacing drinks that make people sick with drinks that are good for them. But if we're going to make packaged goods that are better for people, we also need to find packages that are better for the planet. 99

Even though we had just started working with a new bottling process, we had come up with a plan for an even better process that would enable us to use a lot less energy and a lot less plastic. Unfortunately, achieving that goal would require significant investment in new equipment, and raising that kind of money would be impossible for us as a small company.

"Well, we're going to get a lot bigger," I said, "so we'll be able to do that someday, but right now we need to focus on getting bigger with a process that works. Meanwhile, let's figure out if there is something we can do to improve with the resources we have today."

"Agreed."

So now our mission had broadened to include both personal health and a healthy environment. This company mission aligned very well with our sense of responsibility as the parents of four kids. We want to do whatever we can to leave the world a better place for the children of today and future generations to grow and thrive in.

We took that challenge very seriously, setting a multiyear goal of reducing the amount of plastic per serving of Hint by at least 30 percent. Over the next twelve years, Theo developed a vision for the bottling line of the future and gradually became an evangelist for a better approach. We visited co-packers around the country, trying to convince them they could adopt advanced technology that would save them money and also be more environmentally responsible. We challenged bottle manufacturers to reduce plastic by improving their bottle designs.

We made progress, step by step. In partnership with our suppliers, we achieved significant improvements during the early years. Eventually, we found a partner who could produce a bottle on the manufacturing line and seal it with a cap made in the same building. Today, using a solution that Theo envisioned thirteen years ago, our newest package is 40 percent lighter than our original sixteen-ounce, hot-fill bottle, and our one-liter bottle, launching in 2020, achieves an even greater savings of plastic. We no longer ship empty bottles into the bottling plants, and we've achieved a tremendous reduction in water waste, with our newest bottling plant using a zero-waste, water-purification system.

We're proud to have produced the most environmentally responsible package possible for our products today, while working toward even better choices for the future. But consumers often ask us why we don't use aluminum cans or bottles instead of plastic. Aluminum suppliers, who noticed the tremendous growth of bottled water, have launched a massive campaign attacking plastic and touting the high recycling rates of aluminum, but what those companies don't talk about is that aluminum packages cause up to ten times more global warming than plastic, even after taking those recycling rates into account.

align with a cause.

Many of our competitors, in response to consumer sentiment, are moving to aluminum. But we have no intention of switching to an environmentally inferior packaging solution to sell product to people who don't fully understand the issues and, in many cases, have been misled by irresponsible messaging from self-serving suppliers. (If you want more information on our perspective on packaging, please check out hintgreen.com.)

Our mission has evolved and broadened in other ways, beyond our efforts to make healthy products that people love and to minimize our environmental footprint. One way is by donating our product to initiatives and organizations that promote health. It all started when one of our earliest Hint fans asked us to donate product for a charity bike race. Theo and I agreed, and we asked if we could set up a table so the riders could sample the product and we could get their reactions.

Almost everyone who tried Hint loved it. They commented on how weird it was that it tastes great without tasting sweet. One rider tasted the pomegranate and said that was his favorite. Then he noticed the bottle next to it and looked horrified. He literally yelled at us.

"Cucumber water! Who would put cucumber in water?"

That attracted the attention of another rider.

"Cucumber water? That sounds amazing!"

The two of them got into an intense debate about flavors that went on for at least five minutes. We had never guessed cucumber could be such a polarizing issue. Meanwhile, a crowd had gathered to see what all the excitement was about.

That event made me realize there are endless numbers of charitable events that need to provide water to participants to keep them hydrated—bike races, triathlons, and walks. By donating Hint, we can support a number of important causes while introducing the product. The participants associate the brand with a cause that's meaningful to them, which makes it all the more memorable and valuable.

Theo and I have several causes that are near and dear to our own hearts, but we decided that Hint would be cause-agnostic. We would donate to events of all kinds, as long as there was a charitable purpose. That got the product in front of all sorts of people, and we consistently saw that Hint could be the one thing that they could agree on. (Okay, maybe not cucumber.)

> " By donating Hint, we can support a number of important causes while introducing the product. The participants associate the brand with a cause that's meaningful to them, which makes it all the more memorable and valuable. "

Over the years, we've donated water and provided staffing support for organizations that fight autism, cancer, heart disease, and diabetes, as well as organizations dedicated to protecting the air, water, and climate. Along the way, we've met people all over the country and heard their perspectives and passion on all sorts of issues.

We've also gone on informal research trips to better understand how Hint fits into their lives and complements their values and aspirations. We've driven across the country and up and down both coasts more than once, because we needed to understand not just how my friends and I in Marin County see things, but how people in all sorts of different places see things. As we crossed this beautiful land, stopping in cafés, grocery stores, and restaurants along the way, we discovered that most Americans still share many of the same hopes, dreams, and frustrations. From Seattle to Miami and everywhere in between, Americans aspire to lead healthier lives, but they struggle to do so because healthy choices are rarely the most enjoyable, available, or satisfying choices.

Our focus on water's role in health so thoroughly drives everything we do, I really think of it now as a cause. We knew from the very beginning that the water into which we put our fruit essences had to be clean and as close to 100 percent pure as possible. Over the years, we have learned a lot about water, its composition, and how it can be purified. Water typically contains traces of naturally occurring and harmless elements such as salt, calcium, and magnesium. It may also contain toxins and contaminants. The most common and dangerous ones are arsenic, lead, and human-made industrial chemicals known as PFAS (perfluorinated alkylated substances). These substances can cause damage to human beings, including to our brains.

To get the truest fruit flavors in Hint, we needed to purify our water and get rid of all contaminants. There are a number of different ways to purify water, including a process called *reverse osmosis*. I will spare you the technical details, except to say that the reverse osmosis process results in Hint Water that is exceptionally pure and dramatically cleaner than the water that comes out of your tap at home.

This may come as a surprise, even a shock, to you. It did to me. People understandably like to think that their tap water is clean and safe to drink. In some places, it's a point of civic pride. If you spend any time in New York City, for example, you're sure to hear local residents claim their city water is the best in the nation, if not the world.

But as I educated myself on the subject, I learned these assumptions are mostly wrong. The nation's water supply is poorly regulated, mainly because our aging water distribution systems, the pipes and fixtures that deliver water to our homes, schools, and businesses, have not been properly maintained and upgraded. Only half of the fifty states have a formal process for testing drinking water at the point of use, particularly for the presence of lead. Even in states that do test, there is no regulation that requires them to make the test results public. And, even if lead is present, there are no regulations about what has to be done about it. As a result, people might be drinking contaminated tap water for years without knowing it and without the state taking any action.

In 2014, the whole country caught on to the situation when the water crisis erupted in Flint, Michigan. Flint's residents were exposed to high levels of lead contamination when the city switched its water source from Lake Huron to the Flint River. The water had to flow through aging lead pipes, and the city failed to treat the water with chemicals that would prevent the pipes from leaching the lead into the water. The result: one hundred thousand residents—including thousands of school-age kids—were drinking water that was hazardous to their health. When the problem finally came to light, a state of emergency was declared and the process of replacing the pipes began. As of this writing, the problem is still not resolved.

The Flint crisis got me thinking more deeply about the importance of pure water, not just in Hint but in our society in general. I knew that our water we use to make Hint was as pure as could be. Then, I began to wonder if there was anything we could do to help the public drinking supply be as clean and safe as the water we used for Hint.

After some investigation and exploration of various issues, I learned that one of the key vulnerabilities in our water infrastructure is school drinking fountains. The federal government is an important player in this regard. It administers the $13.6 billion National School Lunch Program, which provides funds to public and private schools to serve meals to about thirty million schoolkids. That's according to the US Census Bureau. What goes on the subsidized lunch tray has to meet nutrition standards set by the US Department of Agriculture. In 2010, a new law required that the nutritional standards be updated to include more healthy options such as fruits, vegetables, whole grains, and prepared foods with lower sodium and fat content.

For the first time, the regulation specified that water had to be available, too.

I thought this might be a good way for us to get involved in the school market, until it was pointed out to me that the water did not have to be *packaged* water. Drinking fountain water, according to this new law, was an acceptable source. I reached out to nutritionists and school administrators who told me the water in their schools sometimes tasted bad and kids didn't want to drink it. When I asked how that could be, they said it was because their state was one of the states with no requirements for testing school drinking water.

Now I was as concerned as they were. My kids attended public school, and I had never dreamed they might be at risk drinking water from the fountains. I couldn't stop thinking about the importance of clean water in schools and wondering how it was possible that there were no state regulations to ensure everyone had access to it. Somebody had to do something, but it seemed the system was so big and ingrained that no one inside was able to take action.

> 66 I couldn't stop thinking about the importance of clean water in schools and wondering how it was possible that there were no state regulations to ensure everyone had access to it. 99

That's when I made a decision—*let's apply our extensive knowledge of water for a greater social good.* I would push for nationwide testing and regulation of school drinking water. That's the genesis of the initiative I am working on now. I'm reaching out to legislators and community and business leaders, and the goal is simple: I want to ensure the water our kids drink in school is as clean and pure as the water we use in Hint. It is my hope that legislation will be enacted to push states to test for substances such as lead in our school drinking fountains—an initiative that would affect more than thirty million students. The legislation would specify that states will lose funding if they fail to comply. Too many kids and teachers are silently being affected by dirty water. This has to stop.

We continue to broaden Hint's mission in service of the cause of health, sometimes in ways that seem unconnected to water. In 2020, for example, we made a leap into a new category: deodorant. Some people found that even more baffling than our move into sunscreen, but to us, it made perfect sense.

The project got into gear when the *Today Show* did a segment with me about Hint, and I got to have a conversation with host Maria Shriver. She told me about her mission to raise awareness and money for research into Alzheimer's and dementia, which had affected members of her family and disproportionately affects women.

That got me refocused on a project I had been thinking about since 2010, the year my dad passed away from Alzheimer's disease. During his struggles, I did a lot of research about the disease and its causes. Given that the disease can run in families, I wanted to do whatever I could to avoid getting it myself and to protect my kids from it. Many doctors pointed to research that suggests aluminum may be a factor in bringing on the disease. I decided I should try to avoid products that contained aluminum, one of the most common of which was antiperspirant.

I started talking with Theo and the rest of our team about the issue, and we went about researching antiperspirants and deodorants. We came to the conclusion that the basic purpose of deodorant made sense—to prevent or reduce armpit odor—but the solution we were living with, introduced in the 1920s, made no sense at all. Antiperspirants work by clogging the pores of the skin in your armpits with microscopic bits of aluminum. Not only does that prevent you from smelling, it stops you from sweating. If such a product went on the market today, would anybody accept it?

Deodorants are different from antiperspirants. They are intended to mitigate odor, not shut down the whole sweat system. I found that most of them are not even particularly good at that. They often use intense odors of their own to mask your own aroma. The very best of them are extremely expensive.

I tasked our team with developing a subtle-smelling, super-effective, odor-fighting deodorant that went on smooth, didn't stain clothes, and didn't cost a fortune. We had to put the project on hold when we came up against an environmental issue. Some of the ingredients we required could not be produced without palm oil, which tends to be grown in areas where the rain forest is cut down to plant palm trees. We did not want to reduce armpit odor at the expense of the environment.

When I met Maria, I decided the need for a healthy deodorant was significant enough that we should get started and take on the environmental issues as we built the business, just as we have done with Hint Water.

In the fall of 2019, I was thrilled to sponsor Maria's "Move for Minds" event in Los Angeles, serving our Hint Water and providing prerelease samples of the deodorant. We not only used our network to bring attention to this horrible disease but also the ingredients that we both believe are not helpful to the disease and to our minds—sugar and aluminum.

Some people told me they think it's odd for a beverage company to offer a deodorant. To them, I simply say, "I'm sorry if I confused you."

But I'm not really.

I have come to believe that it's imperative and entirely feasible to build a successful, profitable, sustainable company that is also committed to social good—in its products, its organization, and its activities beyond the immediate business.

From these adventures in social commitment, I realized the contribution can take many forms, one of which is sharing knowledge. I had gained a great deal of knowledge over the years, knowledge that could be valuable in many other pursuits outside our business. In addition to my understanding of water, I knew a lot about entrepreneurship, as well as how to bring change to long-established, change-resistant entities.

In other words, I began to see I had something valuable to contribute beyond product donations, charitable gifts, and supporting causes. I had a lot of knowledge, combined with an ability to disrupt the status quo, to stand up to people who did not care. Wouldn't sharing my knowledge and creating change for the better be the most valuable contribution I could make?

The answer was, *Probably*. But the question was, *How?*

CHAPTER 20

share your knowledge.

never liked speaking in front of a live audience. I felt much more comfortable with small groups or one-on-one. I liked conversation better than presentation.

But I had been getting requests to do public speaking about Hint at local gatherings and other live events. This seemed like the most obvious and best way to get out there and share what I knew. Now that I saw knowledge-sharing as an important part of my mission, I determined to get ahold of my nerves so I could take advantage of the opportunities that came my way.

My first assumption was that I needed a more polished presentation and that I had to practice my delivery until it was perfect. I soon had my first opportunity to test this theory. I was asked to present a thirty-minute keynote address with PowerPoint slides. The topic was how I built Hint and how entrepreneurs can understand their "why"—their mission and purpose.

I went to work, writing a speech and putting together a deck of great-looking slides. When I got up to present, I was nervous, but I followed the script and the presentation went pretty well. But I have to admit, it felt formal. I didn't feel like I had connected with the audience. I hadn't learned anything new and I wasn't sure if they had either.

A few days later, I got another call, this time from a friend who invited me to present at her company's off-site gathering. I would be one of several speakers.

"Great," I said. "I have a PowerPoint talk all ready to go."

"Kara," she said, "you don't need PowerPoint. In fact, we don't allow PowerPoints for this. Just come and tell us your story."

Gulp! Now I would have to speak with no props, no backup, no security blanket. It would be just me talking. And the meeting was the next day. I was even more nervous than I had been the day before.

I went. My friend gave me a great introduction. The audience clearly wanted to hear what I had to say. I knew the general outline of the talk, and I certainly knew what the important messages were. Before launching into it, however, I looked over the audience and spontaneously started asking them questions.

Has anybody here tried Hint? A lot of hands went up.

Do we have any entrepreneurs in the room? Fewer hands.

Have any of you ever tried to raise money to start a business? Not many.

It broke the ice. Instantly, I had a sense of the audience and they had a better sense of themselves. We had made a connection.

I felt the speech went great, and the feedback confirmed my impression.

The best talk of the day!

She really spoke from the heart!

It was so helpful!

What had made the difference?

First, without having to worry about slides, I was free to talk as the spirit moved. I wasn't constantly fiddling with the clicker and nervously checking to make sure I was on the right slide. I could focus on the audience. I had thought the PowerPoint deck was my security blanket onstage, but it was actually the opposite. Now I looked into the audience and could read their faces and gauge their reactions to what I was saying. It became a conversation, an exchange.

My friend had also allotted enough time for the talk, with a question-and-answer session afterward. I didn't feel rushed. I could relax into it.

Today, I can't imagine my life without the public speaking role. I love to do it and have addressed audiences all over the world, sometimes two or three times a week. I find it's a great way to meet and connect with people. We learn together.

So, as time went along, and as Hint gained more and more customers—and I got better and better at speaking—the invitations to do talks at conferences and events poured in. I started to see the public role as one of the great privileges of leading a company that people care about: they want to hear from you, learn from you, ask questions, and engage in conversations.

I met and talked with people who were experiencing all kinds of challenges in their businesses and careers and had great stories to tell. As I shared knowledge with others, I learned as much from them as they did from me. When I returned to the office after an engagement, everybody wanted to know what had happened and who I had met and what I had learned. I was kind of a proxy—their eyes and ears—for my own people.

The more talks and appearances I did, and the more I learned, the more I felt I had to do more than pass along bits of information and stories in a random way. I wanted to reach out to people beyond my immediate network and do so on a regular basis. I wanted to offer lessons and practices that others could adapt and use for themselves. And I wanted to continue learning from others.

One way I have been able to do that is by joining a number of remarkable networks of people with similar goals, including YPO,

TheLi.st, C200, NACIE, and EY's Winning Women and Entrepreneur programs. YPO is a great network overall, organized around small forums of business leaders who support each other by sharing stories confidentially. As you talk about challenges you face in your personal life or business, other members of your forum respond not by offering opinions, but by sharing relevant stories from their own lives.

While I can't share any of those confidential stories, you can tell that the YPO Forum format has greatly influenced this book. For times when I need specific advice or answers, I often turn to *TheLi.st*, which is a group of amazing women who seem to be able to answer almost any question that might come up in business. No matter what the issue is, I can always find someone on *TheLi.st* who has been there, done that, found a way forward.

C200 is a group of top women executives who meet several times a year to share trending issues, but who also serve as a terrific network. EY, known mainly as an accounting firm, has built their business in part by bringing people together once a year at the EY Entrepreneur of the Year conference. While winning an award from EY can itself be quite helpful, connecting with people from all over the world, with a broad range of experience and perspectives is what brings so many people to their annual event.

Networking is critical. Make time for it. Friendships and good networks, wherever you can find them, will support you and keep you going so that even when you have one of those days, or one of those years, you keep trying.

As much as networking enabled me to connect with more people beyond my immediate circles, I still wanted to reach out to an even bigger, more general, audience. Since I had experience in the world of publishing from my work at Time Inc., it felt natural to begin by writing. I started out with posts on LinkedIn, and one of the first was titled "I Knew I Would Win When He Called Me 'Sweetie.'" You can guess what that one was about. It got a lot of comments and likes and encouraged me to write more. Today, I've posted almost two hundred articles on LinkedIn, and it's proved to be an effective way to share knowledge with a big group of followers.

> " Friendships and good networks, wherever you can find them, will support you and keep you going so that even when you have one of those days, or one of those years, you keep trying. "

Given the response I was getting from my posts, I wanted to make my knowledge available even more broadly, beyond that special base of the LinkedIn community. So we started recording my conversations on video for the website or as audio for a podcast called *Unstoppable*, and it all gradually came together under the name The Kara Network, aka TKN.

For the *Unstoppable* podcast, I interviewed all kinds of experts, thought leaders, and change makers—scientists, educators, physicians, authors, journalists, actors, musicians, and, my specialty, entrepreneurs and company founders. I always asked my guests, "What makes you Unstoppable?" It's so great hearing their responses. The information they provided that rings true for entrepreneurs is also relevant to anybody involved in business, in any way, and at every level.

What I find so fascinating and most enlightening about these interviews is how honest people are about the challenges of entrepreneurship and, in particular, the mistakes they made along the way and how important those mistakes are to learning and growth. The podcast has been one of the greatest learning experiences for me, and I hope for everybody who listens.

I found so much inspiration and motivation and was meeting so many fascinating and committed people, I wondered if I could continue doing the same for others on a bigger scale.

CHAPTER 21

face your fears.

Don't let anyone tell you that entrepreneurs are a special breed of human being—that they, unlike normal people, feel no fear. That is not true and it's not what being undaunted is about.

Quite the opposite. Being undaunted is understanding what your fears are, deciding when it's important to face up to them, preparing yourself to confront them, and then working through them.

When you do, two things happen.

First, you put that particular fear in its place. You might not completely overcome it, but you cut it down to a manageable size.

Second, and even more important, you gain confidence to overcome *any* fear, any obstacle that might stand in your way.

That's the key: the more success you have at taking on your fears, the more confidence you gain to take on others. It's a virtuous circle.

Which is why, a few years ago, I decided to hike the Grand Canyon.

I've always had a terrible fear of heights. I remember visiting the canyon as a very young girl and hearing about people hiking it "rim to rim."

> 66 Being undaunted is understanding what your fears are, deciding when it's important to face up to them, preparing yourself to confront them, and then working through them. 99

Maybe one day I will have the courage to do it, I thought.

But heights gave me the willies. I've always loved to walk and hike, but I never really confronted my fear of heights.

Then one fall a few years ago, I was talking to my sister, Maureen, and she told me she was planning to hike the Grand Canyon from one rim to the other and asked if I'd go with her. She had done it before with her husband, Alex, and wanted to do it again. She had booked the cabins. All I had to do was say yes. My first reaction was terror. If you've ever been to the Grand Canyon, you know what I'm talking about. The cliffs are steep and the canyon floor looks like it's almost straight down. I can feel the palms of my hands start to sweat just writing about it.

But the timing was right. By then I had faced and overcome so many things in my personal life and in building our company, I thought I could do this. Besides, the hike was almost a year away. The plan was to go in October, when the weather would be starting to cool down a bit and the trails wouldn't be as crowded as in the summer. I figured I had plenty of time to get in shape, which would be fun. I'd prepare like crazy. And I'd keep telling myself: *You can do it*. I also figured there was plenty of time to back out.

I said okay.

Let the preparations begin.

First, I read up on the facts. The idea was to complete the route in one day, which is ambitious to say the least. We'd start early in the morning on the North Rim, elevation about 8,200 feet. We'd hike more than fourteen miles down the narrow, zigzagging trail to the canyon bottom. After a break, we'd hike another nine miles across the canyon and then 4,500 feet up to the South Rim. A hike of a total of about twenty-four miles, even on gentle terrain, is an arduous one. The big change in elevation makes it all the tougher. The rim-to-rim hike is well known as a serious physical challenge. Each year, a few people attempt the hike without preparation and have to be rescued by the National Park Service.

Still, I wasn't too worried about the physical part of it. I recruited my daughter Kaitlin to help me train. At twelve years old, she was already fit from sports and was eager to do the hike with me. In that year, we did many training sessions together near our home in the hills of Marin. We also hiked up at Tahoe, where the summits are about the same elevation as the Grand Canyon.

We gradually increased the length and height of our climbs, and I steadily gained more confidence in my skills and my physical strength and stamina.

Meanwhile, we worked out the plan in more detail. We recruited others to join us, so we were a party of six people in total: Kaitlin, Maureen, Alex, our friend Jim, and my nephew Chris. Theo volunteered to take our son Keenan and my nephew Nick on some shorter hikes off the North Rim and then drive around to the south side to pick us up at the end of the day.

We bought and tested all the necessary gear. Hiking shoes. Backpacks. Sun hats. Sunscreen. Layers of clothing. Water bottles. Loads of Clif Bars. I thought I was totally prepared.

Then, just a few days before we were scheduled to hike, I was on the sidelines at Kaitlin's soccer game. I was talking with another mom and told her about the upcoming hike.

"Gosh," she said. "I don't think I could ever do that. I have such a fear of heights. It's a really long way to the bottom and looking straight down into the canyon. How can you handle it?"

It suddenly hit me we would be starting at the very top of the cliff rather than at the bottom, as you do when climbing up from the base of a mountain. I would be staring straight down into the canyon. How could I not have thought of this? It would be like standing at the top of a skyscraper, only worse. The tallest building in San Francisco isn't even a thousand feet high. I had been so focused on my physical fitness that I hadn't thought about the mental part of it. Now I realized I had no choice but to confront one of my biggest fears: heights.

I couldn't back out now. My friends and family had invested a lot in the training. They were all counting on me. My daughter was counting on me. They were all rooting for me. I had set myself a goal I wanted to achieve.

Could I modify the plan somehow?

It struck me that the problem was mostly the first part of the hike, as we started down and I would be looking over the cliff to the bottom, more than a mile deep.

Well, I thought, *what if I couldn't see the bottom?*

We were planning to set off at 6:00 a.m., at first light. Given the length of the hike, we would probably be climbing out of the canyon after dark. I had already bought a headlamp in preparation for that contingency. What if we started out earlier, before the sun came up, so we couldn't see the bottom?

I called my fellow hikers. "I was thinking about the timing," I said. "Maybe it would be better to start earlier so we can finish the hike in daylight." Slight pause. "And I'm really afraid of heights. It might help if I can't see too much from the top."

Everybody agreed. For which I was grateful.

The big day came. We woke up at a hotel in the park at the North Rim. Theo dropped us off and kissed me and my daughter goodbye. We were on the trail by 4:00 a.m., our headlamps illuminating the trail a few feet ahead, the canyon completely in darkness. I felt nothing but exhilaration. No fear.

I've got it made!

Well, just like in business, nothing ever goes according to plan. Or as Mike Tyson famously put it, "Everybody has a plan until they get punched in the mouth."

I didn't get punched in the mouth, but I did almost get kicked in the head. After a couple hours of hiking, my sister and I were together, negotiating our way carefully down the trail. Suddenly, a herd of mountain goats came careening down the cliff and leaped over our heads, coming very close to taking us with them down the cliffside.

> **Well, just like in business, nothing ever goes according to plan. Or as Mike Tyson famously put it, "Everybody has a plan until they get punched in the mouth."**

After the initial shock, Maureen and I started to laugh. It was a shock, an amazing sight, and also kind of a wake-up call. Even with all the training and outfitting we had done, and even with all the care we were taking as we walked, the whole thing came very close to an abrupt conclusion, thanks to a bunch of goats.

Wild animal disruption had certainly not been in the plan.

We kept moving. The encounter with the goats actually relaxed me a little—laughter will do that for you. As the sun rose, we were treated to one of the most spectacular views on Earth. We made it to the bottom by about 9:00 a.m. with no further incidents. We were tired and thirsty and I had a moment of doubt, wondering if we had made the right decision to do the whole hike in a single day. The Phantom Ranch, with its overnight accommodations, looked pretty appealing. My crew, as well as many other people I knew, had done the hike both ways on previous visits—in a single day and with an overnight—and everyone insisted the one-day plan was best. After an overnight, you have to face a second day of walking with your body aching all over. Brutal. Besides, when I gazed back up at the North Rim trail we had just completed, I thought, *Well, we've done the hard part. How much worse can it get?*

After a rest and plenty of Hint, we set off along the Bright Angel Trail that threaded across the floor and up to the far side of the canyon. I hadn't given much thought to this part of the trek, because it was relatively flat and seemed like it would be easier going. The problem was the heat and almost complete lack of shade. Even in October, it gets hot in the canyon, especially at the bottom. The temperatures probably got into the eighties but it felt like it was hotter than one hundred degrees. I was constantly thirsty, and I started to worry I might not have enough Hint to get me through. That would be ironic. The founder of a water company dies of thirst?

After a few miles, I was super-hot, exhausted, dragging, but I just kept putting one foot in front of the other. The crew was all together, but it was Jim who really saved me. He must have sensed something was wrong.

"Are you okay?"

I said something, I don't remember what. Jim stopped me.

"Kara," he said. "You're overheated. You're talking gibberish."

"I'm fine." But I didn't feel fine. I hardly knew what I was doing. My legs felt like rubber and my brain was foggy. And I was hot. So hot.

We were walking along the Colorado River at that point. "Kara," Jim said again, keeping my attention. "Go jump in the river. You have to cool down."

"I'm not doing that," I said. "I'll just get swept downstream."

"No. You'll be fine. Just go in for a few minutes."

I decided I had better do what Jim was telling me to do. He, my sister, and my nephew Chris got me to a calm spot in the river and we all plunged in. It felt fantastic. I started to cool down. My strength came back bit by bit. My mind started to clear.

I don't know what would have happened if I hadn't taken Jim's advice, accepted that I needed help, and did what he told me to do. He probably saved my life.

Sometimes even the Undaunted need a helping hand.

We made it across the canyon floor to the base of the South Rim trail. I looked up at the endless switchbacks we'd have to negotiate. (Pick and shovel work, for sure!) I couldn't even see the top—the end destination.

By this time, I had fallen into a steady pace, and the group had separated into clumps. A few, including Kaitlin, were going a little faster and had gotten ahead of me. Maureen and her husband were taking their time and had dropped behind. That left me alone in the middle. I was more than fine with that. I was just doing my own thing, going at my own speed. It was similar to times I've experienced as an entrepreneur. When you're tired and severely challenged, sometimes it's necessary to take time for yourself. Trust your gut. You don't require advice or collaboration. You need to figure things out and work through them for yourself. At this point in the hike, I wanted most of all to be alone.

Just as I was trudging along, eyes focused on the rocky ground at my feet, thinking that I'd be fine if I just kept moving along, I looked up and there was a rattlesnake on the trail, just a few feet in front. The path was maybe four feet wide at this point. The cliff came down sheer on one side and dropped off even more sharply on the other.

Being from Arizona, I have some knowledge of rattlesnakes. I knew they don't usually make a move toward you unless they think you're attacking them. But I also knew that you needed to stay far enough away from them, at least twelve feet, as they can move fast, jump at you, and bite.

I considered my options. I could have moved backward, but that might startle him. I could try to get him to move somehow, but that seemed risky. I could try to maneuver around him, but the cliff going up was much too steep to climb. If I went around the other side, I would have to look down, and fear might kick in. If I lost my balance, I could easily go over the edge.

I decided to wait it out. Do nothing. Just see what happened.

Ten minutes went by. Twenty. The snake and I looked at each other. My sister and Alex still had not reached me. I couldn't see Kaitlin and her crew anymore, they were so far ahead.

Finally, the rattlesnake slithered off the trail and disappeared into the rocks. Relieved, and a bit rested, too, I set off again. Thinking: *Okay, that's about as bad as it can get. I'll be at the top soon.*

After another hour or so of steady climbing, I came around the corner of a switchback and there, dead ahead, were two coyotes standing in the trail. They looked like small wolves, and I had no desire to mess with them. Another roadblock. Another situation for which I had no plan. Cliffs on both sides. No way around.

I felt like I was about at the end of my rope. I remember thinking, *So this is how it's going to end? A coyote is going to finish me off?*

Then I felt a surge of energy. *No way*, I said to myself. *I've been through too much. I overcame my fear of heights. I avoided heat stroke. I survived a goat attack. I stared down a rattlesnake. I'm not going to let these coyotes get in my way.*

Filled with renewed courage and confidence, I laughed out loud.

The coyotes turned around and sprinted away.

I kept going, my mind essentially blank. I still had quite a way to go, but at least I could glimpse the top. The sun had set, it was dark, and it was hard to see the trail. But I had my headlamp. I lost track of time, but I also knew I wasn't going to spend the whole night in the canyon. Then I heard someone coming down the trail. I felt an immediate sense of alarm. *Who would start the hike at night?* I wondered.

"Kara, are you okay?"

It was Theo. Kaitlin and her group had been at the top for almost an hour. Theo had gotten worried and started down the trail to find me. He could tell I was exhausted, but I was smiling and calm. A few minutes later, I was on top. The ordeal was over.

YOU CAN DO IT

I have thought a lot about that hike and how meaningful it was to me. It turned out to be very different from what I had expected and what I had prepared for. I had trained for the physical part and it had paid off. Although I grew tired, my legs didn't give out. I had sufficient stamina and strength. Even at times when I believed I couldn't go on, I did.

What I hadn't anticipated was the mental achievement of the hike, which was more significant than the physical part. It wasn't as if I had a magical transformation, but I did arrive at a kind of clarity about what I had been through. I came to think of the experience as a nice metaphor for the entrepreneurial journey, a useful way to step back from the day-to-day work and see it with a new perspective.

Building a business or a career is much more complicated and plays out over a much longer time span than a hike. Yet, seen from forty thousand feet, the two look similar in lots of ways. To be successful in both, you have to prepare as well as you can for the predictable challenges while accepting that you can't plan for or predict everything that will happen. You need to decide when to rely on your team and when you have to work things through for yourself. You are forced to look at each new challenge as a problem to be solved, not as a barrier to progress. It's life and death on the trail. And, even though you're not in the same immediate physical danger, it's life and death on the entrepreneurial journey, too. Plenty of companies don't make it. And there is no National Park Service to save them.

Perhaps the biggest factor in success, though, is how you handle the miscalculations, errors, missteps, and threats to progress. We've had plenty of those as we have built our company, from moldy water to losing big accounts. Each time, we had to decide if this was an obstacle to tackle head-on, one to go around and deal with later, or one that could be seen as an opportunity. The challenge of the shelf-life problem was one we could avoid until we were a little bigger, while focusing on making the best tasting product we could. By the time it was mission-critical, the problem had grown simpler. Today, you can buy Hint in all fifty states. The Starbucks setback compelled us to expand our web presence and take more control of our destiny while not being so reliant on other retailers. Our web sales now account for about 45 percent of our business and, with Amazon, 55 percent.

Another factor is being willing to take the big, if well-calculated, risk. In 2019, we filmed three TV commercials in a single day and tested two of them, with a great response from viewers. The third was really funny, but seemed like it might be a bit too polarizing for national TV, so we focused on the other two. Then we had a crazy idea. Let's show the ad during the Super Bowl. Some people would love it. Some might hate it. Either way, it would start a conversation and get us noticed.

This was in the middle of January, only two weeks before kickoff. But, hey, it was worth a try. I reached out to an old friend from my CNN days who connected me with the people at Fox Sports.

Sorry, they said. A single spot would cost $5.6 million. Besides, we're totally sold out for nationwide ads. But have you thought about running the ad in specific, targeted regions? You'll get to audiences who can help you build the brand, and it's much cheaper.

you can do it.

We went for it. For less than $1 million, we bought airtime in two major markets, New York and San Francisco. We got a huge, positive response from consumers, investors, and employees. A major step up for Hint. Over the next few weeks, I heard from several salespeople who were excited to close deals they had been working on for months or years. Listening to them tell the story, I realized that what had changed the most was the salespeople. They walked in with a little bit more confidence than they had before. Their company just ran a Super Bowl ad! Sometimes, when you're ready for it, a big confidence-boosting move is what your team needs to go out and crush it.

When you take risks like that, overcome your fears, manage problems, turn setbacks into opportunities, and withstand outside disruptions, you build resilience. So, when you put yourself in the *next* new situation where you're unsure, challenged, or tested, you think, *I can handle this.* And you do.

In addition to the troubles that are personal and directly related to your business, you will also have to deal with challenges and setbacks that are not of your making and not within your control. We've gotten Hint through deep recession, political upheaval, competitive challenge, and more. On the hike, there were the goats and rattlesnakes and coyotes.

So, along with resilience, you need some plain old persistence— to just keep going, to keep trying, to carry on in the face of doubts and discouragement. I have a deep belief in our mission and that gives me the strength to persist. There were plenty of times in the early days when I wondered if we had made the right decision to start a company. Maybe we should have taken those jobs at Google or some other big tech company. I especially had to wonder "what might have been" when I saw friends and former colleagues who were flying high, making tons of money, moving up the corporate ladder, while we were wedging cases of Hint into the back of the Jeep or trying to talk our way into Whole Foods.

At those low times, I had to remind myself that Hint was the path I'd chosen, because I was building a business I could believe in, one that could change people's lives. Working in tech had been thrilling, but it hadn't been my purpose. The focus on the bigger picture—the reason behind what I was doing—kept me going whatever we were experiencing at Hint, whether it was just a bit of inertia, an outside shock, or a major business setback. As long as we were fulfilling our mission and our promise to our customers, that made it all worthwhile. When I looked at our business that way, I could always see we were making progress in helping people live healthier lives, even if we were going through some temporary business foul-up. That would boost my spirits.

Keeping your eye on the ultimate goal—whether it's the top of the South Rim of the Grand Canyon, giving people a healthy drink alternative, or something else entirely—is tremendously motivating.

Along with the mission, the other driver of persistence is values. They are your best guide. The moment you do something you don't fully believe in because others tell you it's right or because you feel like you have no choice, you put yourself and your mission at risk. If I'd agreed to add diet sweetener to Hint, as one of our board members had proposed in the depths of the recession, I would have been abandoning the fundamental value—our belief in health.

Sometimes it may seem that your values are at odds with your best business interests. For example, when we told Whole Foods we wouldn't go with the two-for-one offer during the bad times in 2008, they might well have said so long, and we would have lost an important account. But we explained how important the values of health and quality were to Hint—and to Whole Foods—and how discounting could damage both our brands. They understood we did not want to compromise our identity or theirs. Hint stayed on the shelf. We still have a great relationship with Whole Foods today.

The greatest source of encouragement, drive, persistence, and confidence comes from the energy and love we get back from our customers. First and foremost, I set out to help people. When I hear stories about how we're doing, I feel a great sense of accomplishment and fulfillment.

When I speak at a conference, a company, a university, or a media outlet—or if someone just notices that I'm wearing a piece of Hint gear on an airplane and starts a conversation—I hear their stories, and I'm inspired. Parents tell me they hadn't realized how much sugar their kids were consuming, and that Hint has made it possible for their families to lead healthier lives. Others tell me that Hint has been a key part of their lifestyle changes, including their ability to lose weight. Cancer patients tell me Hint helps mask the metallic taste from chemo treatments, while other patients say that it helps them control their type 2 diabetes. While we don't make health claims for Hint other than it's water that tastes good, consumers are telling us about positive changes in their lives that Hint has helped them make.

And, of course, some of the most meaningful feedback of all comes from those closest to me.

When my older son, Keenan, was about twelve, the two of us watched Facebook COO Sheryl Sandberg doing a talk on TV at the height of her *Lean In* press tour. She spoke about the obstacles women face in reaching the highest tiers of the business world and what they could do about it.

Keenan turned to me and said, "Mom, I just realized that not many women run companies."

"What do you mean?" I wondered where he was going with this.

"You've been running your company for my whole life. I just thought lots of women run companies. I didn't realize they don't. It's like we're living in a different world. That's awesome!"

That filled my heart with pride. I'm thrilled that, with the help of my husband, Theo, of course, I've been able to create a different world for my four kids. When things get tough at Hint (which, as you've seen, they do), I think about the coming generations. I see my work as more than creating a business, more than helping people live healthier lives. It's a model and a legacy, for my family and for others. That's the reason I established a scholarship for a Hint of Entrepreneurism at my alma mater, ASU.

My kids watch what I do every day, and I hope that what I do helps them become great managers, leaders, and even a wonderful spouse (if they choose that). I hope, too, that they see their mom, a woman, paving the way. I hope I have demonstrated to them the world can be changed for the better, and they have the skills and capacity to do it.

Funny thing. After we finished the Grand Canyon hike and I got back home, I went online to look at some of the websites and discussion groups devoted to the hike. I learned I could become a member of the Rim-to-Rim Club and share my experiences with others who had made the trek, which was cool. On another site, I came across a comment that struck me. It was full of advice about how to prepare for the walk, what to carry, and what routes to follow. One commenter cautioned that it is very challenging to do the rim-to-rim walk in a single day. That would be *foolish*.

That rang a familiar bell. I thought about the Coke exec who had pretty much said the same thing to me. It would be *foolish* to try to sell Americans unsweetened water, sweetie. They'll never buy it. All Americans want is sweet.

If you want to live in a world where things are different—a world where women *do* run companies, where people have choices to make their lives healthier, where staid old industries are disrupted—you sometimes have to do things that others consider foolish, but that you think of as bold, life-changing, and valuable.

You don't have to be super-special, rich, earn ten college degrees, or have front-row seats at the game.

You just have to be *undaunted*. Most of us don't start out that way. We have to learn to be undaunted. Then, if those walls around you ever get too high, you can smash them down. Or if that voice in your head starts telling you that you can't do it, you can tell it to stop.

I believe we all can be Undaunted. It's up to you.

ACKNOWLEDGMENTS

When we launched Hint more than fifteen years ago, I started by telling my own story about what led me to create a fruit-infused water. But almost immediately, I started hearing from people who were excited to have discovered Hint in a grocery store, a café, a spa, a dentist's office, or what have you. And they each had their own story, their own challenges, and their own reasons for appreciating Hint. These stories not only fueled my resolve to make this business work but also helped me answer retailers' most important question: Why should I buy Hint? If you are one of the many who took the time to share your Hint story with me or with a friend or colleague, I want you to know that your passion, your appreciation, and your support have sustained me, my husband, Theo, and the rest of the Hint team through the most challenging times. Thank you!

Throughout my life, sometimes for reasons I don't even understand, I have encountered so many people who have offered a bit of advice and encouragement. I cannot possibly mention you all by name, but everyone who has believed in me and encouraged me has had a role in my success and in this book, and I try to express my appreciation for you all by following your lead and doing my part to encourage others.

Throughout the several years I've been working on this book in my "spare time," I've shared many of the stories with my team at Hint, and they've shared their Hint stories as well. To the entire team, I am eternally grateful to you for the hard work, the passion, and the persistence, without which I would not still be running a company that I founded in 2005 and Hint would not be the brand it is today. A huge shout-out to everyone on the sales, marketing, operations, human resources, and finance teams for everything you do to get the product out there, help people discover it, and support our distributors, retailers, consumers, and one another. There is no better, more dedicated team in the business.

Extreme appreciation for my agent, Carol Franco, and her wonderful and talented husband, Kent Lineback, who were both instrumental in developing the proposal for *Undaunted* and finding a fantastic publisher to back the book. And thanks to the incredible team at HarperCollins Leadership for taking on this project. I owe enormous gratitude to the entire team there, especially Tim Burgard.

Thanks to Carol as well for introducing me to John Butnam, who worked with me over the course of six months to weave many stories together into a book I could be proud of. John quickly understood the vision and need for this book and the structure that would make it all flow. I was very saddened to hear, only a few weeks before we were going to print *Undaunted*, that John had passed away. I want his family to know how thankful I am that he helped to pull so much of *Undaunted* together.

Platon. Thank you for jumping in and creating the cover I was looking for. You are a master, and I will forever remember that day and our lovely chat.

I am grateful to my mentor, best friend, editor, and husband— Theo Goldin. I'm not certain either of us knew what we were getting into when I asked you to pitch in on Hint or on *Undaunted*. You've been a true partner in our life and business, and have spent countless hours reading and editing this book. You really are my North Star, and I am truly grateful for all you do and your unending commitment to me. I love you. You are the best.

Finally, thank you to my beautiful, smart, and witty children and pups—Emma, Kaitlin, Keenan, and Justin, as well as my dogs Sadie and Buster. And to all my family and friends who shaped who I am today, I am so grateful that you are all in my life and allow me to learn and grow with you. May you all live Undaunted as well.

INDEX

ABOUT THE AUTHOR

KARA GOLDIN is a disruptor. She is the founder and CEO of Hint, Inc., best known for its award-winning Hint® water, the leading unsweetened flavored water. She is an active speaker and writer, and hosts the podcast *Unstoppable with Kara Goldin,* where she interviews founders, entrepreneurs, and other disruptors across various industries. She lives in the Bay Area. Follow Kara on all social handles @KaraGoldin.

CALDWELL
on Cross-Country

TRAINING AND TECHNIQUE
FOR THE SERIOUS SKIER

John Caldwell

THE STEPHEN GREENE PRESS
BRATTLEBORO, VERMONT

Photographs 4, 12, 47 and 49 are by Tim Caldwell; 11, the training log, and the two graphs, 45 and 46, were executed by Robert R. Anderson; all other photographs are by the author.

This book has been produced in the United States of America: designed by R. L. Dothard Associates, composed by American Book–Stratford Press, and printed and bound by Halliday Lithograph Corporation. It is published by The Stephen Greene Press, Brattleboro, Vermont 05301.

Library of Congress Cataloging in Publication Data
Caldwell, John H   1928–
   Caldwell on cross-country training and technique for
the serious skier.
   1. Cross-country skiing. I. Title.
GV854.9.C7C3 1975   796.9'3   75–8028
ISBN 0–8289–0255–0

1 2 3 4 5 6 7 8 9 80 79 78 77 76 75

Contents

A Word about the Pictures

Most of the pictures in this book were taken by me with a Pentax motor drive camera. I've never won any photography awards as you may guess, but I've always had some idea of the pictures I wanted, so I took them. Sometimes the choice of background was limited, or the snow wasn't around, or the subjects weren't close by. So it went.

Almost all the pictures demonstrate what I consider good training practice or good technique. Some people have suggested that it would be good to have some pictures which show how not to do it. I've used such a method in teaching skiing and could have done so in this book. But I didn't, for two reasons. First—and the more important—I think we all need to see pictures of the good guys and how they do it, not pictures of people who are not quite so proficient. Second, to show how-not-to pictures would require a lot more space, a lot more film and a lot more time writing explanations. I'm short on all of these.

You may recognize several of the skiers whose pictures appear in the text. None of the skiers asked for or received any remuneration, gift or benefit in return for giving permission to be photographed. They all did it to help the sport and to help me complete this book. We owe them thanks.   J.C.

1. Some Background

This book is intended primarily for the serious cross-country skier.

I've been having fun on x-c—cross-country—skis since 1941, sometimes touring, sometimes walking, sometimes racing, sometimes coaching. I still enjoy it all and my hope is that reading this will make the sport of x-c skiing more enjoyable for you.

There is a wide range of activities connected with x-c skiing and I've covered two aspects of the sport—training and technique—in this book.

The material on training should be helpful to anyone, skier or nonskier, who wants to get in better shape—as long as it is interpreted correctly. As you read through you will see that I am a bit leery of the old numbers game where you plug your weight, height, age, pulse rate and whatever into a formula and come out with a program for yourself. You'll have to do a bit more than that if you want to get the most from the material on training.

The technique section should be useful to anyone who wants to improve his skiing ability. Being able to ski well is a splendid goal for anyone because few thrills surpass gliding over the countryside on a pair of x-c's.

Most of my skiing background has been connected with racing and coaching and I've tried here to bring across material that will help parents, friends, and coaches of racers of any age. Even if you don't ski yourself you could find plenty that will aid you in helping others.

Finally, this book is written as a tribute to all the friends I've made through x-c racing—athletes, coaches, doctors, parents and officials—from all around the world. Most of my memorable experiences have been associated with these people, who are called *sportsmen* in almost every language in the world. They have been friendly and co-operative in sharing their knowledge, especially some of the sportsmen from abroad.

I'm reminded of a story concerning an interview with one of the East German swim coaches during the summer of 1973 after his girls had cleaned up everything in sight at the European championships. An American reporter asked him what the German secrets were. The coach replied that they had no secrets: their coaches simply looked around the world, including the United States, came back and sat down together and planned a national system of training. That approach has been lacking in the United States, and if reading this book helps anyone interested in cross-country to enjoy any part of the whole cross-country scene I will feel I have put something into a program which means so much to me.

1. Magne Myrmo and Oddvar Braa, of the Norwegian X-C Team, pause between chunks of a technique tune-up session in Putney, Vermont, during their 1973 visit to the Caldwells.

Where it started

I've always wanted to write about training and I started this project a few years ago. Two important things happened at that time. First, I got so absorbed in research that I thought I might have to go to medical school in order to understand better what I was reading, or to be able to test some private theories of my own. That would have delayed publication for years and would have been otherwise impractical. In the meantime, two physicians named Peter Caldwell and "Skip" Sheldon came to my rescue. They have been very patient in trying to explain many matters to me. Anything in this book that is medically correct is their due. Any errors are mine.

Second, the more I thought about the training procedures I prescribe—which I have developed in Putney—the more I realized that they tie in directly with technique. So I decided it would be appropriate to include technique as a part of this book. You will see the connections as you go along.

I hasten to point out the nontechnical aspects of this book. I've read countless journals, reports, books and articles on training. Many of them are written in technical language I am not thoroughly familiar with, like Medicalese. In writing this I have tried to make it understandable for the average skier, at the same time using or introducing some terms that I find necessary to use, or terms which will help to raise the general level of knowledge about the subject. However, there are not a lot of highfalutin explanations to go along with many of the statements I make, although I know this poses a danger because some may find it easy to poke holes in what is written.

I'm not going to list many references either. I've read three-page listings of references that accompany two-page reports and I want to avoid anything like that. It's time-consuming and takes a lot of space. Besides, I have not taken much material from any particular source. Most of it is common knowledge to many coaches around the world, but even more of it has derived from my twenty-five continuous years of coaching since 1951.

The Putney Method

I've dubbed the over-all approach to training as described in this book the Putney Method not to be vainglorious but merely because the concepts were jelled and implemented here in this small Vermont hill town.

The system didn't just show up on the scene: it has evolved over a long period of time. Every good skier who has been connected with Putney in any way has had a hand in the formulation of this system. And the system is changing all the time, too.

A few skiers and coaches I know have taken out of context some of the Putney approaches to training, or have failed to understand them. Perhaps

---

Skipersons

Let me set down *he/she, his/hers, her/him,* and all those word combinations here because it's the last time you'll see them in this book. No slight intended: I think women's lib is great, really. I get a thrill along with everybody else when I see Martha Rockwell, an American and one of the top x-c racers in the world, or Toini Gustaffson, Swedish gold medalist in the 1968 Olympics.

It's just a matter of how I was taught to write, and I find it very awkward to haul up short and insert "or her," etc., as though I were one of those writers who religiously follow such usage these days. Therefore "his" is used in the general, and pretty obvious, way hereafter. And "chairman" means the person in charge, whether male or— oops, whether female or male.

to an outsider who doesn't see how they mesh, they do look a bit loose and discombobulated. So it might be easy to get the impression either that the training methods are not vigorous or that we are keeping secrets from everyone.

But of course we have no secrets. For instance, we in Putney were primarily responsible for introducing hiking, biking, and roller-skiing into the training programs used by many people. I can recount with amusement the hurdles I had to overcome to convince many coaches of the value of these three types of training, because their repertory for several years consisted of running and perhaps a few other exercises like calisthenics.

What are the keys to the program? I would say hard work and intelligent training. Sounds simple and maybe it is. Hard work and intelligent training must come from the athlete's love for the sport, which naturally includes training for it. Cross-country skiing and training is a year-round matter: it's all one. And the more you like to train the harder you will train. So it seems sensible to make training enjoyable and challenging, and I have always had that as my primary goal.

Next, we try to make training as specific as possible—but not to the extent that we lose variety. For instance, an athlete doing hill-bounding and roller-skiing during the entire offseason would be doing specificity exercises but he might soon tire of this regime. So every once in a while he should substitute something else—rowing, hiking, biking, running through the woods, skill games like tennis, volleyball—you name it.

There's something else going for x-c in the Putney area and Europeans recognize it as atmosphere or acceptance. The local people are sympathetic to training, they accept the notions and ideas, they don't nearly drive off the road when they see someone roller-skiing, and so on. These are plus points. Also, the geography of the area lends itself to training, for the terrain and the weather are both conducive to good training.

So perhaps at Putney we've been lucky in these respects. But there it is, anyway.

Introducing the Caldwell Principles

You will find statements called Caldwell's Principles of Training (CPT) and Caldwell's Principles of Technique (CPTK) sprinkled throughout. Some of these are stated in a way that may seem funny to you; some are funny to me. But at the same time I am perfectly serious about them; they underlie my philosophy of training. Without further ado I introduce my first Principle of Training:

First Principle

CPT 1: If you read far enough in the sports literature, or talk to enough athletes, trainers and coaches, you can find justification for any number of seemingly conflicting training methods.

A few years ago, for example, word came out that the Germans were putting a great deal of emphasis on interval training and felt it was the best method for building endurance in an athlete. This news roused several coaches and athletes who had been using LSD (please, in track parlance that's short for the Long, Slow, Distance method of training) and they came out with articles and comments citing the advantages of their methods.

Well, the controversy rages on and I hope it's never settled. Wouldn't it be awful if it was conclusively proved that Method X was the best for developing endurance in an athlete? Then everyone would start to train the same way and there would be nothing to speculate about, little more to write and argue about, and much of the interest and variety would be taken out of training.

2. Typical outing with family and friends, on top of Mt. Lafayette of the Franconia Ridge in New Hampshire.

Another example, easy to understand, comes from the weight-lifting crowd. In order to develop optimum muscular strength some of them prescribe lifting very heavy loads for a maximum of three times (if you can lift it more than three times it's not heavy enough, they say). Others shake their heads in disbelief at this approach and tell us we should use three sets of ten lifts each, with much lighter loads. And so on.

Controversy is fine, it's interesting, and it will continue. The danger for the athlete, as I have observed, is this: Too often skiers will get hold of the past season's star performer and inquire about his training methods. Then, after being told, they will exclaim—"Aha! No wonder we were getting whipped. So-and-so used many more short intervals in early November than we did! That explains it!"

Actually it doesn't explain anything. The surest thing you can say after a race, if you get beaten, is that the fellow who beat you took less time on the course than you did. Don't be looking for excuses, don't suddenly decide to change your training methods; try instead to evaluate your own performance with respect to your expectation. Analyze your own training. That's what is important.

3. Sixteen-year-old Jennifer Caldwell knows how to use a splitting wedge for the family's winter woodpile—after much practice.

You have to set up your own program and gain confidence in it. I know this can be difficult, especially with all the literature coming out on training. (I doubt a person could keep up with this reading even if he had it all at his disposal, in his native tongue—it's being produced that fast.) For every champion endurance-event athlete who stresses one particular system of training, another can be found who stresses an *apparently* conflicting method. So don't be psyched out by someone else's program. Remember CPT 1.

Which leads me to make one more observation and I introduce it by way of CPT 2:

CPT 2: Athletes tend to train hardest using methods or activities in which they are very successful, or which they enjoy most.

For instance, Skier A, who is a good road-runner, will tend to do the largest part of his offseason training by running, entering summer road races, etc. He will justify this by saying that running is the best training and this will be backed up by CPT 1.

Skier B, who loves manual labor—throwing logs around, digging ditches, and so on—will spend most of his training time doing this sort of thing. Easily he can cite strength as being important, and, in passing, hint at the good cardiovascular endurance he is gaining by working hard.

However, it is too often the case that A probably needs more muscle-building work and B needs more running. Therefore the corollary to CPT 2 is this: In *training*, athletes should work on their *weaknesses*; in *competitive events* they should concentrate on their *strengths*.

To give examples which will be obvious: A skier who has very good technique doesn't have to spend his offseason doing a lot of co-ordination training such as trampolining, tumbling, diving and skill games. He probably needs some good distance work. He should concentrate on distance.

And during an x-c race, a skier who is very strong on the uphills yet can't ski too well downhill, should really go all out on the uphill sections. Make time here. On the downhill he should take it easy; check rather than take a chance on falling and losing time.

2. Some Definitions

If you know what I mean when I use certain words or terms it will make for smoother going as you read on, so time-out here for a few working definitions. Some are necessarily simplified and many may be different from definitions you are familiar with, and therefore I hope you read these carefully.

A number of the terms will be expanded in the fuller discussions in chapters that follow.

Metric system

The United States is on the verge of adopting the metric system, and I use it throughout the book because all ski distances are measured in kilometers and all the scientific literature uses liters, milliliters, etc.

For the uninitiated, a kilometer is about 6/10 mile and a liter is a little more than one U.S. liquid quart, so watch out when they serve you a liter of beer abroad or you'll get loop-legged in about half the time.

Here are some lengths:

1 centimeter (cm) = .3937 inch (about 4/10 inch); *1 meter (m)* = 100 cm = 39.37 inches (about 1 1/12 yards); *1 kilometer (km)* = .62137 mile (about 6/10 mile); *5 km* = about 3 miles; *10 km* = about 6 miles; *15 km* = about 9 miles; *30 km* = about 19 miles; *50 km* = about 31 miles.

The standard ski-racing distances are 5, 10, 15, 30 and 50 km. It's interesting to note that track people run races of 5,000 m or 10,000 m, while skiers refer to these same distances as 5 k's or 10 k's.

Here are some volume measures (liquid):

1 milliliter (ml) = 1.000027 cubic centimeters (cc) = .061025 cubic inch = .0338147 U.S. fluid ounce.

1 liter (l) = 1000 ml = 1000.027 cc = 61.025 cu in = 33.8147 U.S. fluid ɔz = about 1.06 U.S. quarts.

And it takes 453.5924 *grams* to make 1 pound, or about 28 grams to tip an ounce on a balance.

Physiological terms

Oxygen Transport System

This includes all those processes by which oxygen is inspired and delivered to the tissues. An important part of this transport system is the heart and

4. Mike Gallagher, Bob Gray and Mike Elliott (left to right) sparked U.S. Teams from 1962 to 1974 in the Olympics and all major FIS competitions. Their dedication to the sport made the world's ski powers begin to take America's x-c efforts seriously.

circulating blood. A simple equation will explain further:

$$\frac{ml \; blood \; pumped}{min} = \frac{heart \; beats}{min} \times \frac{ml \; blood \; pumped}{beat}$$

Or, translated from the Algebra:

$$Cardiac \; output = Heart \; rate \times Stroke \; volume$$

Training increases the stroke volume, which in turn permits maintenance of any given cardiac output at a reduced heart rate. This is important because the perfusion of heart muscle occurs during the relaxation phase of the cardiac cycle. Thus, with a slower heart rate there is more time for adequate blood perfusion of the heart muscle.

Training works in other ways to augment the oxygen transport system. Consider:

$$\frac{ml \; O_2}{min} = \frac{ml \; blood}{min} \times \frac{ml \; O_2}{ml \; blood}$$

Or:

$$Oxygen \; transport = Cardiac \; output \times Oxygen \; content \; of \; blood$$

15

Training increases the red-cell mass of the circulating blood volume, thereby increasing the capacity of oxygen in any given volume of blood. This is important because any given level of oxygen transport can be achieved at a reduced cardiac output.

Red Blood Cells

These are erythrocytes to the medical profession, and are often abbreviated "RBC" in articles and books. In a normal human adult there are six million RBC.

RBC's are the cells that carry hemoglobin, the O_2-carrying protein. The hemoglobin content is often expressed in grams per hundred milliliters of whole blood; thus a hemoglobin count of 15 percent—which is regarded as normal for healthy adults—means 15 grams per one hundred ml of blood.

5. He's been running hard uphill for 6 minutes, during a late-summer training session.

Mitochondria

These are the parts of normal cells where the reactions take place which produce high-energy compounds necessary for muscle contractions.

Oxygen Utilization System

This involves the total cumulative metabolic processes in the tissues requiring oxygen. At present there is some evidence that these chemical processes may be facilitated as a result of training.

Oxygen Uptake

This is the equivalent of oxygen utilized per unit-time (usually one minute), and may be limited by the oxygen transport and oxygen utilization systems described above. Hence, oxygen uptake is influenced by training. Indeed, many physiologists believe the measurements of maximal oxygen uptake to be the best index of physical fitness.

If one person has a maximum oxygen uptake (max O_2 uptake) of 6 liters (6 l) per minute, and another person has a max uptake of 3 l per minute, I think you can see what will happen if both engage in an exercise like running which might require 3 l per minute in this case. The first person will be cruising along, working at 50 percent of his capacity while the second person will be working at 100 percent, or all out. And soon the second fellow will be all out—of gas.

CPT 3: Training increases the capacity for O_2 uptake.

Oxygen Debt

Oxygen debt might be expected to occur when oxygen utilization exceeds oxygen uptake for any appreciable length of time.

Only small amounts of oxygen are present in solution in the tissues; the rest is in the lungs (as air) and in the blood. There is little change in the oxygen content of the respiratory system (lungs and blood) during exercise. Further, the volume of oxygen stores (1650 ml or about $3\frac{1}{2}$ liquid pints) is almost insignificant when one considers that it represents only about 15 seconds' worth of the max O_2 uptake of a person who has a capacity for 6 liters per minute. (Peter Harris: "Lactic Acid and the Phlogiston Debt," *Cardiovascular Research*, 1969, 3, 381–90.)

Steady-state Condition

Essentially all the work done in a strenuous endurance event such as an x-c ski race is performed during a steady-state condition where there is a balance between the oxygen consumed by the tissues and the oxygen delivered or transported to the tissues. It's so important that I'll say it again: Training increases the capacity of the cardiorespiratory system for O_2 transport, so the more O_2 you can deliver the more you have available for consumption and the faster you can go.

Aerobic/Anaerobic

Aerobic work is a general—and therefore imprecise—term that is used to designate effort expended under steady-state conditions with respect to oxygen.

Anaerobic work, on the other hand, is that effort which is expended under conditions of presumed oxygen debt, such as a sprint event like the 100-meter dash.

Glycogen

This is the storage form of carbohydrate; readily mobilized as glucose, it is used as a source of energy during exercise. There is some evidence that training and diet may increase glycogen stores in the liver and muscles. (See Chapter 11, on diet.)

Lactate

Lactate (lactic acid) is an intermediate in the chemical degradation of glucose to carbon dioxide and water. Trained athletes maintain lower levels of circulating lactate during exercise than untrained athletes. This suggests that training may facilitate the metabolism of glucose.

It is thought that the disagreeable sensations (such as numbness) sometimes occurring in extreme effort may be in part accounted for by an increased level of circulating lactate in the acid form.

Coaches' terms

Going Under

This term is deliberately descriptive, rather than precise. It refers to the sensations of numbness, clumsiness, stiffness, muscle pain, blurred vision, paresthesia, dizziness, and imminent collapse which come at the limit of effort.

The causes for these symptoms are very likely to be multiple, and may include lack of oxygen, abundant lactic acid, and other circulating metabolites as yet unidentified.

Upper Limit, Limiting Factor

Coaches and physiologists talk about the upper limits of exercise for an individual, meaning as far as he can go, or as intensely as he can work. Some also talk about limiting factors.

For example: "The O_2 utilization system may be the limiting factor in exercise." This means that theoretically an athlete could do more work if he could just utilize more oxygen—the O_2 is there, the lungs can take it in, absorb it, the heart can pump it to the muscles, but the chemical processes aren't efficient enough to utilize all the O_2.

Well, at best this is a gray area. Many of the top physiologists will not agree on what the limiting factors are in exercise, or if there are any at all. Some say that all the factors converge to a limit, others feel that one

6. Tim Caldwell of the U.S. Team at the end of a 3-km sprint uphill on roller skis—but he's actually far from going under.

hundred years from now athletes may be able to run 1500 meters at a rate close to the present rate for 100 meters.

My purpose in this book is not to go into these theories or aspects. Instead I am trying to make the point that a lot is still not known, and that you should not always be drawn to believing that any one physiological system is the limiting factor in exercise.

Optimum

Webster is the best authority here: "The best or most favorable degree, quantity, number, etc."

Nice word. If you race for a distance at your optimum rate it is usually taken to mean that you have gone just as fast as you could; and this in turn means you have done it under steady-state conditions of oxygen supply and demand for the major part of the time.

If you train at your optimum rate you are going at the rate which is most efficient in terms of conditioning. Naturally there is some controversy about the optimum rate of training. Some will say it's 50 percent of maximum O_2 uptake; others think training, at least much of it, should be at 100 percent of maximum; and then there are lots of in-between theories. I'll go into this in a separate section.

Warm-up

I mean "warm" in the literal sense. My standard warm-up is accomplished by running or skiing easily with plenty of clothing on. After I'm warmed I usually feel just a little more alive—you know, I can count my pulse in more places, I begin to perspire gently and, at the same time, actually feel relaxed—then, after that, I stretch occasionally.

You too should always be warmed up before you try any vigorous stretching exercises.

There are all sorts of other warm-ups that involve calisthenics and the like. These are fine but they border on what I term a workout.

It's well accepted that your body will function better after it is warmed, and therefore a warm-up before racing is a must. On the other hand, many people like to incorporate their warm-ups into their workouts. This is easily done and perfectly acceptable.

Warm-down

After a vigorous workout a warm-down is in order. This should be a relaxed, cooling-off period, and could be done in the same way you did your warm-up. A few stretches at this time is a good idea.

Whatever you do, don't come in from a workout under a full head of steam and then just sit down or go inside and rest. Rather, walk around, or ski easily. Cool off. Flex yourself a bit to see how you feel—and then go in before you get chilled.

Distance Training

This refers to a long workout, done under steady-state conditions, where the distance covered is the dominant feature. A 150-km bike ride is a distance workout, as is a run on foot of 15 km.

Endurance Training

All distance workouts provide endurance training for the cardiovascular system. Long bouts of physical work could be considered endurance training for strength. Weight training that stresses many repetitions, even though the time involved is not as great as that of a distance workout or an eight-hour working effort, is also considered endurance training for strength.

Weight or Strength Training

This is any work or exercise that involves resistance, and thus causes great tension in the muscles being used.

Examples are weight-lifting, pulling elastic armbands, doing hard physical labor like logging, digging ditches, etc.

Isometrics/Isotonics

Isometrics is a contraction of the muscles without movement of the limbs or parts of the body involved. Stand in a doorway and push outward against the sides. If the doorway doesn't collapse you are doing an isometric contraction. I will dispose of isometrics here by stating that I do not think they have any part in a good x-c training program.

Isotonics is a contraction of the muscles that involves movement of the participating limbs and muscles. Weight-lifting is an example.

Interval Training

This is a term used broadly to mean any exercise or activity—but usually running—that is interspersed with periods of less intense activity. There are obvious variables in interval training: the intensity of the activity, the length of the activity, the number of repetitions of the activity, the length of the recovery period (or the less-intense activity period) and its intensity.

A standard interval workout might be running 60-second quarters and jogging 120-second quarters after each; repeat ten times.

Or a person might run natural intervals on a ski trail, putting out extra effort on the uphill sections only, and going easier on the downhills and flats. This type of workout is not as regimented as the track workout but is probably more valuable as x-c ski training.

Tempo/Speed

Tempo training in this book will mean going at a pace equal to racing speed.

It is sometimes confused with *speed training*, which, in this book, means going all out. Speed training, if continued long enough, will cause you to go under.

Specificity

This refers to training or exercises directly connected with the movements required by your event. For instance, roller-skiing and pulling on armbands are both specificity exercises for x-c skiing (see Chapter 7). Almost all weight-lifting is not.

Deconditioning Effect

This is just what it sounds like: a decreasing of the physical condition of the body. It is the generally accepted theory that all training effects are reversible. Some physiologists put it this way: If you train for five years it will take you about five years to decondition, assuming you don't train during that time.

A certain amount of deconditioning can occur during sickness, and some doctors claim that too much bed rest during the competitive season may also cause some deconditioning.

Further, if you set yourself a training schedule that is not progressive you may suffer from deconditioning. This is a very interesting point and I want to dwell on it.

Suppose your goal in training is to be able to run a 7-minute mile three times a week. You begin by jogging, walking, running when you feel comfortable, and you progress slowly. You are conditioning yourself during this period because your level of intensity is increasing during this time. Finally, you reach your goal and can run the mile in 7 minutes.

But you continue at this level. And what happens now is that you get more and more efficient at running the mile and therefore you begin to do less work. Clearly, you won't completely decondition yourself if you main-

7. An early fall hill-climbing workout ends (just by chance, of course) in Bill Darrow's apple orchard.

tain this level, but you may eventually come down a bit from your peak at the point of being able to run the 7-minute mile.

In order to continue a progressive training program in this instance you would have a choice between two obvious options: either run the mile faster, or run more than a mile at the same rate. (You could also run the mile with a weighted vest, or run a mile up a gradual incline—the point is to require greater effort.)

Rest Day

This can mean any sort of day that is more restful than those when you train regularly. For some it might be curling up with a book all day, for others some mild exercise. The hotshots talk about active rest days, and for them this might mean going out and running a mere 15 km.

3. General Information on Training

Suppose two people who are alike in all their physical characteristics begin a training program. One walks a mile every day in 20 minutes and the other runs a mile every day in 7 minutes. What changes will take place?

To begin with, if these two maintain the same diets there will be little difference in their weight changes due to exercise. That's because each will expend approximately the same amount of energy in doing the mile.

However, the person who is doing the more intense exercise by running the mile will begin to show the effects of training, and if we could measure all of these effects after a period of time we would probably find at least the following changes: His rested pulse rate would go down, his cardiac output would increase, his oxygen uptake would increase, and perhaps his ability to utilize oxygen would increase.

It's very important to know what training causes these changes, the so-called training effects, to take place. It isn't so important for us to know why they take place. But a few words on these training effects will be helpful.

O₂ uptake

The oxygen uptake of a person is the amount of oxygen he utilizes during a certain period of time. Uptake may not be the best word for this process, but it's the one everyone uses. Actually, a person breathes in and absorbs more oxygen into his bloodstream than he utilizes in the production of energy. Some oxygen circulates through the body in the bloodstream and then is discharged by exhaling, so it's only the oxygen that is utilized for energy that is defined as the measure of a person's uptake. Because of this "extra" oxygen available in the bloodstream, some doctors have theorized that the oxygen absorbed into the bloodstream is not the limiting factor in severe exercise, but rather the actual chemical process of utilizing the O_2 may be the limiting factor. (This would lead into a discussion of blood cells, mitochondria, etc., and it is not my purpose to go into that now.)

To determine their oxygen uptake, thousands of people have been tested while exercising vigorously. The testing method is easy to understand but it does require some sophisticated equipment that you don't find lying around everywhere.

A person runs on a treadmill or pedals on a bicycle ergometer until he reaches the steady state. Then the air that is expired from the lungs is captured in a device called a Douglas Bag, and is compared with the surrounding air (from which he inspired) for the difference in O_2 content. That difference is the O_2 used by the body, or O_2 uptake.

If the intensity of the exercise is increased until the person has to stop from exhaustion, a good measure of his max O_2 uptake can be determined.

Measurements for max O_2 uptake are given in two different ways. You might read that a person's max O_2 uptake is 6 l/min, meaning that he can utilize 6 liters of oxygen per minute. In the section of definitions I compared two people, one with an uptake of 6 l and another with an uptake of 3 l. Imagine what would happen if both were engaged in exercise that required more than 3 l/min. The person with the lower uptake would be forced to stop very soon, and from his example is learned the advantage of having a high O_2 uptake.

You might expect a person weighing 80 kg to use more oxygen to carry himself around than one who weighed 40 kg. And you'd usually be right. Thus, the measurement of O_2 uptake in terms of liters alone is not as meaningful as another system of measurement—one that expresses O_2 uptake in terms of milliliters per kilogram body weight per minute. An athlete's uptake might be expressed as 65 ml/kg, meaning that he can utilize 65 milliliters of O_2 per kilogram of weight per minute. With this measurement we might find that our 40-kg person mentioned above had a higher uptake rate than the one who weighed 80. From there we could be led to assume that the lighter person had a higher capacity for endurance work.

All max O_2 measurements are for the exercise being performed—that is, usually biking or running on a treadmill. Since skiing x-c requires the use of more muscles than biking or running it's very probable that if a person could be tested for skiing and then for biking, his uptake for skiing would be higher. But you can see the problems of attaching a lot of equipment to a skier in order to measure his O_2 uptake. It has been suggested that skiers be measured on the treadmill, using roller-skis instead of running, to see if their O_2 rates would be higher. But I don't know many skiers who would be willing to risk roller-skiing on a treadmill. And can you imagine the damage the pole tips might do to the equipment?

Measurements of O_2 uptake can be significant if they are done on the same subject under exactly the same conditions over a period of time, thus allowing progress to be charted. If a batch of skiers is tested for O_2 uptake on the bicycle ergometer, then relative measurements can be determined for that exercise. The correlation between O_2 uptake for biking—the ergo-meter—and for skiing would be expected to be high. However, there's more to being a successful skier than having a high O_2 uptake. There are little items like strength, technique, motivation and intelligence. The champions on the Douglas Bag don't always show at the top of the results list, so let's not "run our races" in the laboratory.

Some Socialist countries measure their youngsters at an early age for max O_2 uptake and then program them for particular events. A kid with a high uptake might be encouraged to go into distance events, for instance.

This approach is tied in with a certain theory—or perhaps it's a con-jecture at this point. And it is this: that athletes are born with sprint/strength muscles or with endurance muscles. If you happen to have en-durance muscles it means that the muscles' cells are more suited for utilizing O_2 by those chemical processes that take place during exercise, and there-fore your uptake would be above normal. In other words, O_2 uptake, to a degree, is inherited. I don't know about this. If O_2 uptake is inherited it ought to be possible to predict an athlete's uptake by measuring his parents and I haven't heard of any experiments along this line.

Science and test scores

As we get more scientific about our training for x-c skiing we must at the same time caution ourselves not to become too dependent on medical tests,

---

Women's Lib Again

There are a couple of interesting items concerning O_2 uptake.

Women's lib notwithstanding, it's a fact that women have average max O_2 uptakes of about 25 percent less than men. (At the same time, a few highly trained women athletes have max O_2 uptakes only 10 percent below those obtained in comparably trained men.) It's very important for women to realize this and accept it. If they try to train, ski, and race on an equal basis with men, they are going to have a very discouraging time of it. However, the enjoyment and the in-spiration to be derived from women and men training together should not be underestimated. Many of the world's top skiers of both sexes, and plenty of the tour-racers, take their workouts together to the benefit of everyone.

scores, and the like. I've seen treadmill and ergometer scores, results of tests for body fat, arm strength, leg strength, etc. All these make for good conversation and they are certainly an indication of potential. But don't read too much into these scores. The doctors are the first ones to warn against this.

One of the first things you should ask yourself about an experiment or a test score is this: What are the variables? Consider a bicycle ergometer test used to determine a person's O_2 uptake. If everything else was equal (and it never is) wouldn't you expect a person who had biked extensively to score higher on this test than someone who had not biked at all? The veteran biker would be more efficient and could therefore carry a heavier load—this would mean a higher score. However, his actual O_2 uptake might be lower than the other fellow's.

Suppose it becomes possible to take care of these variables (such as experience in biking) by plugging certain factors into some formula. What then? Couldn't we do a pretty good job of predicting race outcomes? Well, you still must consider other variables in a race situation. How about motivation, technique, ability to pace, good wax, the breaks that often occur during a race, and so on? These will always be variables and no one will ever be able to predict results in good competition by looking at the test scores. Isn't it a lucky thing, too? There wouldn't be any point in having a race if we could figure out the winners in the laboratory beforehand.

But enough of this heavy stuff. Let's be sure we know what training increases your O_2 uptake, a matter that is important for endurance events like x-c skiing.

Cardiac output

The more blood your heart can pump through your body to the working muscles, bringing a fresh supply of oxygen, the more work you will be able to do. As you might expect, there is a high correlation between cardiac output and O_2 uptake.

Tests have shown that during vigorous exercise the maximum pulse rate of a well-trained athlete and an untrained person is about the same. But there is an important difference in the two heart-stroke volumes. The athlete may be able to deliver as much as 40 l of blood per minute whereas the untrained person may deliver only 20 l. In other words, with each stroke or beat of his heart the athlete is pumping twice as much blood. Proper training will increase your stroke volume and this is another of the training effects.

The reason people with low pulse rates are often good bets for endurance events is this: Let's assume two people who are nearly alike in body weight, make-up, etc., are sitting around and we check their pulses. One is 40 a minute and the other is 80. It isn't stretching it too far to assume that the demands for blood are the same in each person and therefore the fellow with the low rate is pumping twice as much blood per stroke. More than this, his heart has twice as long to fill with blood before it is pumped out. This implies a bigger and stronger heart, a better machine!

But having a good machine that can really pump blood isn't the end-all either. The blood has to get to the working muscles, and for this it is necessary that the muscles relax. Try carrying a bucket full of maple sap up a hill with one arm. Soon your arm gets that numb feeling because the arm muscles are not relaxing and permitting a free flow of blood (this is probably due to a build-up of lactate in your arm). Anyway, what do you do? You stop and rest, or switch arms. In other words, you relax the muscles, fresh blood comes into the numbed arm with a new supply of O_2, and at the same time the blood helps to carry off the lactate.

So it is with skiing. If your technique does not allow your muscles to relax sufficiently the blood will begin to bypass those areas that are constricted—the very areas where you need continuing supplies of blood (and therefore oxygen). In this case it doesn't matter what your cardiac output or your max O_2 uptake is. What does matter is your technique.

Pulse Rate

In general there is a correlation between a person's heart rate, his O_2 uptake at that time, and his cardiac output. This means that the faster your heart beats, within certain limits, the more blood and oxygen you will deliver to your muscles.

It is also generally true that during intense exercise a person's O_2 uptake reaches a maximum, or levels off, before his heart rate reaches a maximum. For instance, if your max heart rate is 200, you might reach your max O_2 uptake at 180 beats. After this point an increased heart rate would not deliver any more oxygen (blood) to the system.

This leads us toward trying to determine the optimum intensity of exercise, or training. Most physiologists and coaches around the world think that an athlete should work very often at his max O_2 uptake. One reason given to support this notion is the belief that, the body being such a wonderful invention, it adjusts to stress situations, and therefore if you train hard your body will learn to function better at these high levels.

If we agree to this theory of training at max O_2 uptakes quite often, the next question is: How do you know when you are at max uptake? First, we can say that it is not when your pulse rates are at maximum. Next, it's probably safe to say that if your max uptake occurs at 180 beats per minute, a rate slightly lower than this will be associated with an O_2 uptake which is 85–90 percent of your max uptake; so this isn't bad.

But there still remains the problem of how to determine this max O_2 uptake intensity, or an optimum intensity for training, and then how to pinpoint when you are working at this rate. If there is anyone in the crowd who can claim to know definitely, will he please step forward?

How Hard?

There have been attempts to specify an optimum average heart rate for distance workouts. I'll throw out a couple of examples for you, but I cannot recommend only one method over the others with any finality. However, they might serve as a guide.

8. Mike Elliott's super conditioning permitted him to train at high-energy output for distances of 20 to 30 k's.

Try This

One method for determining your *optimum average* heart rate for a distance workout is to multiply your rested pulse by 2½. For me that might be too fast: my rested pulse is about 60 and the formula indicates I should average 150 beats per minute during a distance workout. I don't think I could do it, and that may be because I'm too old.

I know some skiers with rested pulse rates of 40 and if they followed this formula they would work out at 100—hardly worth the effort!

If you are somewhere between these two extremes the 2½ factor might work.

Or This

Perhaps the simplest method is to run your workouts at a specified pulse rate below your maximum. For distance workouts, try 40–60 beats below max, for intervals try 20–40 below max. For speed workouts you don't measure your pulse. For tempo workouts you should try and determine your optimal pulse rate. This is what pacing is all about. But more about that later.

The Problems

There are two main problems with any formula for pulse-rate averages for exercise. First, it's quite difficult to measure your pulse accurately, particularly your maximum. The instant you stop to count your heartbeat—you know, you feel on your wrist or your neck or over your heart to get the thumps, and then you wait for the second hand on your watch to come to a convenient point—your heart starts to slow down. By the time you finish your count your heart rate might be down as much as 5 to 15 beats a minute from its maximum. Second, supposing that you could get accurate readings of your heart rate at any time (you might have a monitor attached to yourself, or some such), then you are faced with the problem of trying to determine what your average rate is during your workout. On uphills you would expect a rate higher than average, on downhills a rate lower than average, and on the flats——? From a strict mathematical approach you would have to determine how much time you spent at each heart rate in order to figure your average. Of course it's not intended that you try: these are just guides for heart rates.

Common Sense

I'm going to suggest another guide.
  It's you.

Don't get too hung up on pulse rates in determining intensity of exercise. However, you can take out a watch occasionally and time yourself. See what you are working at on a tough uphill. See how soon your rate recovers considerably. Sometime when you seem to be going along very comfortably, in a steady state, check your pulse. Log all these figures; then in a few weeks do it again.

If you get a fair amount of information on your own heart rate during different bouts of exercise you can use these casual data as a check on yourself. You might be out plugging along, thinking you were working hard. If you took your pulse you might find it was a fair amount under what you had been able to tolerate previously, and hence if you want to get a better workout you should step up the pace in this instance.

General theories on intensity

A very good rule to follow during training is—

CPT 4: During a training period or season, increase the duration of your training first, and then as the training period nears an end, increase the intensity of training.

For instance, many skiers train steadily by running, beginning late in the spring and continuing until snow comes. During this time, under this schedule, it would be a good approach to build up the amount of distance done during spring and summer, even perhaps into early fall (this last would depend in part on when you were expecting to get on snow). Thereafter and until snowtime, the distance should be held constant and the intensity increased. Thus if your distance workouts got to around 15 km by, say mid-September, you would not increase them, but run them faster.

Or, if you worked up to a certain number of intervals you would then keep the number steady and increase the intensity, by running them faster or cutting down the rest periods in between, etc.

An athlete who trains this way, with a steadily increasing intensity, will probably be able to perform fairly consistently during the racing season.

There is another approach to this idea of increasing extent and then intensity, and for that I invite you to read the discussion on peak periods in Chapter 10.

CPT 5: One of the characteristics of all living things, including the human body, is its ability to respond to a stimulus.

You train hard and in doing so send a signal to your body, which in turn

31

reacts and adjusts to the load. You work harder and harder and your body responds more and more.

Well, that's what it's all about, this training.

CPT 6: It is easier to stay in shape than to increase your fitness.

Some physiologists have determined that a decent workout twice a week will do a good job of maintaining the status quo. I believe this, and it's an important precept to remember during those periods when, for one reason or another, you can't train more often. But remember that you will have to train harder in order to up your conditioning. Don't get lulled into a state of complacency if you want to improve.

Value of anaerobic training

Recalling the definition of anaerobic work as that which produces so-called oxygen debt, or causes you to go under if continued long enough, the question arises: How much of this kind of training is good or necessary?

There is no clear answer to this.

Since nearly 100 percent of a long-distance race is run under steady-state conditions, it makes sense to train in steady state (or aerobically, as many refer to it). I tried hill climbs with poles for the U.S. Team for many years, thinking these anaerobic workouts were good. There is no doubt that 40–90-second hill climbs, done hard, are the toughest exercises going and can bring anyone to his knees. One theory holds that by training the anaerobic processes you can increase your ability to go faster under such extremely demanding conditions. Or you can build your tolerance for lactate in the system—lactate equaling pain in this case.

I don't know. There is probably some value in doing these tough hill climbs. Specifically, there is a mental toughening that is good for some people. But I now believe that if too many tough hill climbs are done there are the following risks. First, it's easy to build a dislike for this workout; and if you begin dreading the workouts that isn't good. Second, you may begin to ease off in your hill climbs in order to avoid pain; and then you are fooling yourself. Third, this sort of workout is termed a destructive one, where some of the cells of the body are actually destroyed; and there is real doubt as to the value of such destruction. Finally, and though it is a bit way-out, I believe that if hill climbs are done in excess the body will build in an automatic, psychological reaction which will force it to slow down to a point where the speeds can be tolerated more easily. This reaction is not to be confused with a conscious effort to slow

32

9. Each of these international racers trained specially for such a sprint start as this women's relay at the Swedish Ski Games.

down: I think the body just says, "Enough of this."

There are still plenty of situations where extreme efforts are called for. In a race, if you know the course and know you have the ability to recover adequately, you really should attack the last parts of the uphills, and then recover on the downhill sections. Of course if you go under and do not recover you will lose time. So you train by sprinting up and over the tops of the hills, and then checking your recovery.

But after those tough hill climbs we used to do we were so tired that all we could do was stumble back down the hill, or rest. This is too intense, or going under too far, and I think it should be avoided in racing and in training, both.

The best place to use an anaerobic effort is at the end of the race. You sprint for the finish and then take the consequences.

Finally, I highly recommend 10–12-second hill sprints (described in Chapter 9). These are primarily speed and strength builders, but they may have as much value in improving the anaerobic processes as the longer periods of anaerobic work—if there is any improvement to be gained at all.

Aerobic training

As I have said, most of your training must be done in a steady state, where you don't go under. One nice way of putting this is to say that a reduction of speed means less fatigue (lactate, going under, etc.), which in turn means you can increase your volume of work each training session. There's no doubt that the volume of training is important.

The trends are toward increasing volumes. It's almost unbelievable. For example, during November 1972 one Swede skied 2000 km. Now that's a lot of work! (He went in for an oil change at the end of the month.) In fact, it may have been too much for him. And it certainly is too much for almost anyone reading this book. At this writing, the top skiers in the world are averaging about 1000 km of training—mainly roller-skiing, hiking, running, and snow skiing—a month for eight months of the year.

There is a fine line we must recognize between volume and intensity. You might say that you were going to walk 20 miles a day, which would be quite a volume. But it wouldn't do much for you, and it would take a long time too. A fellow would be better off running less far, but running with some intensity. I'll suggest some schedules in Chapter 13.

Best kinds of training

Most sports or exercises which utilize large muscle-groups are more pleasurable than activities which use fewer muscles. Wouldn't you rather get a workout by rowing, running, skiing, etc., than by pulling on arm-bands? You just can't get that feeling of over-all body relaxation after an armband workout.

Further, physiologists have actually determined that the best exercises are exactly those pleasurable ones which do use the largest muscle-groups. Lucky thing for all of those people who run, row and ski. In rowing a shell, for instance, it's quite easy to reach your max O_2 uptake. In fact, the demands of rowing are probably higher than those of running, but both exercises use the large muscle-groups, and hence mean more requirements for O_2.

And this in turn means better training.

Motivation

CPT 7: Ya gotta wanna do it.

Most of the exercise programs set up in this country are determined by coaches or school situations. From a young age on we are told, "It's time for Phys. Ed class . . . Now we are going to train . . . When I blow the whistle you begin . . ." And so on. Students, especially, are given little latitude in the types of training they can do, or in choosing the periods of time to do them in.

Since most of the instruction comes from paid coaches (who usually double as teachers in a school situation), most athletes think "this is the way it is, this is the way it should be"; and they even seek similar situations after leaving school. If some student athletes do try to strike out on their own they are often thwarted in one way or another by so-called top-level coaches. (And that's the subject for another discussion, but it can't be covered in this book.)

There is a very fine line to be drawn between coaches and athletes in the setting-up and performing of a training program. Coaches should offer suggestions or point out areas of weakness that need work. Coaches should be able to help organize and inspire the athletes, and to pick out technical flaws. But if you as an athlete go too far in accepting a coach's recommendations, or in depending on him to coax you out to train, or to bark orders and blow whistles for you, pretty soon you won't be doing it for yourself. Worse: If you rely on a coach who leaves the area, or if your opinion of him changes, your own program will suffer.

The feel of it

The human body is a very wonderful, complex mechanism and every day exercise physiologists are making strides in learning more about the body and how it performs under stress of work. Yet there will always be some unanswered questions. It's very unlikely that anyone will ever be able to explain fully the psychology of it all, even if doctors do figure out the physiology of it.

What allows an athlete to go out and have a fine performance one day, and then, several days later, apparently under the same circumstances, to go out and falter badly?

You may, better than anyone else, be able to figure out some of the answers to these questions. At any rate, you must try to, and one method

10. Motivation. Period.

which will help is to keep a training log like the one described in the next chapter.

Some of the top skiers of the world train themselves by feel. For instance, if their regular workout calls for some distance running and they don't feel up to it, they do something else. They are not bullheaded to the point that they follow through with their plan regardless. Nor are they ordered out by an inflexible coach.

However, the danger here is obvious. If athletes go soft on themselves and operate by a debased feel, they will lose out. Clearly, then, the top athletes don't go soft on themselves. They can tell the difference between feeling bad during a workout because they need the work, and feeling bad because they are run down or sick. If our top U.S. x-c skiers were to be judged as a whole I think we would find that they too often go out and bull it. This is partly because they do not know themselves well enough, or they are operating "under orders," like Watergate boys.

So I think there is quite a bit of room for that business called the individual approach to training. If there is one message I want to get across, it is this: Your own training program must be suited for you. Obviously it must be demanding, feasible, and all that, but the emphasis should be on the *you*. YOU gotta wanna do it.

4. Precautions, Progression & Paperwork

No matter what your age, you should have a thorough medical examination before you begin any intensive training program. The doctor should be able to tell you of the need for any restrictions.

If you are young and in average health there are probably very few restrictions you have to worry about. Some physiologists believe that healthy people in their teens, or younger, cannot harm themselves by hard training. Their theory is that when a person gets into an extreme exercise stress situation he will simply slow up, naturally or otherwise. I generally agree; but I do warn against competitive situations where young people might be spurred beyond acceptable limits by crowd stimulus, or by a desire to satisfy the emotional parents who might be on the scene, etc.

I remember a theory prevalent several years ago which held that one's growth could be stunted by hard exercise during the formative 'teens. Today the belief is quite the opposite. And many physiologists think that an athlete will develop his oxygen uptake the most, or completely, before the age of 20.

If you are middle-aged (and I'm not going to try and pin *that* one down) and have been used to an active life with a fair amount of exercise, and if you are normally healthy, you can undertake quite a program. In fact, the limiting factors might be your own time and interest. But get a medical check and keep doing so regularly.

People with some form of heart disease should not attempt anything described in this book. Doctors are turning to certain forms of exercise as rehabilitation in many cases of heart disease, but physicians are the only ones to make such prescriptions.

The progressive program

You'll hear that training programs should be progressive, and I want to explain what is meant by that.

Generally, if your program is progressive it means that your over-all workload or intensity increases during the months that you are training. Here are several statements which might sound contradictory, but actually should help to clarify things.

1. I recommend 2- to 4-week periods during the year when your pro-

gram will *not* seem to be progressive. More about peaking in Chapter 10, but for now suffice it to say that during these periods your over-all load will not increase.

2. A progressive program does not mean one that shows an increased load *day by day:* this would be disastrous.

3. During certain seasons, such as the spring, your program might be hard to measure, or it might actually slack off in terms of workload. But with a progressive program you would expect to do more during one spring season than you did during the previous spring.

4. If you are advanced in age there is some point where you should stop worrying about progressing in pure workload terms. Think of it in another way: "If I can still do things at age 50 that I'm doing now I'll feel I have progressed." As I've said before, training is an individual matter, and the older you get, the more you should rely on yourself, not charts or graphs.

The Increments

One of the biggest disappointments for people beginning a training program is the apparent lack of progress. Often they try to up their workload too soon. For example, one person might start out jogging 5 km three or four times a week, then after two weeks try to cut down the time for that distance by as much as a minute or two. This in turn might be quite a strain on his body; he might go under or come home with sore muscles, and all that. Such results are discouraging and are not what I consider part of a progressive program.

So take the increments slowly. You shouldn't even think of a crash program. If you want to race, or train to get in shape, it won't be very meaningful to you unless you train for at least a year. After that time you can look back and see what you have accomplished and then judge your progress.

In the meantime, set up your schedule so that the increments—the jumps, progressions, or whatever you want to call them—come once a month. A month is a good unit of time and easy to associate with. "I'll be running 5 k's this month and next month it will be 7 at the same speed." And so on.

In the beginning if your program seems too easy, don't worry. There are advantages to establishing yourself at an exercise level. Your muscles adapt to that load, your body can take it, you are less likely to get tired, run down or discouraged. I don't think there is much chance for deconditioning if you take an increment at the beginning of the month, reach it easily within two weeks, and then hold it for the last two weeks of the month.

If you can gain confidence in your ability to do the workload it will mean a lot for your whole program. It's called stabilization.

Number of Workouts

It's better to go out three times a week for six weeks than six times a week for three weeks. It goes back to the stabilization process I just mentioned. Don't rush things.

It's also better, if you have the time, to split the workload, after a point where you are doing a fair amount, to two workouts a day. Many top athletes take two workouts a day for an average of five or six days a week, right through the year. Normally the workouts are of different types: the athlete might do strength work in the morning and running in the afternoon, rather than doing everything in one wrap-up session.

Day On, Day Off

Probably the simplest, most easily understood method for determining the intensity of your workload on a given day is to follow the formula of one hard (or harder) day, then one easy (less hard) day. After a tough workout one day it's pretty hard to bounce back the next day for another grinder, so take it easy.

As they say, "Train, don't strain."

If there is any question now regarding harder days *vs.* easier days, you'll soon learn to distinguish them as you train more.

Training Log

One of the most important parts of anyone's program is the keeping of a log or journal. I'll address the advantages to the athlete who wants to peak for certain races during the winter.

The log should contain, as a minimum, the following information: each day's workout and some comment on how it felt, hours of sleep, weight taken about once a week, and rested pulse rate. In addition, some athletes keep a running score of their various workouts in terms of time and distance. The kilometers run each day can be added weekly, then each week's sums can be totaled at the month's end, etc. (See sample sheet from a training log on the next page.)

WEIGHT 170 lbs.

RESTED PULSE 48/38/38/38/—/40/40

DATE	DISTANCE	INTERVAL	ROLLER SKIING	TEMPO	OTHER	RACES		COMMENTS
6/9	2 hrs.						25 km.	AM got skis ready — skied late in day — felt pretty tired and a little clumsy
6/10	4 hrs.						45 km.	AM skied 25 in tracks near pass — good skiing — afternoon slept 2 hrs, then in evening toured up Daisy Pass — slow snow
6/11	4½ hrs						50 km.	AM skied 25 in tracks about 2 hrs — good skiing — slept 2 hrs after lunch, then toured Daisy Pass again — good vertical
6/12	4 hrs						50 km.	AM skied a good 35 ks, nice skiing, felt good slept 3 hrs + went skiing — bad snow, slow — slugged out 15 ks then quit
6/13	4 hrs						45 km.	up very early — skiing 5:15 feet terrible, tired, sluggish, just skied slow + easy, nearly in a coma — 2 hrs sleep after lunch
6/14	1 hr.		3/4		½		34 km.	AM roller skied up from park — went too fast afternoon hike, real slow — skied 1 hour evening, slow snow, felt OK
6/15			1⅓				21 km.	roller skied 21 km — nice steady speed, feet tired but was OK — up, fast, up — good trip — slept 2 hrs after lunch, rested
TOTAL FOR WEEK	19½		2+		½		270 km.	quite a week of skiing + training — had a few bad days toward end of week, but am first going easy now.
TOTAL TO DATE	38	1	7⅓		7			

11. One week in June from the training log of a U.S. Team member. The camp was high in the Montana Rockies, so he could alternate between roller-skiing on hardtop roads and getting on snow. It is usual to log distances in terms of workout hours, rather than in k's covered.

The Day's Workout and How You Felt

There are very good reasons for keeping a log. First, you can look back in your log after a few months and see progress for yourself. Next, if you make some comments on your own condition it will give you some guide to the consequences of your workouts. For instance, "Those hill runs were real tough, especially after the fifth one." If you had a distance workout the day before and found your hill runs the next day too tough, your entries tell you something you may be able to apply to a racing situation.

That Super Day

If you train long enough you're going to begin to have what I call super days every so often. These are the days when you run right away from the people you're training with, or when you just can't seem to tire yourself by going at top speeds.

Put a star in your log for these days. The whole idea is to try to program these super occasions so they fall during race days. Sounds simple, but it may take years to learn this. You'll have to study all the days that led to your great effort, then try to duplicate it again and again. You might not get the formula right off, but keep working at it. Competition is so tough at the top levels that no one wins unless he has a super day.

Rested Pulse

The rested pulse can be a very valuable bit of information if it is used correctly.

First, you must always take your pulse under exactly the same conditions. The best time to do so is immediately after you wake up. If you lie in bed, roll around, and begin thinking about the day's events, it's likely that your pulse will elevate and a reading of it might alarm you. Some athletes know their heart rates go up automatically when thinking about a race and therefore they don't even bother to take it on race days.

After you train for a few months your rested pulse rate should go down . . . unless it's already at its low.

The lowest pulse rate I'm acquainted with is Mike Elliott's. He went to a doctor one day for a check-up and his heart was bleeping along in the low 30's. The doctor thought Mike was a candidate for sick bay rather than for the Olympic Team. A fair number of athletes on the U.S. x-c team register rates in the 30's when they first wake up. But don't fret if yours isn't that low. I never got mine even into the 40's—it seems to plug along at 60 no matter how rested a state I'm in.

If you wake up with a slow pulse it generally means you are rested and ready to go. You can again check back in your journal and see what events preceded this low-pulse day. Then try to plug that information into your race schedule during the winter. You can experiment on this during the offseason too.

If you wake up and your pulse is higher than usual it could mean any of three things. First, you're excited about something or just woke up from a wild dream; second, the previous day's workout was a "bear" and you're tired; or third, it may be the onset of some sickness.

Whatever the cause, though, don't get psyched out by a slightly high pulse. If all athletes allowed their pulse rates to program their workouts and dictate race participation we would see a lot of inactivity and lots of did-not-starts.

Body Weight

Keeping an account of your weight should lead you to figure out your best skiing weight. It's also the simplest way to know if you are getting enough calorie intake. There's a simple principle: If your calorie intake exceeds your calorie output (the amount of calories you burn up by existing and exercising) you will gain weight. If the process is reversed you will lose weight.

Some of my doctor friends tell me that during a good training program your appetite decreases relative to your caloric demands, and this is the best, healthiest way to get your weight down to "a fighting trim." I'll buy that.

I'll say more about food in Chapter 11.

Hours of Sleep

You should find this useful in your over-all approach. If it seems necessary to get so many hours' sleep for two or three days preceding a good workout, plug this fact into your program.

Also, learning your sleep pattern over an extended period, particularly during travel, will help you to diagnose the reasons why it may vary on occasion, and you'll be less likely to get uptight about sleep before a race.

Memories, Too

If you keep an accurate and, I hope, helpfully descriptive log, it will provide you with a lot of pleasure as you look it over in the months to come. There just has to be a psychological boost in looking back and

12. And don't forget that family tour in your training log . . .

reading about those workouts which stood out in your mind.

I wonder that I ever did some of those things—like hiking 30 miles a day for nine days. But there it is, in print, and it makes fine reading.

And More

If you're the mathematical type, or like to draw graphs and charts, you can plot your pulse rate against your weight, your distance totals, and so on. This can prove very interesting.

Theoretically, your pulse should go down as you train, your workload should go up, and, if you're overweight, your weight should go down. If your weight doesn't go down it might be because you've lost fat and gained muscle, which is heavier, so don't worry about *that*.

In sum: A training log should be kept to provide you with useful information. The important matters are your progress, your over-all conditioning, and your ability to program or predict the circumstances which lead you to your best efforts. Body weight and rested pulse rates are not as important. I've seen lots of winners of the rested-pulse sweepstakes who don't come out on top of the finish list, so don't get obsessed with your facts and figures, *or especially anyone else's.* Use all this information as objectively as you can.

5. Interval Training

Interval training can be thought of as a series of fairly hard efforts interspersed with periods of less intensity. Intervals can be done on foot, on skis, while biking, roller-skiing, rowing, or during many other kindred activities that require a large O_2 uptake.

The most generally accepted theory for the efficacy of interval training is that the body's system can be worked at near-maximum power for a longer accumulated period of time than one would believe possible. Since the best way to improve one's condition is to work at or near maximum effort, the argument goes, interval training is good.

Sample workout

A typical interval workout might go like this. A 4- or 5-minute loop is run at about 80–100 percent effort, putting the body under a stress that could not be maintained for so long as, say, 10 minutes. Then the loop is jogged once, rather easily, to give the body time to recover; then it is run again at the higher intensity. And so on.

The standard method for determining the number of loops to be run is by taking times. When the running or recovery loop times fall off quite a bit it's probably time to quit. Or, when your muscles feel stiff, tired, numb or sluggish. (If you run intervals on the same loop you won't need a watch after a while: you'll know when your times are slacking off and it's time to stop.)

There are hundreds of different interval workouts and this is just one example, but it will serve to continue the argument, which goes like this. A cross-country ski race can be considered a series of intervals. On the uphills the skier is working near maximum effort, continually flirting with the danger of going under. On the downhills he has a chance for partial or complete recovery. The flats are run at efforts in between these two. So why not train by running intervals?

As applied to x-c

Well, I have to agree. But I think that distance training is the most important kind of training for skiing. Distance training by my definition necessarily contains a series of intervals. (Try running around the countryside of the Green Mountain State, Vermont, without getting into some stress situation on hills, which are followed by recovery periods going downhill.) I'll say more about this in the section on distance training, but for now I would like to summarize some of the important differences between x-c skiing and track-running. So many interval-training programs are laid out for track-runners that it is worth noting these differences:

1. X-C skiing has more ups and downs, of irregular distances.

2. X-C skiing has more-nearly-complete recovery periods on the downhills.

3. X-C skiing requires more strength, especially in the upper body.

4. X-C skiing is usually done over longer distances. Except for the marathon, 10,000 meters is the longest official Olympic running distance, while 10,000 meters, or 10 km, is the shortest men's x-c racing distance.

One problem some of our skiers have had is that their training schedules were patterned after those for track-runners. As you can see, I think these are best left to the track people, especially in the matter of interval workouts.

Distance in interval

However, I have a hunch that lots of the people who have been arguing so long for one method of training or the other—interval or distance—have actually been doing both kinds of training, but simply haven't defined it that way. If a runner goes out interval training and runs 10 hard loops, taking 4 to 5 minutes each, and takes a recovery loop between each hard one, it might be understating it to say he had a distance workout. And if a skier went out for a distance workout and bounded around the countryside for about two hours, at a pace slightly faster than the recovery-loop pace of the first runner, he would probably get into quite a few stress situations on uphills which would be followed by recoveries, just like interval training.

Call it what you want, but let's agree to get into some stress situations during training. In running, biking or roller-skiing these will best be done on uphills.

How many, how far, how hard, where

For x-c ski training you must run intervals of at least 3 minutes, preferably more. It's fine to run loops and use the same one for a recovery loop. If jogging this loop seems too easy, run it a bit faster, or run a recovery loop that is shorter. Running a recovery loop is much preferred to standing around waiting to recover.

You should run the loop fairly hard, but not so hard that you go under, or that you cannot recover by jogging the loop afterward. Many athletes use pulse rate as an indicator of recovery. When the pulse is back down to 120 it's time to run another hard loop.

I don't recommend timing every running and recovery loop, but if you do so occasionally you will see some advantages. First, you can tell when your times fall off—in the event you can't feel it. Second, you will have some record for your log and something you can refer to for comparison in the months to come.

I run a little loop in the woods and about every two weeks I time myself just to see how it's going. During the spring and summer I simply try to increase the number of loops I run, and they take about 5:30 each. During the fall I hold the number of loops steady and try to run them faster. This is in line with the theory I expressed previously.

When you run intervals you should do them on varied terrain. This is most important. Stay away from flat-running situations if you can.

Next try to get a loop in the woods or on other soft ground. It is more like the terrain you find in racing situations and it is also more rewarding, psychologically. Compare running in the woods with training on a hardtop or gravel road. The footing on the hard surfaces is firmer and requires little concentration, whereas in the woods it's likely to be a little uneven.

What Pain Barrier?

Some coaches and athletes talk about the pain barrier, and training or conditioning oneself to be able to push back that barrier—i.e., to be able to take more and more pain.

I think that word *pain* should not be used in talking about training and racing. I've never heard the world's top racers talk about it, and the reasons they don't are easy to understand. For one thing, pain should not be considered an automatic ingredient of training: if it were, it might be too destructive, both in terms of physical conditioning and mental outlook. Next, in a race, pain is something to avoid. It usually means you have been running too hard and may be about ready to go under. And if you go under your time is bound to suffer.

But I say this unevenness is good, because it is more similar to a skiing situation where you have to concentrate with every stride. Running on slightly uneven ground will also develop the muscles that help you to maintain better balance. Soft ground is easier on the joints too.

Build a loop

Every training setup should have available a little training loop. I have seen these all over Europe and they are quite easy to build. The standard approach is to lay out a track of about 1 km through terrain in the woods. Then clear it, smooth it by digging out roots and rocks if necessary, and mark it. On some of the fancier loops a trench is dug to a depth of about 6–10 cm all the way around, which is filled with a combination of gravel and sawdust, or a similar mixture. This makes for very nice footing. Markers are placed every 50 meters along the trail and then if runners want to go hard for a couple of hundred meters some added incentive is right there.

I've watched athletes training on these loops in Europe and they really

13. An old logging road, clipped and raked, makes an ideal training loop for any season.

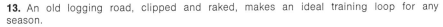

seem to enjoy it. Often two runners will alternate setting the pace, or one will run the fast loop and the other the recovery loop.

Naturally these loops also can be used for distance workouts, but a longer track would be preferable.

Various intervals

A *natural interval* is one which utilizes the terrain. For instance, you might take a run through terrain and go hard on the uphills, even walk the downhills, and run easily along the flats. This sort of workout puts the same stress on your system as skiing does and it is therefore highly recommended.

Many skiers run natural intervals in snow, skiing the uphills very fast, coasting the downhills, and cruising the flats. This is similar to a distance workout, even though, strictly speaking, a distance workout over the same terrain might call for less effort on the uphills.

Strength-speed intervals are designed to improve your strength and speed, and I will cover them separately in chapters 8 and 9.

The *tempo workout* is an interval at racing speed and is usually done on snow during the winter. Because it is the purpose of the tempo workout to adjust the body to racing speed, the skier usually skis uphill for 5 to 10 minutes, then takes a complete recovery before doing it again. As a rule-of-thumb, tempo workouts should not exceed 1/5 the distance you are training for.

6. Distance Training

Distance training is the meat and potatoes of any good training program for x-c skiing. Strict interval training, weight or strength training, co-ordination exercises, etc., are all good activities, but they aren't shortcuts or alternatives to this most necessary part of a correct program. The evidence of the value of distance training is simply overwhelming. It develops the ability to maintain a steady state of exercise at continually higher rates of intensity, it develops endurance, and it develops the ability to withstand fatigue. No successful x-c skier is without these attributes.

I have already covered interval training and have remarked that proper distance training includes intervals or series of differing periods of intensity. This is very important to realize, so you'll know what I mean if I refer to distance/interval training hereafter.

There are all sorts of distance workouts and I will handle them separately. My list is not exhaustive. But first there are a few general points to cover.

Pacing, intensity

Pacing is inherent in the idea of distance training. Many athletes have difficulty pacing themselves during workouts or races. I am a prime example. I usually start out too fast, or hit the first hill too hard, and go under. Then I suffer for a long time afterward, trying to recover. I might add that I go pretty slowly during that time of recovery, too!

So don't go out and blow it right at the beginning. If you're taking a running workout it's quite easy to warm up by jogging slowly. After you heat up a bit do a few stretching exercises, jog some more, then increase your pace—slowly—slowly. If you feel yourself starting to go under (my legs get numb, my chest feels constricted or my breathing increases and gets very loud), slow down.

Don't hesitate to walk up a steep hill. The best skiers in the world walk or ski-stride up hills during their distance workouts, especially in the summer. So don't feel like the Lone Ranger if you walk occasionally.

The Key to Pacing

Remember the most important part of pacing. It's better to finish your workout feeling you could do more, or that you could have gone a bit harder, rather than to finish struggling, tired, or hanging on. You've got to put yourself in a frame of mind that will make you "wanna do it" again.

49

How long

The length of a distance workout depends on the intensity and the type of exercise, of course. It is also very dependent on your own conditioning.

In general, for a running workout you should consider a time twice as long as a short event you're training for, and a time up to as much as you'd need for a race of 30 to 50 k's. Sounds broad, but let me explain.

If you are training for a 20-minute race, a workout of 40 minutes' running wouldn't be excessive. However, if you are training for a 50-km race, where the time runs close to three hours, a training run of six hours would be a bit much, to say the least. Something less intensive than running—hiking or biking—would be better for these longer workouts.

Where

The best place to take a distance workout is over terrain similar to x-c trails, or on x-c trails themselves, if that is possible. (I'm going to talk about biking and rowing and naturally you wouldn't get very far on most x-c trails on a bike or in a shell.)

Most x-c trails in this country are not suited for running. This is because the footing is hazardous or because skiers think road-running is better and therefore don't prepare the trails for foot-running. In time this attitude will change. Running over a trail offers the advantages I have mentioned before—it's similar to skiing terrain, it's easier on the joints, and it's psychologically more rewarding. The advantage of building foot and ankle strength by running over terrain can be somewhat offset if the terrain is rough and you are likely to twist an ankle. I'm not recommending you run through rough stuff: just that you fix yourself a nice running track in the woods, or over good terrain.

Long loops are preferable to shorter ones because you get less bored. The feeling of accomplishment after a long trip is important too. Come in and think about where you have run (or look at a map, if you have to) and it will give you a sense of well-being.

Still, many skiers pound the roads for training. This is tolerable at a young age but it isn't too imaginative. And when you get older you'll be looking for that softer ground. I can guarantee that.

Lighter people can withstand the jarring produced by road-running better than heavier people. If you want a good example of this, study some of the marathoners. Not many of them weigh over 140 pounds and few, if any, are in the 180-pound bracket. In x-c skiing, though, there is an interesting trend toward bigger skiers. Many of the top racers in the world now look like split ends for a professional football team, being well built, tall and rangy. And I don't see many of them running long distances on hard surfaces—they can't take it because of their body weight.

The Three R's

CPT 8: The three best distance workouts are running, rowing, and roller-skiing.

Each of these involves the use of a large mass of muscles in the body, each can be psychologically rewarding, and each has certain direct connections with skiing. If you stuck to the Three R's during the year you would have plenty of variety and I'm sure you would get in good shape. I'm not eliminating such activities as biking and hiking either, but I think you get more for your money's worth with the Three R's.

Running

The distance-running workout is the most popular form of training and there's little doubt that it will continue to be so. It takes less equipment than any other form of good distance training, anyone can do it just about anywhere, and it's intensive enough so that it doesn't require long periods of time to complete. Intervals, natural or other kinds; speed play (unscheduled bursts of speed; what the Swedes call *fartlek*)—ski-striding and ski-bounding all can be incorporated into a running workout. These latter exercises are discussed more

14. Dianne Holum—1972 Olympic gold medalist in speed skating—and Joe McNulty of the 1970–74 U.S. X-C Team match strides in a distance workout.

fully in Chapter 7 and in Chapter 16 on uphill technique. If you're worried about the arms and upper body you can station a few Putney armbands—those blown-out, bicycle-tire innertubes—along your route and stop to yank on them.

It's easy to go out alone, and then it's all you. No equipment to get in shape, no weather to worry about, no skis to wax. You can leave your worries behind and go. Running, done properly, is a free expression and nearly addictive.

The only disadvantages are that long distances or running on hard surfaces can cause stiffness, sore muscles, or slight damage to the joints; running is not the best activity if you're recovering from some lower-body injury.

For long runs try a variety of running forms. Don't just go out and pound out the kilometers, come in and say "There, that's over." You have to train with a difference.

Uphills

Because uphill skiing comprises about half the time spent during a

15. A good program of foot-running pays off during the next winter's competitions.

race you should concentrate on hills. Do your "think-training" here.

After a warm-up establish your pace. Then do some ski-bounding on the first uphills. If this bounding gets tiring, do some ski-striding—which is a bit like an elongated walking step. Old-fashioned straight uphill running, especially off a flat foot or off your heel, will not do so much for you as ski-bounding and ski-striding. I think that you will find ski-bounding strenuous enough so you won't feel you are cheating yourself in terms of a good workout. Another interesting method for going up the hills is to try to use the muscles in your upper leg and abdomen as much as possible. This is best done walking or bounding along at a fairly slow pace, and involves a slight straightening at the waist with each step. The largest, strongest muscles in your body are located here and if you can use them to climb hills, all the better. There is a skiing technique for climbing hills which utilizes these muscles too.

It's a good idea to hyperventilate before starting up the hills. Many skiers do this until they get dizzy and they claim it helps with their oxygen supply. Then try to pace yourself on the hill so you come off the top with more speed than you started with. For a long uphill you might use several different running techniques. You could start ski-bounding; and if this affects you as

it does me your knees will get tired. You could then shorten your stride a bit and use the calf muscles more, until they get tired. Then perhaps some vigorous ski-striding would be in order; then maybe that walk or jogging bound using the abdomen muscles as much as possible. Then you could start all over with ski-bounding, perhaps. You will be able to adjust and use different movements according to the steepness and length of the hill—but try to tax every muscle in your lower body. It's just like shifting gears in a truck in order to get up the hill.

Downhills

There isn't much point in rushing down a hill during training. If you're on hard pavement it can be especially jarring. If you're on slightly rough terrain you run the risk of a fall. An easy jog or even a walk down steep hills is fine. The training effect gained from running down hills is not significant.

If you slow up for a long time going down a big hill you may need to start in again at the bottom rather slowly. You might also be fooling yourself if you counted this time as part of a cardiovascular workout.

The Flats

When you are running along in a steady state, through the woods, you should have a flowing feeling. It's wonderful to be at one with the surroundings when even every breath seems to fit in with part of the landscape. Really. Sometimes I imagine myself as actually part of the trail, the leaves, roots and rocks on the ground, the trees and ridges around the area, and I hate to tear myself away. I suppose runners can get the same feeling out in the open, or on a track, but I've been lucky enough to have woods to run in.

If you come onto some long flats you can do speed-play or *fartlek,* and run at high speeds for as long as you feel good.

Or you can pick out a point ahead and sprint for it, then gear down a bit and continue at your old established pace.

A very interesting, popular set of intervals that many runners use is a progressive system of harder runs. They might start and go hard for 200 meters, then ease off; go hard for 400 meters, ease off; and so on, up to 1400–1600 meters, then come back down the scale. You wind up steadily, then wind down, just like a giant engine that you don't want to treat wrong by stepping it up too fast, or slowing down too fast.

Precautions

There is plenty of material available on equipment for running and I don't want to spend much time on that here. Naturally your shoes should be broken in before you take any long runs. Some runners have special arrangements for socks—some need tape to prevent blisters. Some use special powders or ointments to prevent chafing. These are all tricks you can pick up if you get in with the running crowd.

Most important of all, take running for the good things it offers you. Don't get hung up if you run with a group and can't keep up. Some of the best runners in the world can't ski, and some of the best skiers in the world can't run well either. If ski races were decided on foot-running abilities there wouldn't be any sense in having ski meets, would there? So remember, running is an excellent cardiovascular workout. If you can combine it with ski-striding and ski-bounding, all the better.

Rowing

Rowing in a shell with a sliding seat is one of the Three R's because it demands the use of so many of the body's muscles. The pulling and pushing of the arms is probably more valid for x-c than most weight-lifting exercises. There is little question about the value in using the abdomen and back muscles in rowing. And the real sleeper is the use of the legs: When they straighten out during the stroke the motion is very similar to the straightening of the legs in skiing.

The Central Europeans have long

Value of Rowing

16. From the top frame down in this single-scull sequence, rowing involves all parts of the body. Compare the leg flexion here with the confinement of the kayaker's lower body in the photo below.

used rowing in training, but some of our skiers interpreted "rowing" as kayaking, or paddling—where the legs are immobilized, and hence don't get the needed workout.

17. Here the legs are rigidly braced.

Some purists criticize rowing because the body, as in biking, is supported, while in running or skiing the antigravity muscles—the ones that hold us upright—are being used all the time. However, it's probable that more muscle mass is used in rowing than in any other sport, and this factor is very good for training purposes. It goes back to the old example: Are you going to get a good workout sitting in a chair and lifting something fairly heavy with one arm, or will you get a better workout using nearly all the muscles in the body rather vigorously? You know the answer. Chalk up one for rowing.

Since there are no uphills and downhills in rowing you have to make your own, in terms of intensity. That's easy. You can go hard for a while, then ease up. You can control your own distance/interval training.

If you use rowing for a lot of your training it would be a good idea to add a good ration of toe rises for the ankle and lower leg muscles. These are not used in rowing as much as in skiing or running. They are small muscle groups, but very important. (See section on toe rises in Chapter 9.)

The biggest disadvantage to rowing is the equipment and accessibility. Not everyone lives close to water, and of those who do, not many have access to rowing shells. However, the sport is increasing in popularity partly due to the fiberglass construction, etc. (as in kayaking). I think that in time many more skiers will be taking up this sport.

It's fine to hitch a fishing line on the shell too. See if the fish can catch you!

*   *   *

The third R, roller-skiing, is covered separately in Chapter 7, the one on specificity.

For extra variety

Hiking

To go hiking in the mountains is a privilege not enjoyed by enough athletes. If you have access to good hiking terrain you should take several jaunts a year, for pleasure and for training. Hiking is one of the great exercises that has practically no disadvantages, and it will always be that way.

If you are alone you can set your own pace. I remember that doing the distances in ⅓ the prescribed guidebook times seemed to give a good workout. But that was quite a rush. Now I would prefer to take a pack with food or other weight in it and go at a more leisurely pace, yet still get a good workout.

If you are in a group you can be the one to take the pack. And if there are all sorts of eager beavers who want to carry the pack for extra training, take along one of your

18. Skiing on a hardtop road.

56

own and fill it with rocks. How many mountains have you been up where some people were making an effort to raise the altitude a few feet by carrying rocks to the top? I know mountains which fall a few feet short of an even thousand feet and it has always been one of the jokes to try and raise the level. Well, it's a gimmick, but all good programs have a few gimmicks.

The uphills provide the best test, as usual. Ski-striding and ski-

19. Hairy terrain (in Bessengen, Norway) adds flavor to any hike.

bounding are in order for these sections. The downhills should be taken with caution. I would advise against carrying heavy loads downhill: the continual holding-back can cause too much strain on the legs.

Hiking is so much fun that you almost feel that it can't be good training. I remember one kid who used to hike a lot and then he took up x-c skiing. His coach told him that he had to train hard, get out there and suffer, and that hiking was good for ski training. Well, the fun went out of it for the kid when he started to be so concerned with the training aspect of hiking, rather than the pleasures of hiking; so he gradually quit it. Now he's stopped skiing too.

Hiking a few mountain ranges ranks with taking a long tour on skis. These are some of the supreme moments in exercising and the more of them you do, the happier you'll be. (Psst! You'll get in shape too.)

Orienteering

Orienteering combines running or hiking through terrain with map-and-compass reading. This sport has long been used by the Scandinavians for ski training and it's just beginning to catch on here in North America. The sport will get another big boost from World championships, scheduled for 1976 in England.

You'd be well advised to try orienteering, if you haven't already. It is marvelous training and puts you in another frame of mind. When you're competing, or after you're finished, you just feel different. It's difficult to explain that feeling but it isn't anything like the other normal training you do. One reason for this might be the requirement for thinking during orienteering. Don't underestimate the need for using your brain or for concentrating. Many a skier, eager for a workout, has been lost while orienteering. And if you're lost in an orienteering race, well . . .

Ice Skating

Although not many skiers do much ice skating, this is another good exercise. In our area we often have good ice (especially the "black ice") before the snow flies and we always try to get out. The rhythm in skating is similar to skiing, it's wonderful for your balance, and it provides another good diversion in the training schedule.

Biking

The use of biking as training for x-c skiing is a wonderful illustration of CPT 1 and CPT 2. I don't think it offers the training potential that the Three R's do, and my belief is based on these reasons:

1. In biking, the body is supported and you do not use the large group of muscles required by any of the Three R's. (In rowing, recall, even though the body is supported, many of the upper-body muscles, as well as those in the legs, are used.)

2. A lot of biking is likely to develop large thigh muscles, which are of little use in x-c skiing. In fact, excessively large muscles can be a hindrance to the skier. Biking can also lead to a stiff back.

Other Disadvantages

There are other disadvantages to biking. Let me list these, before I turn around and tell you why so many skiers do bike as part of their training program.

Biking can be dangerous. Many of our top U.S. skiers have suffered injuries through spills.

Biking is not really a specificity exercise.

Weather is a prohibiting factor. During cold or wet weather, biking must be avoided.

Equipment is expensive and equipment problems themselves can be frustrating.

Nevertheless . . .

However, lots of skiers take to their bikes during the early spring and summer months for all the advantages that biking does offer.

Biking is a very good diversion. Some athletes get tired of running all year round. Biking can be more exciting and enjoyable. Large distances can be covered in a day. (During a bike tour the U.S. Team skiers were able to cover over 160 km a day with ease, for eight consecutive days.)

Since the body is supported in biking this means less strain on the ankles and knees. Therefore it's a marvelous exercise for someone who may be recovering from certain leg injuries, or for someone who has brittle joints that suffer from a lot of running.

During long bike rides there are two features remarkably similar to x-c skiing. One is the need for feeding, or replacing liquids and food burned by the body. So biking is a good way to train yourself for feeding. The other feature which is often overlooked is the need for concentration during biking. If you're riding in a pack you must be alert at all times, being sure to stay in position, to be in the right gear, to watch the road for small bumps or ruts, and

20. U.S. Team members take food on the fly during an 800-mile (over 1300-km) training tour.

21. Co-operation and concentration make 100 miles each day an easy trip.

to be ready to take the lead and expend a high amount of energy. (See section on concentration in Chapter 15.)

Hilly terrain can offer the distance/interval training demands necessary for x-c. We have some courses around home which are ideal for that. There are several short uphills followed by flats and downs which require that straight-ahead, steady, hard effort.

Some skiers claim that standing up on bikes so as to pump uphill utilizes the same muscles and motions used in skiing uphills. You will notice that you can get quite a bit of power off the ball of your foot when standing up on the bike.

In sum: Biking is a good form of exercise. Since following a biker, or utilizing his windbreak, makes it 15 to 20 percent easier to pedal, biking is an event where the stronger bikers can go ahead and break wind for the weaker ones and everyone can hang together and still have a good workout. It is quite an equalizer.

7. Specificity: Training with a Difference

There is a fairly new trend in most sports toward specificity training. Previously—to give an example of nonspecific training—some coaches and athletes who thought strength was a vital factor in the performance of their event would lift weights according to well-designed programs, but without reference to the specific muscle movements used in their events. Now of course, if they believe in specificity training, they do weight-lifting that applies more directly to the movements required by the particular skill sport.

The x-c skiers have always been in a peculiar situation. For training, if you're a foot-runner you can run all year, if you're a swimmer you can swim all year, but if you're a skier the only way you can ski all year is by going to the Southern Hemisphere during their winters, which are our summers. And this is a bit impractical for most x-c'ers I know.

So quite a long time ago skiers began their own specificity program, although then it didn't have the fancy name. First it was simply the use of armbands during the summer. Then ski-striding and ski-bounding came along and were incorporated into hikes or runs during the offseason. Now roller-skiing is here, and you can't get much more specific than that without actually being on snow.

There is no question of the value of specificity training. The more of it you can include in your schedule the better. And this brings up the following related point.

Which Exercises?

In training you should concentrate on the dominant feature of your event.

There may be disagreement between coaches and athletes as to the dominant feature of x-c racing. Is it endurance and conditioning, or is it technique and pacing? If it were simply endurance and conditioning one could train for x-c skiing much the same way an x-c foot-runner does, adding a few exercises for the upper body. If, on the other hand, x-c racing were primarily a technique and pacing event, an athlete would be well advised to train on these aspects during the year. Clearly, a good racer is strong in *all* aspects and he cannot slight any of them.

If there has been a fault with our program in the United States, I would say it has been with the lack of emphasis on technique and pacing. There has been too much emphasis on intensity at the expense of learning good techniques in training and skiing. By training on technique and pacing there is bound to be some spin-off value in conditioning (often quite a bit, in fact), but the converse is not always true.

It goes back, in part, to the corollary to CPT 2—you should put emphasis on training your weaknesses, especially during the offseason.

First Things First

The specificity exercises I list below are the best offseason training routines you can do. Most of the exercises qualify as strength builders, most of them will tax your O_2 uptake, and all of them will help your technique. They are really bonus exercises.

But remember, pay close attention to developing the proper form for the exercises first, then later building up the intensity with which you do them. This is training with a difference.

Ski-bounding

Ski-bounding is an uphill running exercise usually done at a tempo slightly slower than that of regular skiing. But an effort is made to simulate as much as possible the actual skiing movements. This means

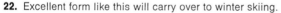
22. Excellent form like this will carry over to winter skiing.

Ski-bounding Uphill

coming off the ball of the forward foot with a certain amount of aggressiveness and momentum, reaching forward with the arm as in diagonal (single stride) skiing, landing fairly flat-footed on the other leg and almost simultaneously rolling forward onto the ball of that foot and springing off it, etc.

One small error is to land on the ball of the foot instead of landing on a flat foot. In skiing uphill one of the keys is to set your wax and this is best done by having the ski flat, in contact with a maximum amount of snow. Then you press down on the ski . . . and hope. All this is done very quickly and automatically by top skiers. In fact, it's done so quickly that it may escape notice of the casual observer. If you land flat-footed while ski-bounding you will be more nearly imitating the skiing motion. On steep uphills it will not be possible to land with a flat foot, so don't worry about landing on the ball of your foot.

As you ski-bound pay particular attention to bending the forward ankle and collapsing or compressing slightly on the forward knee. This cushioning is an important part of

23. The vigor of his ski-bounding has him virtually airborne in the three top frames of this sequence. (Flags are used to measure the length of each bound in later videotape analysis.)

uphill skiing. Some skiers straighten the rear leg behind to simulate the so-called kicking action of the diagonal technique. This is O.K., but I think it's more valuable to try to straighten your leg as much as possible while it's still underneath you.

Poles may be used, or not. I prefer them since it is more like skiing.

While you won't be getting up the hill quite so fast as a foot-runner in a hurry, I think if you do a little ski-bounding you will find it rather challenging as an exercise. We have a little hill here called Caldwell's Backyard Hillclimb and a few trips up this one, ski-bounding, seem to be enough for the toughest guys around.

Ski-striding

This is more similar to a walking motion but the effort here is made to simulate the body position and movements that are made during skiing the single stride. The tempo is slower than that of ski-bounding and many place the emphasis on a strong rear-leg kick.

Ski-striding is probably one of the most underestimated or least-used exercises in training. It's really one of the best. Consider running up a long hill, so long that you be-

24. This Junior girl shows especially good form by the use of her arms in this ski-striding sequence. Note the foot always in contact with the ground, as compared with ski-bounding on the preceding page.

gin to tighten up or go under. Do you think you will gain by continuing to try and run? Definitely not. But if you break into a ski-stride you will be more able to keep going and keep your cardiovascular system working at a very high rate. The spin-off value gained is that you will be exercising your skiing muscles instead of *trying* to exercise your foot-running muscles.

Naturally, ski-bounding and ski-striding can be done during almost any part of a hike or run. If you want to make ski-striding more effective just put a pack full of weights on your back.

The most important techniques in these two exercises are getting the thrust, or next move, from a rolling forward of the body, and specifically the appropriate leg, over the ball of the foot. This implies a certain amount of forward ankle-bend in the exercising leg. The most typical fault is bounding or striding off a flat foot. This won't do. Good skiing technique does not permit this motion, and therefore it's taboo in specialized training.

Armbands

Armbands—those elastic cords, or ropes which are pulled against some traction device—are a good training device because they can be set up almost anywhere, anytime, and using them will improve the strength and technique of your poling action.

The usual controversy exists about the use of armbands: Is it light resistance and many repetitions, or few reps and heavy resistance? It is most common to use armbands with a higher degree of resistance during the summer "to build strength," and then as the snow season approaches to lighten the resistance and increase the number of reps "to increase endurance."

As you might guess, I don't completely favor this approach. I prefer using armbands with a fair amount

25. Tracey Thompson, 1975 Vermont high-school girls' 100- and 200-yard dash champion, skis x-c during her offseason. Here she works out on the Norwegian nylon line to strengthen her poling action.

of resistance—about as much as I can handle for 2 or 3 minutes—all year round. There are two reasons for this. First, I have never found endurance the main limiting factor in poling during an x-c race: rather, it has been strength. Second, in the interest of time I think it is more efficient to use armbands with a good deal of resistance. I've seen skiers work with armbands for 30 minutes and I'm not sure they get much out of it. They might have been better off doing an exercise that used a larger group of muscles, or resting.

Kinds of Armbands

Factory-produced shock cords are available, some with good handles, others that you have to adjust or fix yourself by putting on a ski pole handle. Some skiers buy their own shock cord and make up a few sets of armbands.

The Norwegians have come out with an interesting rig that's nothing more than nylon line wrapped around a metal device. The more wraps, the more resistance.

The Exergenie is also a good rig, because it can be used at almost any setting of resistance. It's easily carried and set up—door jambs are good places—and therefore is a favorite for taking on extended trips.

Then there are the "Putney armbands"—homely, but cheap and expendable. Just get over to the

nearest bike dealer and pick up a bunch of his blown-out bicycle innertubes and nail them up wherever you want them. We scatter them around trees in the woods and when we're out running we can stop and give a few yanks on them.

There are two basic differences between types like the shock cords or Putney armbands and the ones like the Exergenie and the Norwegian fixture. First, friend, there is no double-poling possible with the Exergenie type. (If you want to penalize skiers who are late to a workout, give them twenty double-poles on the Exergenie!) Second, the initial pull required for the shock-cord type is very slight, but then the resistance increases as your arm passes the body. This is quite unlike real poling action, where the main effort is expended at the beginning of the poling stroke.

Well, you can't have everything.

How to Do It

Most skiers have their armbands set up too low. It's a good idea to have them hitched up at head level, or higher, since this will develop the stronger poling motions, whether it's single-poling or double-poling.

Single-poling

Keep your elbows in as you use armbands. Don't cock your wrist to start the action. Make the initial effort with a strong pull *downward*,

66

26 (left frames) **& 27** (right). Martha Rockwell, foremost woman x-c'er in North America, uses her Exergenie both from the front and from behind in a single-poling training session. Note how strongly she pulls downward.

not backwards. Some skiers get into the bad habit of pulling backwards because there is too much tension on the cords.

It's a good idea to have someone watch you once in a while. He can observe these things and also see if you have any extra quirks such as upper-body motion, a dropping of the shoulder, a twist of the hip, side-bending, etc. All these should be avoided: they're flaws (i.e., losses in efficiency) that can be carried over to your skiing technique.

Double-poling

During double-poling exercises you should get an upper-body motion. I tell skiers to pull with their arms to a point where their hands are about level with their hips and then to "statue" it the rest of the way: meaning to get the upper body into it—at least until the arms are past the body.

On-snow Applications

You can do all these exercises on snow and provide yourself with any amount of resistance. Simply stand on your skis on the level and single-pole without using any leg motion. Or double-pole. If this is too easy, get on an uphill section and repeat. You'll get the message.

Roller-skiing

I don't know who invented roller skis but someone probably saw kids roller-skating or skate-boarding and figured that with one or two adjustments he could come up with a device for summer training that would approximate x-c skiing. The adjustments are easy to picture. On a skateboard put an x-c binding and some ratcheted wheels, which spin in only one direction. Grab your poles and you're all set to go.

If an x-c skier had to choose only one type of training to do during the offseason he would probably be wise to roller-ski. In our corner of Vermont we have been roller-skiing for many years, and the more we do it the more important it seems. Interestingly, the Scandinavians have been slower to take this up than the Americans or some of the Central Europeans. The Scandinavians also believed for some time that the primary benefit of roller-skiing was for training the upper body and arms, so they spent most of their time on roller skis doing the double-pole. But now they appear to be doing more than that.

The Types

There are all sorts of roller skis, and to list the ones available at this time would only pose a problem to you, because in a year or so there will be newer models on the market, and some of the ones presently in vogue will no longer be around. Ski coaches are the best source of information for obtaining roller skis since

68

these items are not carried regularly by many ski shops. Meanwhile, suffice it to say this:

You can get roller skis that are quite fast and easy to push along. You can get them with different sets of wheels which can be switched according to your needs. (Generally, these skis come with two sets of wheels and the smaller ones are used when you want more resistance in moving the skis.) You can get roller skis that are easy to maintain balance on, or ones that are difficult. Some skis can be used on smooth lawns or fairways, while most of the others are suitable for hardtopped pavements only.

Given a choice, you have to decide what will best suit your needs. If you have technique problems—particularly if you kick late, or ski flat-footed—you should not depend on skis that are easy to balance on, or ones that are slow and steady, because using these types will just compound your problem. On the other hand, if you ski well, or if you are just beginning, this type of roller ski would be O.K. If you need strength training, or a more powerful stride, you should not necessarily get the skis that are easy to move. (Although you can practice the diagonal stride on fairly steep sections of road and thus develop more strength this way.) And so on.

Of course a good way to check out advantages of various skis is to swap brands with someone else.

Some Tips on Beginning

I will list a few procedures that we have found useful.

1. In beginning to use roller skis, start with short sessions of 10 or 15 minutes three or four times a week. Get used to the skis and balance problems before you go off on longer trips. This may take a few weeks.

2. Find roads that are smooth and that have a minimum of traffic.

3. Do most of your skiing on uphill sections. This is really the only place you can practice the diagonal technique. In fact, you can probably practice the diagonal on any hardtopped uphill section of road in North America. You can also practice the double-pole on easy uphill sections.

Use the flats for double-poling only, and don't use the downhills at all unless they are fairly gentle, smooth and have good runouts. Then you can coast down, or double-pole. It's easy to get out of control on a downhill. Flipping onto the pavement or the shoulder of the road is not as pleasurable as flipping into the snow during winter when you're on ski skis.

4. Get special carbide tips for your x-c poles if you use the roads. The Swedes and Norwegians have a couple of different tips that work well and do not wear out as fast as conventional pole tips. Or you can braise snow-tire studs on your own pole tips.

Binding Placement

Most skis are marked to show you where to put the bindings. Some skiers I know move their bindings so their feet are closer to the wheels that hold the ski from slipping, hoping to get better kick, or purchase. I think this is a mistake because, as I have already said, you tend to get spoiled and overconfident about your technique.

It's better to place the bindings at the recommended marks. If you do slip a bit now and then, analyze the reasons why. Probably you're skiing too flat-footed. Or kicking too hard. Different skiers react the same way to roller skis as they do to waxed skis. Some can handle almost any roller ski and not slip, while others have troubles with the same skis.

Advantages of Roller-skiing

It is the best form of specificity training you can do during the off-season. If the terrain is suitable and you can make a circuit beginning where you started—this means that the downhills aren't too steep, and that there are some uphills as well as flats—the demands on your system will be very similar to those of skiing a course, even though the techniques used in roller-skiing will not be exactly the same. (On roller skis you will double-pole the flats instead of using the diagonal, and

probably coast the downhills instead of double-poling.)

By stressing roller-skiing uphill, using the diagonal technique, you can develop a stronger stride than you would otherwise on regular snow skiing.

Roller-skiing will prepare your muscles, particularly those in the groin area, for on-snow skiing. In this regard, when you start on snow you will be a week or two ahead of skiers who haven't done any roller-skiing. You will easily make the transfer to some good snow workouts right away.

Roller-skiing requires at bit more concentration than regular skiing in good tracks. It's easy for a roller ski to go askew and if one crosses in front of the other it can be very awkward! Some might list this as a disadvantage but, as before, I claim it's an advantage to have to concentrate on every stride. Good training!

There are no tracks to set, no skis to wax. (But you'd better oil the bearings once in a while, and keep all the screws and bolts tight. Did

28 (near strip) **& 29** (frames in right strip). These vertical sequences demonstrate the close relationship between roller-skiing and x-c skiing. It's the same skier—and going at the same pace in both—training in early fall on a hardtopped road, and working out later on snow. Compare each left with each right frame to see the striking similarity of form throughout.

30 (strip far left) **& 31** (near strip). The vertical sequences opposite show two members of the U.S. Team—Tim Caldwell at left and Bill Koch at right—roller-skiing uphill. They're both using a very strong, and similar, diagonal technique, but there are subtle differences in style: in general, Bill's rear-arm and rear-leg carries are higher than Tim's, while Tim's are more classical. The point is, though, that individual styles are to be expected—and they're fine with me, as long as the basic technique is good, and totally efficient for each skier. (The actual pitch of the hill is shown best in the fourth shot from the top of each strip, by the way.)

you ever lose a wheel while roller-skiing?)

Since roller-skiing technique has so many similarities with snow technique, you can take videotape pictures of roller-skiing and analyze your problems. All this can be done during the long days of summer and fall, at a relaxed time, and when you won't have the standard winter problems of the video machine or operator freezing up.

And roller-skiing is a pretty good substitute for snow skiing during the competitive season if for some reason you can't get on snow.

Disadvantages

I've already hinted at the danger of injury. If you try going too fast too soon, or take some downhill sections you shouldn't, there is a danger of spraining an ankle or getting

scraped up. One girl from our area wore the knees out of three pairs of sweatpants before she got accustomed to roller skis, and she was using them on just the flats. But hers is an extreme example.

Roller skis don't maneuver very well. Generally, you should avoid situations where turns are necessary. The step-around turn is the best way to change direction.

There have been some isolated cases of sore arms or elbows caused by the jarring of poles on the pavement. If you feel soreness, especially in the elbow joint, ease up on roller-skiing until you determine the cause. Then proceed accordingly.

Sometimes long downhills are too fast to roller-ski with safety and thus pose slight problems: how to get down them?—how to get home? Most skiers happily walk, jog or hitch-hike back. Some are in situations where they can actually depend on public transportation to bring them home. In Oslo, for instance, a skier can start downtown, take any number of routes that will eventually take him high above the fjord, then take a train or bus back.

And then there are the law enforcement officials. In some areas roller skiers using the roads have been hauled in for operating without brakes, without lights, without license plates—you name it. I can't give you complete advice for this situation. You'll have to snoop around yourself.

73

Uphill Roller-skiing

The diagonal technique is used on all uphills and the length of the stride depends on the steepness of the hill. In any case, you can get quite a bit of power into your stride and thus develop good strength for skiing. A word of caution, however. With the ratcheted wheels you have that superwax job that almost never slips. Under these conditions it's easy to begin to horse it too much —and if you do so your technique will begin to get rougher and rougher. Don't do it. Ease off and ski smoothly, correctly.

Some roller skis with a ratcheted front wheel will slip occasionally on the uphills. Sometimes the wheel may need tightening, but more often it's a problem with your skiing. If you don't have enough weight over the front wheel you won't get the necessary traction on it to help hold you from slipping. You can correct this slipping by getting more forward ankle-bend and by not trying to go quite so hard. It's just like skiing.

Roller-skiing the Flats

Double-poling is the best technique to use on the flats. You can make the motions exactly the same as you do on snow.

Occasionally, for a brush-up or review of your diagonal, you can cruise along on the flats with the single stride. It will be very easy, so if you aren't careful to go with a certain amount of smoothness, you'll get snarled up. But you can see how your rear ski is coming through or check how you are riding the front ski. Maybe this will require you to change the timing of your poling motion slightly, since you will glide longer in each stride. On the whole, though, it's very easy and relaxing to ski the flats.

Downhills

If you can roller-ski a downhill section I would recommend that you begin by standing up straight and relaxing. Occasionally the skis will wander a bit and you have to be ready to make small corrective steps to straighten them. This situation arises on snow too.

When you get good on the roller skis you can crouch or tuck and train the same downhill muscles you will use on snow. If you're skiing with someone else you will be able to see the advantage of a tuck over an upright stance that presents greater wind resistance.

If there's any question about your ability to negotiate a downhill on roller skis, take them off and walk.

8. Tempo & Speed Training

Speed and tempo workouts may be classified roughly under interval training. Some people consider them as the same, but I want to emphasize a distinction between the two.

Tempo training can be thought of as *pace-training at racing speed*, and it is usually done under steady-state conditions.

Speed training, by my definition, is an *all-out effort at maximum speed* —which, if continued long enough, would cause a person to go under.

A few examples will help clarify.

The most common tempo training is done by skiing at racing speeds on predominantly uphill terrain for periods of five minutes or more. This is a steady-state effort, and after it the skier usually takes a complete recovery before doing another run. (Usually, in interval training, the rest after each session is not complete; and also the speeds used in interval training vary.) The object of tempo training is to adjust the body to racing speeds and to learn to pace oneself.

There's no doubt that racers should go harder in the shorter races. If you go under in a sprint race, chances are you'll finish O.K.—though

---

Pace: Q.E.D.

The 1974 Holmenkollen 50-km race is a made-to-order example of the need for pacing in long-distance events. In important races like this, by the way, the interval times are calculated and broadcast to the crowds over radios and through the public-address system in the start-and-finish area. It was apropos the PA announcer's interim comments that Magne Myrmo, the winner, made an interesting observation on his performance.

Contrary to the broadcast announcements to the effect that he was gaining on everyone, especially during the last 10 k's of the circuit, he said this just wasn't so. His lap time for the first 25-km loop was within a few seconds of his time for the second lap. Thus he paced himself perfectly—and the others did not. Instead of his gaining on the field, he said, they all lost to him.

Nice summary.

probably not in the money. On the other hand, if you go under near the end of a 50-km race, you may have to be carried back to the finish. Moral: Pacing is more important in the long-distance events.

Speed training

Speed training can take many forms, but in general it consists of doing some skills at top speed for a very short period of time. My favorite off-season speed training is running 10–12-second uphill sprints (discussed in Chapter 9). I try to stress some of the features of the diagonal technique when doing this, especially coming off the ball of the foot and reaching forward with the hands.

In rowing you can do a "big ten" and go at it full force for those strokes. In roller-skiing you could either go at sprint speeds doing the double-pole, or the diagonal. And so on.

There is some controversy about the value of skiing at top speeds, speeds so fast that your technique may begin to break down. But I firmly

32. Bob Gray at top speed (doing a change-up) in a 30-km spring race.

believe it is important to do ski sprints of 100–200 meters occasionally. This will train the body to be able to ski faster, and eventually skiing at racing speeds will seem easier. I have seen a lot of relay races lost on the home stretch because the anchor man couldn't ski fast enough. This is reason enough for speed training.

Just pick out a good track, perhaps slightly uphill, be sure you are warmed up—and then go. I mean, really go at it! We've had match races for 150 meters at Putney that have left the track pulverized and the air full of snow from the thrashing given it by the racers.

Speed training has spin-off value as a strength-builder too. To put your muscles under stress in a high-speed situation is so taxing that I list some of these speed sessions as strength workouts.

Bicycle Bumps

Another variation for speed and strength training is practicing on "bicycle bumps." Shovel a series of mounds of snow of varying heights and at varying distances, pack them so they are smooth enough to ski over and put in a track. Then shave down the left track on the first bump, the right track on the second bump, and so on: the idea is to have the opposing tracks at different heights. You may have to water the snow slightly to help it set up firmly. When you ski into the first bump with a little speed you'll find that the track forces your legs to simulate the full pedaling motion of a bicycle rider. If the bumps are spaced close enough you should be able to accelerate even without poling. The different spacing between bumps offers syncopation that does wonders for your timing, especially at high speeds. A track of about 100 meters, full of these bumps, can provide a very strenuous and sometimes amusing ride. (Shoveling the snow is a bonus strength workout too.)

9. Strength Training

The various kinds of strength training remind me of long skirts—they come and go with the passing of the years. At this writing, many coaches and skiers in the United States are on an upswing with weight-lifting while other countries are avoiding it. Most of the weight-lifting programs I am familiar with in this country have been adopted on general principles rather than on the results of tests for efficacy: I know of no scientific study of weight-lifting programs for skiers.

There is no question of the value of strength for the x-c skier. And it's not enough to be strong; you must be able to use that strength with a certain amount of speed. This strength-speed combination is referred to as your power. You might be able to do certain strength-building exercises under tremendous loads at slow speeds, but unless you can transform this ability to a movement with faster speed—and specifically a movement used in x-c skiing—your strength will be of little avail.

The different kinds of strength training

1. The most common type of strength training is lifting weights. Done correctly, this sort of training develops the muscles used in the particular lifts you are performing.

2. Another type of strength training consists of doing ski movements against resistance. The object here is to develop the same muscles used in skiing. Roller-skiing and pulling on armbands are two examples of this kind of exercise (both described in Chapter 7, on specificity).

3. A third kind of training is what I call over-all, co-ordinated strength training, which fosters the ability to use muscle groups from various parts of your body in harmonious effort. Weight-lifting and ski-movements-against-resistance will not necessarily develop this skill. I'm sure you have seen many a strong person who could not use his strength in a co-ordinated way, and many a co-ordinated person who had no strength to use: neither has what I define as co-ordinated strength.

It's this kind of over-all strength that really separates x-c skiing from distance foot-running—and the sheep from the goats. A good skier must be able to use so many different muscles in skiing uphill, around corners, over bumps, through poor tracks, on bad wax, downhill, etc., that learning one set of concerted movements by roller-skiing alone, for instance, is not enough. There's always some new situation to cope with in x-c skiing.

You might be off balance, you might have just slipped on one ski, your pole may have missed its mark, and so on. I'll say more about this later.

Areas of agreement

It's generally agreed that strength-building programs should be progressive and should be done at stress loads.

A schedule of strength training three times a week, with at least a day off between each session, is indicated.

During the competitive season you can probably keep your strength level by training two days a week. It should not be necessary to try and progress during the season.

There is probably a high correlation between strength and muscular endurance. However, there is not full agreement on the relationship between increasing one aspect by training for the other. For example, do heavy loads with few repetitions, as in the case of weight-lifting, build muscular endurance?—or should it be lesser loads with many repetitions?

33. Martha Rockwell, pressing.

The *Pro's* of Weight-lifting

There is a lot of literature about weight-lifting and I am not going to get into detailed descriptions of various programs here. Lack of space prohibits it and, as you might have guessed, I prefer other approaches to strength training.

The advantages of weight-lifting are as follows:

It can be made progressive. The weights are easily measured and adjusted. The results are easily seen and therefore are gratifying.

Special muscle groups can be developed by weight-lifting. This is particularly advantageous for patients recovering from injuries or surgery. I have had firsthand experience with this and there is no doubt in my mind that for rehabilitation, weight-lifting is the best method.

The *Con's* of Weight-lifting

Some of the disadvantages of weight-lifting are:

There is a chance of developing some muscles you don't need for x-c skiing; in fact, if weight programs are not done correctly there is some danger of losing flexibility and gaining too much weight at the same time.

Lifting weights can be dreary work.

You can't take weights with you everywhere, and if you are going to continue strength work during the competitive season you may have to develop another program for yourself.

Instead of barbells

I have to put in a plug for logging since I live in the country. I use the term logging to include cutting brush, cutting and splitting firewood, and hauling it to my stoves and the sauna.

In the 1950's and early '60's several of the world's top skiers were loggers and many aspiring x-c'ers believed that in order to win races you had to be a logger. Nowadays that notion has changed, but the validity of it has not.

More and more skiers come from areas where it is not possible to do things like logging so they must do something else for strength-building. That's O.K. And we know there is less and less logging going on anywhere these days. Finally, can you imagine some coaches sending you out to log for your strength training? That might take away a part of their job, especially if they feel the need to be checking up on weight-lifting progress all the time. Well, here's one coach who still recommends logging, anyway.

You show me a skier who has been doing a lot of logging and I'll show you a guy—the same person—who is really strong and who will be able to use his strength better than the person who has been lifting weights.

You might wonder how logging can be made progressive, according to the established rules for strength-training. It's actually pretty simple. You go out and thrash around the brush, clear it, cut your trees, limb them, section them, split them, throw them into a pile and pick them up—oh, you're tired? Your legs, arms and back ache? O.K. Knock it off for the day.

Come back again another day and continue. Keep it up. Then after a few weeks, if you think you aren't progressing, get one of your friends out there with you and ask him to pitch in, and see how long he lasts. Or compare the volume of wood you last cut with the first product of the few days you were out.

Actually, it isn't hard to measure your progress. You can just tell when you've had a good workout.

This co-ordinated strength approach is very interesting. I give the example of a couple of boys who were training for skiing. They occasionally attended training camps where they were tested in such things as the bench press. One boy did a fair amount of rowing one spring, following the ski season, and without lifting weights since November, showed up in June and pressed 20 pounds more than he had in the fall. Another one, doing a lot of brush cutting and "piddling" work like that, raised his bench-press maximum by 20 pounds in a period of two months, again without lifting weights formally.

Maybe rowing and logging (or cutting brush) do increase your ability to lift heavier weights. The interesting question follows: Does weight-lifting increase your ability to log or row? How transferable is the strength gained by weight-lifting?

Logging—marvelous work. It's outside, in natural surroundings; and, as we say in Vermont, "The man who cuts his own wood gets warmed by it twice."

Ski motions against resistance

Too many strength-building programs, especially weight-lifting ones, stress the development of the upper body, the arms and shoulders. There are two problems with this approach. For one, the strength gained by lifting weights is not necessarily transferable to skiing. For the other, programs of this sort slight the use of the legs.

9. Strength Training

But you ski with your legs, with most of your skiing strength coming from well below your shoulders. Therefore you should train your legs and lower body. I have already described such specificity exercises as roller-skiing, ski-bounding and ski-striding. In addition, there are several valuable exercises that use extra resistance to build strength—for skiing.

CPT 9: You should train the muscles that will be used in skiing and, as much as possible, train them by using the same movements that are used in skiing.

Running in Water

This is very good for leg-lifting strength, quite similar to that used in skiing uphill. An ocean beach is the best place for it, because you can intersperse running in thigh-deep water with sprints along the shore, following the waves' high-water mark as they roll over the beach in uneven patterns. If you feel the workout isn't tough enough get into deeper water and then run up a few sand dunes for variety.

34 (near strip) **& 35** (opposite strip). These vertical sequences offer fascinating similarities between running in thigh-deep water and skiing uphill. Rolf Kjaernsli, Norwegian coach, regarded his romp in Long Island Sound as a training exercise; Oddvar Braa of Norway is the skier.

Leg Workouts

Be aware of blisters that may develop on your feet from running barefooted. Running in old shoes or sneakers is out, since they fill with sand and become quite uncomfortable.

Legbands

Using legbands—a logical variation on armbands—is a good exercise for developing forward knee-drive. In working with legbands be sure not to initiate the forward leg-drive with a slight swing from the hip, because doing so could lead to bad x-c technique habits.

The *foot* should lead the power

36. New idea for those shot bicycle inner-tubes called "Putney armbands": use 'em as legbands.

stroke forward, in a pendulum motion, and then the rest of the leg, from the lower part up, joins in the effort. This happens very fast and it is quite a subtle movement which may be hard to discern.

Hill Sprints

This is a good anaerobic exercise to build strength and speed, which combine to form power. There may be some other value as an anaerobic exercise which has yet to be determined.

The best approach is to get warmed up, then run sprints up a hill for 10–12 seconds. Go just as fast as you can! If you walk back down you should be ready to start again when you get to the bottom. Try to maintain good forward-body position and come off the ball of your foot with each step (rather than leaning back slightly and running flat-footed, as you would if you ran slowly): if you think about slanting your whole body forward it might help. Make a conscious effort to reach ahead with the arms and not just run with them tight or making very small arcs.

In time you can work up to 15 or 20 of these, quite easily.

Sit-ups, Back-ups

Sit-ups and back-ups are very good strengtheners for the stomach and back muscles.

You all know what sit-ups are like and how they are done. The best ones are done with bent knees and with your feet anchored by a strap or by someone holding them down. After you get fairly proficient at these you can make them more effective (difficult, too) by holding some weights on your head. Then, the next degree of difficulty involves doing them on an incline, with your head low of course.

Back-ups feel more restrictive because you just can't bend as easily or as far when you're lying on your stomach. But put your hands behind your head, get some means of anchoring your feet or ankles, and lift up—legs straight this time. When it gets easy, hold some weights on your head. Continue.

Finally, if you're feeling really tough, do them on an incline with your head low again.

Pull-ups, Dips

Pull-ups (also called "chinning") are a stand-by whose virtues are well known for arm and shoulder work.

A recent addition to many skiers' repertory is the dip, in which the

37 (frames at left) & 38 (above). Martha Rockwell does her sit-ups with a 10-pound weight for overload, and with feet anchored; the pillow protects her coccyx, and flexed knees prevent the wrong kind of strain on her lower back. Her back-ups in the strip above strengthen the muscles so vital in maintaining a strong single stride in racing (components of the stride are described at length in Chapter 15).

skier does a sort of inside-out push-up from behind—if you follow me. The muscles used in lifting the body are the same ones as those used in the most vigorous poling, thus making dips the single most valuable exercise of the four shown right here.

Toe Rises

Stand a little less than a meter from a wall, lean on the wall by placing your hands slightly above your head height, then while keeping your butt and your head parallel to the wall, do toe rises. When this gets easy

39 (left frames) **& 40** (right). Strong arm and shoulder-girdle muscles mean strong poling action (again, see Chapter 15), so Martha does pull-ups—and, at right, dips, which are even more demanding, and are much the most valuable of her strength-training exercises.

Strength-training Dividends

Around my neck of the woods the success of a good strength workout is measured not by kilos lifted, pressed, etc., but by that feeling in your body at the end of a day's hard activity, whatever it may be. When you come in and have a "bone-tired" feeling as you collapse into a chair, or when you climb into a sauna at 140 C. that feels only warm-like-toast, then you know you've been at it. These are some of life's most pleasant, relaxing moments.

start over again with two legs but wear a weighted pack. Then shift to one leg. And so on.

As usual, the technique here is important. If you rush ahead too fast with your weights, or by getting onto one leg too soon, you may end up doing toe rises off a flat foot, or by initiating the action with a little twitch of the abdomen. The point is to strengthen the foot, ankle and lower leg muscles, so these are the main muscles you should use. When you come down your weight should be on the forward part of your foot and you can actually do a slight kneebend before going up again into another toe rise. Concentrate on the ankle and knee flexion.

In sum: All these ski movements against resistance are probably more enjoyable than standard weight-lifting. I think they are better. But they have one disadvantage and that is this: these exercises are sometimes hard to measure for progress. The best way to discover your progress is by keeping a descriptive training journal, the log I talked about in Chapter 4.

10. Inseason Training

Many skiers have a real problem knowing what to do for training during the competitive season. There doesn't seem to be any commonly accepted routine and this fact is perhaps one reason for erratic results. The schedule I propose below is based on several points, or beliefs, which I will go into first.

Some of the dangers

I've seen too many skiers take to snow in the beginning of the season and never do any more foot-running or strength work. As the season goes on, they lose part of their pulmonary (breathing) capacity; they lose some of their strength; and finally, they lose some of their speed—all conditions that were probably at higher levels at the very beginning of the season.

Most of the coaches and athletes I've talked with admit that they should continue with some sort of foot-running and strength program during the competitive season, but they just slide into a routine of all skiing and then begin to suffer a deconditioning effect.

Traveling, or Training?

Travel plus an intensive race schedule can practically ruin a skier in a matter of a few weeks. Suppose you have a race coming up which requires some travel; you rest up and travel, then race. Next thing you know, it's time to travel again to the next race. Meanwhile the food is different, you're in different sleeping situations every night or two, and after a while you begin to wonder what happened to your training program. Well, it went out the window when you first took on a schedule requiring you to travel and race so often.

"Training" Races

You should spend a great deal of time in planning an intelligent schedule for the whole winter, with emphasis on just certain, important races. The other races should be counted by you, in your own mind, as training races or progress races.

For instance, in the beginning of the season you might travel to your first race, knowing you haven't had much skiing. It's rather pointless, under the circumstances, to put a lot of value on your results in this one. Furthermore, you might be better off to plan your day so you could race and then take another spin around the track in order to get in some extra kilometers. Your plan might even call for arriving at the race site a day early and getting in a good workout, one much more intensive than you would normally take before a race day.

If you are committed to some awkward schedule of travel and racing you must try to make the best of it. This might mean taking a good run at the airport; or if in the city, at some park far removed from the ski scene. This isn't so bad, and in fact it fits in with my recommended schedule.

A minimum schedule

It's generally agreed that three good cardiovascular workouts a week will be ample to keep that system at its present level. For strength, probably two workouts a week will suffice to maintain level. So here are a couple of minimums to take into account during the winter season.

The cardiovascular workouts would usually be accomplished by skiing. Practice during the week is one example. Certainly a race would qualify as a workout of this type.

Instead of Weights

If you've been on weights all year you might find yourself in a situation without weights. (Can't you see the fellow at the airlines counter lifting your box of weights onto the conveyor belt—and then figuring the excess-luggage fee?) The alternative is other kinds of strength work. We've tried all sorts of ideas and most of them have merit.

The Exergenie is a marvelously versatile device for carrying along on any trip. As noted earlier, you can set it up practically anywhere.

If you like the out-of-doors you may find yourself in a situation where you can go chop wood or shovel snow. Or you can go out with one of your buddies and take turns carrying each other piggyback.

You should find situations where you can do some of your regular strength work at least twice a week. It doesn't take long.

In addition, you should continue with your sit-ups and back-ups on a regular basis. Many skiers recently have been plagued with back problems during the season and I find that most of them had stopped doing all their back exercises once they got on snow. After a while, something is likely to give, and if it's your back that fails, then you are in deep trouble.

Work on the Weak Link

Many of the younger athletes I train complain occasionally about some part of their anatomy giving out during a training session or a race. I tell them that everyone has a weak link and that usually, when you go hard, something will give. If it didn't, we'd all be Olympic champions.

Recently I've seen more backs "torn apart" during the fall and winter than seems necessary. I think many more athletes are training harder and getting stronger. In particular, they are doing a fantastic job of building their leg and upper-body strength. But their lower-back and stomach muscles have not been trained in concert with the rest of the body and therefore these muscles are suffering from the strain that is sometimes placed on them. It's almost always the back that gives out when you do any excessive amount of hard work, so heed the warning and train your back muscles.

Some Foot-running

I would include two days of foot-running every week. This should be rather short and intensive, maybe only 15–20 minutes, of course after a good warm-up. The foot-running offers several advantages. By going at it hard you will keep your breathing capacity up. I've always found that I breathed harder foot-running than skiing. (Maybe it's because I didn't know how to run, you say? Doesn't matter, it's good conditioning.) Also, it helps to keep your speed of movement high if you run hard.

Finally, it's assumed that at the beginning of the snow season you came off a program of running. To continue twice a week, even running fairly hard, is just a drop in the bucket, and if you keep it up during the season, come spring you will find yourself a week or two ahead of the fellow who doesn't run during the winter. I might also mention that sometimes you will be forced to run, maybe even longer distances, in order to get a workout. You might be traveling, or weathered out, or living too far from snow to ski every day. Then running (or roller-skiing) is a must.

Rest Days

There are rest days and there are rest days. What might seem to be a very imposing workout for you will be considered a rest day for another.

41. Vermont version of a late-season strength workout: gathering maple sap in the sugarbush. Many U.S. Team members have been brought to their knees by a day of such sidehill work in old corn snow.

Most top skiers in the world take some exercise every day of the week. The easier days are called rest days, or active rest days, and they consist of easy, no-strain skiing, or an easy jog of some sort. Even during travel most athletes get in a bit of exercise, maybe just enough to break a sweat.

If you aren't sick, you should exercise every day. Keep the motor tuned up. Besides, you never know what the next day will bring. It's possible you won't be able to train, for some reason. A bird in the hand . . .

Other skiers prefer to simplify matters during the season and they "tour" about 25–35 km a day for training, then take it easy the day before a competition. Otherwise, they rest and skip strength work and foot-running.

In sum: As a minimum during the competitive season I recommend for each week two days of foot-running and three other cardiovascular workouts (preferably skiing), and two days of strength work.

Peak Periods and Overtraining

The goal of every competitor who trains seriously should be to hit a peak for as long as possible, particularly during the most important races of the season. It does little good to be up on top for the December meets only to fade out during some championship races later in February or March.

Another theory for peaking

There is a very interesting theory being practiced now by many of the top skiers in the world. It hasn't caught on in the States yet but perhaps it will. It goes like this: You should train in intervals of 4 to 6 weeks and time your peaks according to the important races.

For instance, let's suppose you plan to get on snow at the beginning of November. You ought to reach one peak, in your dry-land training, at the beginning of October, and then use October as a maintenance month without trying to increase your intensity of training. In fact, you might ease off a bit.

When you get on snow you would start in easily and gradually increase the intensity of training for, say, 6 weeks, then take another 4-week "breather" from the middle of December to the middle of January. With the Holiday season this is a good time to ease up a bit anyway.

After the middle of January you start on another upswing, hoping to peak in the middle of February when your big races might be scheduled.

Weak Results are O.K.

This method would mean accepting some weak results for a period of 3 or 4 weeks from the middle of December to the middle of January. The problems with this arrangement are obvious. Many so-called point races in the United States are scattered throughout the season, and there is pressure from some organizers in the Nordic world to expect racers to be on top for almost the entire season. It's always been clear to me that this sort of expectation is too much for a racer. If there are point races sprinkled all through the winter, and if they all count approximately the same toward making a state, divisional or national team, there is bound to be too much pressure on all the racers. Perhaps we will get more sophisticated and make it possible to relieve some of this constant pressure on our racers. I'm sure their results will improve.

How to Plan

Meanwhile you as an athlete will have to live with this situation the best way you can.

One of the surest ways to have a dreary season is to try to get up for every race on the schedule. If you live in the eastern United States and have a large choice of races you'll probably get all worn out and discouraged before the end of the season. I would suggest picking out the important races during the season, and then programing your training so that it fits in with the idea of 4- to 6-week periods of increasing intensity during training, followed by 3- to 4-week periods of holding even, or easing up.

Here is another situation where your training log can be so valuable, especially after you have finished the year and are looking it over for general trends. Set yourself a plan, try to stick with it, evaluate it as you go along, then sum it up at the end of the season. This leads right into a discussion of overtraining.

Overtraining

Overtraining generally means training so hard that you tire yourself out or tear your body down so much that you turn in weaker performances. Also, some athletes who feel sick, bored, or tired often attribute these symptoms to overtraining.

In the first instance of too much training, this can be checked. Look at your log, check your pulse rate and your weight. If your rested pulse rate is going up and if you're losing weight it's probably time to pull back and ease up on your program, or to take a few days off. Maybe you *are* doing too much.

A State of Mind

On the other hand, the situation where the skier feels sick or bored is often a state of mind. If you find yourself losing interest it's probably time to make a few changes in your schedule. It's rather unlikely that you are working too hard in this instance. In fact, if you stepped up your program it might be just what you need.

Another solution would be to change your schedule in an attempt to attain a different outlook. A couple of tours wandering through the countryside might even make that difference.

93

42. A good inseason diversion is fooling around perfecting your *Quersprung* so you can get ready for the ultimate test of vaulting stone walls and barbed-wire fences during the spring tours. There are other esoteric maneuvers that can be practiced, but the most important advice is this: use expendable skis.

Use of Free Time

This gets into the whole matter of psychology and approach to competition.

From what I have observed, the successful x-c skiers focus each of their days around skiing or training, and everything else takes a back seat, especially during the competitive season. During their free time these skiers relax with very low-key activities unrelated to skiing, like reading, playing cards, listening to music, or writing letters. A high degree of concern for testing new equipment or different waxes, sightseeing, spectating, etc., can be distracting influences on one's racing performances.

11. Diet

The information available, including studies and folklore, on food and vitamin intake and its effects, is mind-boggling. If you want to create a panic situation for yourself, research this area by talking with different athletes, one at a time, and then try to figure out what you should be eating and how many vitamin pills you should be popping. I haven't known many x-c skiers who weren't at one time serious about special diets or vitamin supplements. I never got too hung up on diet myself, probably because I like to eat so much that I don't want to give up any particular food in order to concentrate more on another kind. But, so be it.

If you want to rest easy, be assured that if your diet is normal and well balanced, you will be getting all the food and vitamins you need. It's normal to expect growing kids to want more food, or for athletes who exercise a great deal to want more food. So if your diet is balanced and you aren't gaining weight, chances are very good that it's O.K.

Two warnings

The first: If you think that some year-round special diet or vitamin supplement is going to improve your performance, you are almost certainly wrong. There is no strong evidence to warrant this assumption.

The second: If you begin to depend on an overbalance of special foods or on vitamins for improved performances you are probably over the hill. I have seen some veteran skiers turn to this approach during the twilight of their careers.

CPT 10: You improve your performance through your training and technique programs, not through your eating and pill programs.

The *Con* and *Pro* of Supplements

Now I'm going to backtrack slightly.

Taking many of these extra foods and vitamin pills probably will not hurt you if they are taken in proper amounts; they probably will not help you either, in a pure physical sense. But they might help you psychologically. So if you think you can't get along without, say, your vitamin supplements, it would be a good idea to check with your doctor to make sure that the dose you are taking is actually not harmful, and that the vitamins contain nothing that might show up in a drug test.

Apropos the latter, in the doping-control tests being given after races now, certain vitamin supplements, because of some of the additives they contain, will produce positive results. Of course the intent of the doping test is not to disqualify an athlete for taking vitamins: the test is so sensitive that it picks up the additives, whose mere presence is enough to register Positive, no question of degree.

However, almost all the doctors I have talked with around the world think that vitamin supplements may have an influence in preventing disease among athletes, particularly those who travel away from their own environments. Therefore all the team doctors I know prescribe vitamin pills for their skiers. But, to repeat, these are not given with the intention of improving performance. The doctors hope they are *preventive* in regard to catching colds, or getting some other sickness.

There are certain adjustments in the diet that can be made during the pre-race days, and on race days. I will say more about these in a minute.

Doping

I have never been associated with anyone who has taken pep pills or anything else like them in order to try to improve his performance during a race. There was quite a bit of speculation during the FIS meet in 1970 about one country's skiers who were alleged to be taking dope. This was never proven, and I think they were just skiing better than anyone expected them to; in fact, they kept winning for the rest of the season—and this indicates they were *not* on dope.

Since 1970 the Fédération Internationale de Ski has provided for more and more doping controls. Now after World championship events, the top three finishers, and other skiers picked at random, are subjected to doping tests to see if they have used any form of illegal stimulant. You can occasionally read about doping of athletes, or countries who have perfected some drug that will not show up in a doping test, but I think x-c skiing is clean so far. Every doping test on an x-c skier I know of has proven to be negative.

Pills

No paper or account I know of certifies to the advantage of taking some form of pep pill or dope. In fact, the studies show the adverse effects and indicate clearly that this is an area to avoid. Most of the drugs stimulate the heart to excessively high rates which could lead to dangerous situations such as damage to the heart or even death. The invulnerability-of-the-heart theory goes out the window under stimulation by drugs. Unfortunately, some athletes in other sports have died, apparently from a result of drug usage during competitions.

The most important argument, really, against any form of doping is a philosophical one. An x-c race is a contest between individuals to compare their strengths in endurance, technique, motivation and even waxing ability. You can think of all these as skills gained through training. It's a highly individual event: it's *you*, how *you* can perform, utilizing the skills you have developed during your training program. To bring in elements in the form of pharmacology or medical aid (if I can call doping that—in the medical profession they're called "interventions"), or elements not natural to the body, is contrary to the whole idea of competition.

Or look at it this way. Suppose a vote was taken among sportsmen regarding the use of drugs. Do you think they would vote in favor of the idea?

If there are some elements connected with the sporting world who want to use dope for one reason or another, perhaps they should have their own events, no holds barred. I wouldn't even be interested in hearing the results.

Blood-doping

There's another interesting approach to improving performance that involves doctoring the athlete's blood. Many weeks before a competitive event an athlete gives up a certain amount of blood; it is centrifuged, and the plasma, containing mostly RBC (red blood cells), is stored in a blood bank. Meanwhile the athlete starts in on his training program again and rebuilds his own blood supply. Then, a short time before the big race the athlete is given back his own blood, thus significantly increasing his RBC and hemoglobin count, and therefore increasing his O_2 transport facility.

The proponents of this method argue that it's the athlete's own blood, isn't it? And so on.

Well, the more the athlete depends on medical teams, or things like blood-doping, in order to improve his performance, the more we will be taking something away from him and from the meaning of his training and racing. Soon he will begin to wonder whose race it is.

Blood-doping is difficult to detect and the rules are not clear regarding its legality. Most countries have an unwritten understanding that they will not resort to this tactic, for reasons of sport.

Pre-race diet

There is a training-eating schedule used by thousands of athletes for a number of years and there seems to be more and more evidence to show that it is effective. Essentially, two or three days before the race the athlete takes a long workout, one hard enough to deplete the glycogen stores in the body. Then he feeds himself primarily on carbohydrates from that time until the race. It has been found that using this regime will actually build the glycogen stores to a higher level than existed before.

Some bikers I know go a step further and take a week of protein diet, then a tough workout which really depletes the glycogen, and then they go onto the carbohydrates for several days preceding the race.

The most important thing to remember about pre-racing eating is that you should not experiment during the big races. Work out a system for yourself during training sessions much earlier in the year, then hold with it during the race season.

43. Ernie Lennie of the Canadian National Ski Team feeds during the North American Championships' 30-km race in March 1975.

Race-day food

Since carbohydrates are easily digested and readily utilized for energy it is a good idea to continue eating "carbos" on the day of the race. There is room for quite a bit of personal preference here with regard to the timing of the last meal before the race, and the content of the meal. Naturally, about everything has been tried, and most athletes like to eat about three hours before the event.

This is an item you should keep track of in your training log. Don't be alarmed if you have some of your best days, or workouts, shortly after a meal consisting largely of fats and proteins. That's O.K.; others have had this experience. On the other hand, some athletes have very definite needs for restricting the food they take in before a race.

Liquids During the Race

The liquid balance in the body is very important. Before a race you should drink a normal amount of whatever you prefer. Don't sell yourself short—but don't stock up, either, in anticipation of heavy sweating. If the race is over 15 km, or if you are going to "feed" (take in liquids) along the way, I think it is a good idea to begin your feeding a few minutes before you start. This certainly is something you should practice during your longer workouts so you can learn your body's preferences in feeding.

The whole idea of feeding during a race is to supply some energy and liquids to replace those you burn up. It's highly probable that none of the top racers in the world could finish a long-distance event like the 50 km at a pace consistent with good performance without feeding during the race.

How Much of What

The amount and content of the drink is another subject for long discussions around the potbelly stove. Before we knew any better, we used to take straight honey during a race. This did not provide liquid enough—in fact, in order to digest honey the stomach calls on liquid from other parts of the body—so we ended up thirstier than before. The honey also provided more energy than we could possibly utilize in a short time.

So a few guides are important. Since a person can absorb only about 50 grams of glucose an hour, and only about 4/5 liter of liquid an hour, it does no good to exceed these limits during feeding. If your stomach is bloated (the doctors call it "gastric overfilling"!) you'll be uncomfortable, and your reaction might impair your ability to ski at an optimum pace.

Some theories hold that fruit juices, especially ones containing citric acid, are bad for the stomach during competition and therefore should be avoided. However, I have always had pretty good luck with a touch of lemon juice in a mixture of tea and dextrose. The acid juice helps cut through that mucky feeling in the mouth.

The old, standard drink of coffee with sugar wasn't far off the mark either. If you believe in replacing some of the minerals in the body—which is one of the features of commercial drinks like Sportade and Gatorade—and get a feeling of being stimulated by the caffeine, you might prefer this.

Sometimes I add a little salt, just enough to be noticeable but not unpleasant when tasting the drink before the race. Then, during the race, the added salt actually tastes good.

Feeding every 15 minutes during the race seems to be indicated. At this rate, and remembering the body's capacity for absorption, you should try to feed a little less than 6 ounces a stop. Actually, this is quite a mouthful.

Time out for Tea

During distance training or long-distance competitions the break provided by feeding is almost always welcomed by the athlete. Nevertheless there is that danger of losing one's concentration right after the feed, and in a race this usually means a slowing in speed. I love those feeds myself, and if someone else—like another athlete training with me, another racer arriving at the food station, or a coach standing there yelling at me—wasn't around I might just linger and have seconds and thirds. But even if one "double-feeds" as some racers do, it's important to get one's mind, as well as those skis, back on the track.

12. Travel, Altitude & Sickness

If you stay with competition long enough and get proficient, someday you may be making a long trip away from your immediate area in order to race. This is one of the thrills that comes with being a competitor, and every skier I know gets excited about travel.

That long trip

We have learned a few things about extended travel and if you can avoid some of our early mistakes you will be the gainer.

Begin the trip well rested. Some skiers used to take very long workouts just prior to the trip, knowing that they might be a day or two in transit and hence would not be able to ski. That's a mistake. A trip is a workout in itself, and if you go abroad, or go through more than a couple of time zones, your whole daily schedule is going to be thrown off by the time you arrive at your destination.

Sleep in transit. If you are taking an overnight flight, or if you change several time zones, ask a doctor to prescribe some mild sleeping pills to help you make the transition.

Regard your flight as a race. After you arrive, regard your trip as a tough race, and figure that every time zone you changed is worth 5 kilometers. For example, in going to Scandinavia from the East Coast we usually go through five time zones. That means that after arriving in Norway, you should behave as if you just finished a 25 km race.

Start training gradually. As an obvious follow-up to travel, you begin skiing slowly in your new surroundings. Don't let your excitement, or the sight of competitors unknown to you, carry you away to the extent of hard workouts too soon. If you wonder how much you should be doing, it's better to do less than more. If you take it easy for a few days you won't suffer. But if you go out and hump it, you may get worn down and increase your chances of catching a cold.

Training and Skiing at Altitudes

In 1964, soon after the 1968 Olympic Summer Games were awarded to Mexico City (which has an altitude of about 2300 m), physiologists earnestly began studying the effects of athletic performances and training at higher altitudes. Now, more than a decade later, altitude training is still quite a controversial subject. (CPT 1 again: but who expects unanimity?)

With some fear and trepidation I make the following introductory statements, hoping there is little argument about them. From there we can go on.

1. For endurance events you can expect weaker or slower performances at high altitudes from around 1600 m and up, as compared to sea level. And you get them. For standard running distances there is a marked increase in times at altitude, and it is quite close to a linear relationship. At 2000 m the running times for distances will be off on the order of 7 percent; at 3000 m, 10 percent; and at 4500 m they will be off by about 20 percent.

2. The basic reason for decreased performances at altitude is that the air contains less oxygen and therefore the body cannot take in so much to utilize in the production of energy.

3. The FIS—the world governing body of skiing—rules state in principle that world championship events in x-c skiing cannot be held on a course any part of which is above 1650 m. The generally stated reason for this rule is that since the lowland athletes would need so much time to acclimatize themselves to altitude the expenses would be prohibitive. Probably another reason the rule went in was that the lowland countries felt they might be at a disadvantage, physically and psychologically, if they had to run at altitude.

4. The thinner air at altitude does not inhibit sprint or so-called anaerobic performances. In fact, sprinters find that there is less air resistance. You may have noticed yourself that it's easier to throw a baseball hard or hit a tennis ball with good velocity at higher altitudes. However, this lack of air resistance does not compensate for the lack of oxygen needed for endurance events.

5. Prior to the 1972 Summer Games in Munich, athletes from many countries were training at altitude for endurance events. Newspapers in Europe at that time made note of the fact in much the same way American papers refer to so-and-so being a good hot-weather baseball player. In other words, the knowledgeable sports fans were led to believe that altitude training was a good thing for those distance runners or rowers.

CPT 11: Doctors, coaches and athletes usually justify training in conditions and altitudes peculiar to their own surroundings.

Since so many countries and their coaches had their athletes training at altitude it's apparent that they at least believe this sort of training is beneficial. I do too.

The Controversy

The Swiss, with their mountainous terrain, have published a lot of information on altitude training, and they believe in it. On the other hand, the Scandinavians are a bit skeptical about altitude training—but we know their terrain is not like that in the Alps. In the United States you can hear both arguments, depending on where you live or who you talk with.

The controversy here goes like this: The high-country group tells the lowlanders that racing at altitude doesn't make any difference. After the lowlanders catch their breath, they argue the point. The high-country group then says they get logy when they try to perform at sea level. Nonsense, reply the lowlanders. And so it goes. Well, they're all right, if you look at it in a certain way.

44. Rest during an altitude training session in Switzerland (Uli Wenger, Swiss coach, at right).

Training and competing in surroundings natural to you is no doubt a psychological boost and is the major factor for the efficacy of CPT 11.

My own feeling

Here is a wrap-up of mine, based on my experiences at altitude and sea level, and from studies and conversations with some of the world's experts on altitude training. Thus:

1. A lowlander, going to altitude, will find it necessary to slow down his pace of training or racing. Pacing is so important, as always.

2. A lowlander, going to altitude, will probably be at the biggest disadvantage between the fourth and seventh days. Before the fourth day the effects of altitude, on the whole, are not so bad. After the seventh day there is a slow improvement in performance.

3. A highlander, coming to the lowlands to train or race, may feel logy for a few days and an adjustment period is recommended. A highlander will eventually have to increase his pace of training or racing in this situation.

4. Training at altitude is unquestionably good if you are going to race at altitude. There's no way around it for the people who live at altitude, so it has to be good.

5. In order for a lowlander to acclimatize fully to altitude, a period of about three weeks is recommended.

Another Altitude Approach

Doctors from Switzerland have gone as far as to determine the optimal altitude for training and they say it's around 2300 m. The theory is that at this altitude the athlete can work hard enough to minimize the danger of deconditioning. (An extreme example might help explain this. Suppose you were situated at very high altitude for a long period of time and that previous to this you had been accustomed to doing a large amount of training at lower levels. You would probably find your capacity to do the same amount of work at high altitude severely hampered, due to the lack of oxygen, so you would do less. After a time you would begin to decondition.) At the same time, at 2300 m, the chemical changes that take place in the body are probably favorable enough to warrant training there. The body produces more red blood cells and hemoglobin at altitude and on coming down to sea level these "extra" RBC will probably increase your oxygen carrying capacity.

The recommended periods of training at altitude are as follows: First an uninterrupted bout of at least three weeks followed by a return for two to four weeks to lower levels for competitions or training. Then, another trip to altitude for about ten days, followed by the final trip to the lowlands for the major competition you have been pointing for. The adjustment period at lower levels will vary with the individual, but a few days should be allowed for this.

Some Disadvantages of Altitude Training

I don't think that altitude training is all peaches and cream. From my own experience watching skiers from this country I have noticed that many skiers who have lived or trained for long periods of time at altitudes have different techniques. These techniques are characterized by slower tempos and more vigorous body movements. I think both traits are natural reactions to altitude. First of all, it's impossible to ski as fast at altitude as at sea level, therefore the slower tempo. The extra body movements like hip wiggles or shoulder twists probably follow for two reasons. If your tempo is slower, especially on a fast track, you have to do something with your body during the gliding phase and even if you have to wait just a fraction of a second, a little extra movement of some sort may help to provide a sort of rhythm. Second, and more arguable, I think the altitude skiers have to "hump" it more in order to get the power they feel necessary for a good stride and thus they put more of their body into each step.

And, since it is difficult to work as intensely at altitude as it is at sea level there is danger of losing some over-all body power at altitude.

In sum: A study of the results of x-c skiers in this country could be interpreted in many different ways. If you are inclined to favor altitude training you could point to any number of cases where it seemed to benefit skiers. Probably the lowlanders who can train occasionally at altitude are in the most favorable situation.

For the future it's likely that opportunity and belief will be the determining factors in our altitude training.

Injuries and Sickness

Getting sick or injured has to be about the most discouraging thing that can happen to an x-c athlete. You train hard for a long period then come to the big event, catch a virus and can't race. In 1972 virtually the whole U.S.

Team was sick and could not ski in the Olympic Games at top form. It would take quite a bit of space to recount the details leading up to that experience and I'll just say that what follows is based on talks I've had since then with scores of doctors. Let's look to the future and better luck for all of the competitors.

The best medical coverage

While only a small fraction of the world's top skiers are receiving the necessary medical attention it's instructive to outline what is being done in some of those instances. Unfortunately, we haven't reached this point in the United States yet.

The complete organization has a doctor who is in charge of the athletes. He compiles records of the athletes' medical histories, calls in other specialists as needed (for instance, an orthopedic man might be able to help with one skier's particular problem, or an infectious disease doctor could recommend immunizations), and travels with the team to all important meets. He is the person in the best position to know the skier from a medical point of view. It's quite different for a doctor who is not familiar with the athletes to come along on a trip, armed as he is with all the up-to-date medical information. The new doctor is still missing that important ingredient of familiarity with the athlete.

The team doctor advises the coach on travel and training schedules, diet, vitamin supplements, immunization shots, and prescribes what he feels is necessary. If the doctor is worth his salt, the athletes will gain confidence in him and this team will be better suited to produce optimum results.

The best for the most

As I have said, most of you reading this book will not be lucky enough to have such a situation. So you'll have to listen to Father John's little bits of advice, picked up over the years.

1. If you are sick, for heaven's sake see a doctor. Find out what it is—common cold, flu, virus, etc., and try to determine the recovery period.

2. If you get injured, or pull a muscle, lay off it. See a doctor or a trainer. Get advice.

3. Talk to your doctor about immunization shots. I know all the arguments for and against flu shots. And I look at it this way. Even though I think the shots may not do any good, it's one of those cases where I'll never know. How would I know if the flu shot prevented me from getting

the flu? More important, if there is some chance it will do some good, and if I'm real serious about my training program and hoping for good results, it's worth taking the shot as insurance. I know there are people who disagree, but there, I've said it.

4. Aspirin is a wonderful medicine and has all sorts of good qualities. I know one top skier who was on a high dosage of aspirin, prescribed by a doctor for a tendon condition. The aspirin helped the tendon, all right, but the skier started having nosebleeds; and this was very distracting, especially during races. The nosebleeds were caused by the excessive aspirin, because aspirin has anticoagulant properties. Further, the skier developed moderate anemia. "It's not a perfect world," the doctor said. And he's right. The point is this—if you take a cure of some sort you may have other, and unwanted, consequences. Be prepared.

5. If you travel abroad you should be very careful of your diet. The Norwegians visited France in 1967, a year before the Olympics, and found out what the French vegetables did to their digestive systems; so in 1968 they stayed away from vegetables. Well, you can't whip over to a race site a year early just to taste the food, and so you have to take some ordinary precautions. If you stay away from uncooked food and vegetables, that's a good start. I think you are well advised not to drink water in most of the foreign countries you visit. You can sort of gain a feel for the water and the food, depending on the country you visit. It's an easy thing to boil the water, or have tea or coffee, instead of cold, raw water (and it may be very raw).

6. Remember that extreme fatigue and cooling lower your resistance to disease, especially colds. You have to avoid this situation. There's no reason for extreme fatigue during the season, except after a long race, and then you should rest up anyway, right after the race.

7. Take care of yourself. I know this sounds simple and obvious, but it isn't that simple for most athletes. Look at it this way: You've trained hard for years and now it's boiling down to a few important races during the winter. Think about what you're doing at this time.

8. Avoid exercises and games that haven't been part of your regular schedule.

9. Avoid crowds as much as possible.

10. Keep on your regular schedule. If it has been producing good results for you don't go off half-cocked on some wild schedule.

11. Saunas are great but there's no firm evidence that taking them will help you sweat out a cold, get rid of that scratchy throat, or otherwise cure you of any infection.

After Sickness

No matter what, you may get sick sometime during the season and then will be faced with the problem of what to do after you get back on skis.

Some gentle training is in order as soon as you feel you're ready to go. If you have three or four days before a scheduled race, take the first couple of days feeling yourself out. Don't overextend, don't get tired. Do some easy distances, then if you feel better, do some short intervals of a few minutes. Sometime before the race you should give yourself a test. In the case of a senior skier this test doesn't have to be more than 3 to 5 kilometers, but it should be taken, after a warm-up naturally, at racing speeds. If you feel O.K. during this, you'll probably be O.K. for the race. But, in the meantime, don't do any more than this.

One of the most difficult situations that arises for a coach is trying to decide who should race on a given day. To take a tough situation, imagine having to decide who will run the 4 x 10 men's relay in the Olympic Games. Two of your best men have been down with colds and are in various stages of recovery. Do they race? In Japan, during 1972, over half of the coaches were faced with some problem of sickness on their team. If the athlete is mature, he will go out and give himself the test I mentioned above, then tell the coach yes or no. Norway's most famous relay skier did this in 1972 and told the coach he was not ready. His loss in this race probably meant the difference between first and second place for Norway. But he was very likely correct in his evaluation of his condition. He had been competing for several years and knew himself well.

If you are just coming off some sort of sickness and have an individual race coming up, you could actually postpone your test until you get in the track, with your number on. If you do this, you must show the maturity to ease up, or even quit the race if you are not feeling well. It does absolutely no good to go out and punish yourself when you are sick. In fact, you might do yourself some further harm.

13. Suggested Training Tips & Schedules

Here are some training schedules to study. If you think about the task of suggesting schedules for everyone who'll be reading this book you can appreciate the difficulties. But I've rushed headlong into areas like this before, so let's see what happens.

First of all, we can narrow things down a bit by saying that these tips are for the fairly serious racer.

Now let's talk again about the individual approach. You are the one who must learn to know your best schedule, your best approach. If you are doing eight hours of heavy labor every day it won't do for me to tell you to concentrate on strength work in your training.

A regular forty-hour work week will impose certain limitations on your training schedule. Being a student will also make a difference: during the summers you may have plenty of time to train, but, come fall, things change drastically; then you run into studying for exams, writing papers, and so on.

So after reading this section you should sit down and figure out a program for yourself, using the information you gain here. I've suggested to lots of skiers the following procedure: Calculate the amount of time you have available, especially during the fall and pre-season. Knowing that you will be working at a fairly intense rate just before the heart of the racing season, cast back through the fall and then back through the summer, and plan your program that way—beginning in the spring with easy workouts, in terms of time and intensity, and then slowly increasing during the summer and fall until you work into a schedule you know is realistic for you during the early winter. Make it progressive, in other words.

For sure, every person should have his own schedule planned in advance. It just won't do to look at the day, the weather, or who is doing what, and then decide on the spur of the moment what you are going to do. You must have a well-thought-out plan, and you should follow it. If it doesn't work after a spell, well, of course, make adjustments.

Here goes with a typical schedule I have given to some of the country's top, senior skiers, recommending the hours of training to spend per week on cardiovascular workouts. These figures do not include time for strength work, for two reasons. Strength training is very important but it is also the most individual aspect of any program: you should figure out your own best program and go at it. (See strength training Chapter 9.) Second, as I've hinted above, it doesn't make much sense to include two to four hours of strength training per week for the fellow who is already doing forty to fifty hours of manual labor each week.

Cardiovascular Workouts

The following does not include strength workouts (q.v. Chapter 9 and Chapter 10).

Month	Hours per week	Comments
May	4–6	Relaxation, ease into training
June	6–8	Distance and "other"
July	8–10	Distance and "other"
August	10–12	Distance and "other," introduce some roller-skiing
September	12–14	Same as August, more roller-skiing
October	14–16	Same as September, introduce intervals
November	16–18	At least half of distance training on roller skis, more interval work
December	16–20	On-snow distance work, technique work, some continuation of intervals and some tempo work (or races)
January	14–20	Same as December, but more tempo work or races; continue intervals
February	12–20	Racing season, easy distance training plus tempo work (or races)
March	12–20	Same as February
April		Race and relax

As you can see, I have suggested upper and lower limits for each week. Even these are not binding of course. During sickness you would not expect to come up to the lower limit, and during a training camp you would probably exceed the upper limit. But notice the average graph. If you plot your program on a weekly basis, instead of a monthly basis as I have done (in the interests of typography), you will soon be able to check your own trends. Colored pencils work better for differentiating the kinds of work-

45. Typical amounts of time apportioned to each type of training activity.

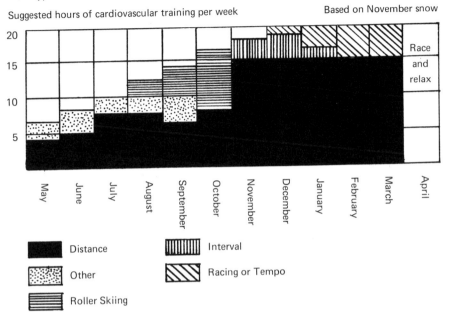

Suggested hours of cardiovascular training per week

Based on November snow

Distance

Other

Roller Skiing

Interval

Racing or Tempo

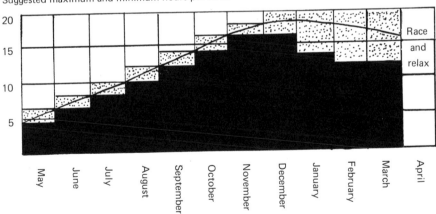

Suggested maximum and minimum hours per week

46. Here the curve shows the average hours per week spent in all training over the year. Notice the increased load in November and December, just before the racing season starts, and the expectable decrease in training sessions during midwinter competition.

111

outs too. You might use blue for distance, black for roller-skiing, red for intervals, yellow for tempo work and brown for other. It doesn't matter, really—but colors do look nicer.

O.K. You start to plan your program. And here come the questions!

How Much Time?

We can run into apparent complications here. Many of you reading this are students and the natural question is: How can I follow this progressive program idea, the one suggested by the average graph, when I have much more time available in the summer than I do during the fall and the winter?

Well, to answer, it's not so bad.

First let me say that a lot of exercise (training) is good for young people and extra hours spent during the summer, as long as it is enjoyable, will pay off.

Next, if you're in this sort of situation with time limitations in the fall and winter, pay very close attention to the intensity of your workouts. Be sure they increase in intensity. In fact, you could substitute a pulse rate scale for the hours-per-week on the vertical axis of the average graph, and then follow that. In other words, increase your average pulse rate instead of the hours-per-week. But since pulse rates vary so much I hesitate to do that for you. However, I have suggested some pulse rates in Chapter 3, and there is the following table.

Type of Workout	Beats per Minute Below Maximum
Distance	40–60
Interval	20–40
Speed	Not taken
Tempo	To be determined by athlete

A few comments about using your table:

First, pulse rate is an individual matter and even the general guidelines given above may not be appropriate for everyone.

Second, in all workouts you should not consciously try to go under. In fact, you should try to avoid it at all times unless you are experimenting, trying to learn the feelings associated with the onset of going under. If you experiment during training you will soon learn your capacities. But, aside from the experiments, don't go under. If this means running a distance workout at more than 60 beats below your max, so be it.

Third, you should expect to be able to work at higher pulse rates as your conditioning improves. For instance, in the early summer your comfortable distance pulse rate might be 60 below max, but in the fall it might be comfortable at only 40–45 below maximum. (This will of course mean that you are going faster, as you would expect.)

Fourth, there is no point in taking your pulse rate during a speed workout. In this kind of exercise you are supposed to go just as fast as you possibly can—usually for a short time period—and knowing your pulse rate is not important.

Finally, when you learn to run your tempo workouts at optimum pulse, you have it! That's pacing.

What Is "Other"?

You will notice an allotment of two to four hours a week for "other" during the summer months and up until roller-skiing begins to take on a significant time block. For some, "other" could be playing tennis or some skill games. I know that many athletes have their own favorite workout

47. Joe McNulty knows his own capacity better than anyone else.

48. Example of "other." And the girl at right wing always holds her own.

especially suited for the summer months, and they include that. Still others concentrate on an area of their weakness, such as hill climbs, and this would be included under "other."

How about Junior Racers?

I have already hinted that juniors do well to take a lot of work, providing it's enjoyable for them. So it's possible some juniors could easily spend as much time as I have suggested for the seniors here. Of course I would not expect them to exercise with the intensity the seniors do.

How Intense?

This is a very individual matter. I have repeatedly said that the intensity should increase, however slowly, during the training season. The pulse rate chart gives some hints. You can take a test run occasionally—remember those? Your times should gradually improve for the test runs (it could be a hike, a bike, a row, some intervals, or whatever) and this is usually indication enough that your intensity of training has increased.

114

And remember the rule-of-thumb that you should not get really stiff during a workout. If you do, you're probably going too hard.

How about Distance *vs* Intervals *vs* Tempo, Etc.?

I feel that distance training, as I have rather loosely defined it, should constitute 60–80 percent of your training time. The bar graphs bear this out. Keep in mind that distance training should be done on x-c terrain and that it necessarily will include periods of greater stress, followed by recovery periods. During the fall and early season you should increase the formal amount of interval training and this is indicated on the graph. But there are no clearly defined percentages to go by, mainly because of the close connection between good distance training for x-c and good interval training.

You should introduce roller-skiing about two to three months before on-snow skiing. Normally this will be counted for distance training unless you have some very special terrain and transportation features which allow you to do strict interval training. I would not suggest this, at any rate. As you begin roller-skiing you will ease off in your other distance training, but don't give it up completely. Roller-skiing three to four times a week just before the snow flies is adequate.

You noticed that tempo training had crept in on the bar graph earlier. Recall that this is training at racing speed. I would include also, therefore, time spent in races as tempo training.

What about Weather?

The weather, especially in New England, is an important factor in any program. I like to think we have it licked here in Putney. Aside from the problem of over-all snow conditions, which are probably not as good as those in some other parts of the country, there are the vagaries of daily weather to contend with throughout the year. No matter where you are, it's a temptation to postpone or cancel a workout because of inclement weather. This is bad.

There are a few situations which would preclude an out-of-doors workout but I can't think of many. (If the weather is very cold and windy the risk of exposure could be dangerous, for instance.) However, athletes and coaches too often change their plans because of weather.

"It's raining and I don't like to run in the rain."

"It's too hot."

49. But sometimes it's even more fun in the rain . . .

"It's too cold, too slippery, too something."

Bah-h! Who's in charge here, anyway? You or the weather?

I observed some U.S. Combined jumpers waiting-out "bad conditions" for a week preceding a World Championship event. First, the inrun was too slick and the boys did not jump. Next, it was too windy. Then a day came along when the conditions were perfect and everyone trained. However, the next day produced slick inrun tracks again. "No jumping for us." Everyone else was jumping, however. The competition day came and the conditions were identical with those of the "bad days." Naturally, our team did not fare so well.

A good rule-of-thumb is to proceed with your scheduled workout unless it poses a high risk of injury or harm to the body. If you cater to the weather you'll never learn to be a mudder. On the other hand, if you train regardless of weather you'll feel better for it—and will also gain an advantage on the fellows who are fair-weather athletes.

"Neither snow, nor rain, not heat, nor gloom of night stays these athletes from the swift completion of their appointed workouts."

116

Alone, or in Groups?

There's no doubt that training in groups is beneficial to most athletes. And there are advantages to training alone, too. The intelligent athlete will do both.

In a group there is usually some added incentive or competition which makes people train harder. Group trips or runs, bikes, hikes, etc., are often more fun than solos. But there are two obvious dangers to relying solely on group training. First, if you depend on a group, or even on someone else to go training with, there will come a day when you won't go out, or you will be delayed because the other party isn't there or isn't ready. Second, if you train in a group all the time you will find that the range in abilities tends to telescope in. The weaker athletes get pulled along faster and this is good for them. But the stronger athletes lack the incentive to go harder because they are already riding on top, and so they often don't develop as much as they might otherwise. (To be on top and to stay

---

Honing Co-ordination

Co-ordination exercises and sports are very good training for improving your technique. I'm not talking now about specificity exercises or actual on-snow skiing, but other types of exercise which require a high degree of co-ordination. Tumbling, diving, modern dance, team sports, tennis—these are just a few. Good coaching in these will increase their value to your skiing. The advantages of these types of exercise are evident.

They are diversionary, often a good break from the rugged routine of training.

By getting coaching in movements not necessarily specific to your sport you nevertheless improve your ability to respond to directions or coaching, and this will probably aid your technique. I've seen lots of skiers improve their technique over the summer without doing any ski-related exercises. (I think your own thinking processes can be improved by co-ordination training of this sort.)

Finally, certain elements in these co-ordination exercises are good for anyone. Some increase your flexibility, your reaction, your strength and your enjoyment of sports.

on top is tough. It requires extra effort and push all the time. You can't stop too often to look over your shoulder, either.)

There are two clear advantages to training alone. First, you can go out whenever you want to. You don't have to depend on anyone else. Second: as they say, when you're racing you're usually alone out there, so you better find out what it's like.

If you can train alone and increase your work load, push yourself harder, and all that, the chances are better that you will be more successful than you would be after most often training in a group.

Back to peaking

If you know yourself well enough to know you are near peak condition, you will do best to concentrate on easy distance skiing during the rest of the racing season, and just taking the races as they come. If, on the other hand, you feel you need more "tuning up," you should include some interval work, and even a little speed work, during the racing season, until you feel you have peaked.

"Sounds easy, don't it?" as we hill folk say. "Well, it ain't! The fella that figures out this peakin' stuff is gonna be near the top of the heap."

Nothing here changes my recommended minimums for inseason training. To review, these include strength work twice a week, short foot-runs twice a week, and three other cardiovascular workouts (these would include races). Most skiers do much more. My minimum is a sort of hang-on situation that will keep you in shape during periods of travel, holidays, etc. The minimum will not increase your capacity if you have followed the program I have suggested.

14. Introducing Technique

Most experienced skiers can recognize good technique when they see it: fortunately there isn't much disagreement on this. Yet the average Sunday x-c'er in this country looks a bit like a bumpkin when compared with, say, a Norwegian tourskier—who probably has technique about equal to our average collegiate racer. Why the difference?

There are a couple of good reasons.

First, at this writing the United States has still not come out with a unified approach to technique. I'm reminded again of the East German swimming coach who emphasized sharing information, because somehow the rivalries among various American groups, coaches included, have been an inhibiting factor to a spirit of co-operation. As a result most coaches and instructors, or regions, have their own ideas of proper technique, how it should be taught, where the emphasis should be put, and so on. No doubt each has a point, but the whole business sure can be confusing to anyone who moves around the country taking it all in, or trying to learn to ski. Some qualified outfit should step into the gap—the U.S. Ski Association, the Professional Ski Instructors Association, or some sport-minded association of businessmen.

Second, we over here don't have the tradition to draw on that exists in Scandinavia. The average Norwegian skier studies x-c skiing as closely as our sports fans assess the fine points of baseball and pro football. As a result, Norway has highly proficient skiers who can be called up to coach or serve as examples for others to learn from. By comparison—and unfortunately—in the United States we are on the verge of getting into a vicious circle that sees more and more skiers with weak technique for more and more beginners to imitate.

"Our tourskiers shouldn't have to bother with technique . . ."—maybe the trouble starts here. Technique to many people is a dirty word or a finicky embellishment to a simple, basic sport. I've heard all the arguments. But whether you're a tourskier or a racer, doesn't it make sense to get the most out of your effort? I've seen too many beginning tourskiers lose interest in x-c either because they were misled deliberately into adopting the notion that with little or no effort *anyone* could "make it," or because they simply decided for themselves that technique wasn't important—that improved skill would, somehow, spoil the fun.

Examples of this abound. It was exciting—and, after a while, a bit saddening—to see the explosion of x-c that took place in this country around 1972 and '73. Exciting, because who could fail to be delighted at

50. Flawless technique, for Norway or any other country: Oddvar Braa cruising by the Putney Elm.

watching a sport that has been a part of one's way of life for more than thirty years suddenly appear to be gaining the widespread participation it surely deserves?

And saddening a little? Well, as the new enthusiasm leveled off, I couldn't help but be sorry for many newcomers to the sport who, beset with misconceptions about nearly automatic expertise, floundered, and soon became disenchanted with x-c. I hope they'll give it another try, perhaps with another approach.

The pity of it is that tourskiers don't have to train like racers in order to learn good technique. It's a lot easier than that. If they take some instruction from competent teachers, study good examples, and practice, they soon will find very exciting the business of learning to ski with a bit of savoir-faire. Nor do the benefits end there. If we follow the normal evolution in most sports, our racers will soon be coming from the ranks of the groups interested in the sport primarily as recreation.

To sum up, then, in general the value of technique is tremendously underestimated even by racers in North America, many of whom train as hard as anyone in the world, but with results that fall short because they can't ski. Well, of course they can ski; I mean that they can't ski with finesse—which means with skill. Some of these racers need less time pounding the pavements and more time spent on roller skis, or co-ordination exercises, or concentrated on-snow sessions to hone their technique.

Yet some racers and coaches remain bullheaded and cite as examples the Norwegians, who rarely practice technique. (Remember CPT 1—the disarray in approaches to training?) And it's true, the top Norwegians rarely do practice their technique. It should be understood, however, that Norway has so many good skiers and the competition for her teams is so fierce, that if anyone does make the team it can be assumed he has good technique. Or else he wouldn't make it to the top.

For years the situation in the United States favored some of the older skiers who had been on deck a long time, who skied fairly well—and, most important, were the strongest guys on the scene, the fellows in the best shape. Now, though, there are more racers around, so technique is becoming an increasingly important factor. It's no longer possible to train your way onto many of the teams in this country.

I feel confident that eventually our technique in the United States will improve. That's one of the reasons for writing this book. So here's the first Caldwell Principle of Technique (CPTK):

CPTK 1: All the best kinds of training will not be a guarantee of good race results: you must know how to ski well.

And It's a Wonderful Feeling

Anyone who has ever skied rapidly over the terrain with seemingly fluid motion knows what it feels like to be at one with the trail and the surroundings. There is a certain flowingness, almost as if the ups and downs in the track are unrolling under you, and you're just waiting for more to come along. The effort required to ski fast with good rhythm adds to the rewards of that feeling.

I've done all the types of skiing events there are, and each has its special flavor, but x-c is just something else! It's the most natural and the most diversified, full of new experiences, and the healthiest. There are more thrills than you can count. And the feeling of accomplishment after an outing is unmatched, whether it's been a cruise through the woods with my family, or a 30-km tour with visiting members of a national team from Scandinavia.

15. Technique for the Flat

Any knowledgeable racer will tell you that the main power for the single stride is derived from the kick of the leg, downward and back. This is obvious. And the trouble is that it's too obvious and many skiers and coaches stop thinking right here. They don't consider the extra power that can be gained from the pendulum-like, forward swing of the nonkicking leg.

To consider the kick alone as the propelling force is a bit like thinking in terms of a cyclist pushing only down on the pedals and ignoring the pulling up. Or, it's the same kind of thinking that leads one to believe that in operating one end of a two-man crosscut saw you should only pull and not push a little as well (at the right time of course).

Several years ago I began to approach the single stride by putting emphasis on what I called forward leg-drive. I'm convinced this approach has worked well and now I have one method of teaching skiing which emphasizes forward leg-drive alone.

The best skiers in the world do kick down and back—*and* they also drive their opposite leg ahead, simultaneously and with great power.

The not-so-good skier relies on kick alone; and he's the one in trouble

---

Impact of Fiberglass

The impact of the new fiberglass skis on technique and waxing is being felt by virtually all the top racers in the world. I have taken the latest technique changes into account throughout, especially in the section on uphill skiing.

The most obvious effect of these skis (as compared with wooden ones) is the increased speed resulting from their design; and this construction in turn accommodates a different waxing system.

Fiberglass skis are generally stiffer in their midsection, so racers need climbing wax only under the foot. The tips and tails are waxed for speed, often with Alpine wax, which is one reason why the skis are noticeably faster on flats and downhills.

But this is not a book on waxing, and I'll merely assume that, when you go out for practice, your skis are properly waxed. (And I hope you don't rely solely on the local weather report in choosing your waxes.)

51. Here's what it's all about—but don't spoil its beauty with a bunch of analysis. Just come back to it again and again.

when his wax slips, or the track disintegrates beneath him. Generally the kick-type skier, as I'll call him, is good on klister snow, or on granular conditions where he can kick like a mule and go like the wind. But get him out on some loose stuff or a soft track and he often looks like a beginner. This is because he does not sneak up on his kick gently: instead, he almost pounds his rear ski into the track. So it is with skiing; and you can't always come down hard on the track, and you shouldn't.

There is an added inefficiency in being a kick-skier. Lots of times the extra kick does little more than break down the snow in the track, thus wasting some power. In a race, this costs you.

One good method for testing how much you depend on your kick is to ski with slippery wax, or with no wax at all. Then if you kick too hard, you just slip and don't really go anywhere. I've experimented with teaching people about more forward leg-drive by having them use slippery skis, and the example often helps.

It might be easy to get the impression that I am endorsing a pussyfoot sort of technique. Not so. See if you can determine for yourself the differences between the top skiers, the ones who kick hard only and don't have any forward leg-drive, and the ones who have forward leg- or knee-drive in addition to a good kick. It all happens so fast that advocates of either system by itself, as being the sole method to use, might be convinced by watching a good skier that he is using the method they opt for. But chances are he's using both the forward drive and the kick.

I'm going to talk about three or four important components of good technique for skiing on the flat. In addition to the forward leg-drive and the kick, there are other aspects such as the arm-swing and momentum. I'll cover each separately.

Forward leg-drive

In each stride the rear leg begins to swing forward with a relatively slow, pendulum-like motion. This slow movement doesn't last very long, though, and it accelerates. I often describe this forward swing of the leg as being similar to the arm motion used by a fast-pitch softballer. Some pitchers poise briefly, with their pitching arm high over their heads, then the arm swoops down, accelerating, and swings forward with a very fast motion just before the ball is released. So it is with the leg in skiing. It swings down, accelerating all the time, and then drives forward.

Common mistakes in the leg-swing are to accelerate too fast and then stop the forward drive too soon; or to have no forward drive at all; or not to accelerate but rather just to swing the foot and leg through in a lackadaisical manner. None of these will get you very far very fast.

The "Level-feet" Problem

Some coaches place occasional emphasis on where the foot should be when the ski hits the snow on its forward swing. They will say the feet should be exactly opposite before the ski really hits the snow— an injunction that sometimes leads skiers to lift their forward leg slightly as it swings through. This lifting is a mistake and will detract from your power. I've seen all sorts of top skiers whose forward-swinging foot hits well before the opposite, more stationary, foot. They don't have any secrets. It's just that their foot is coming through so fast that it doesn't matter where it hits. It's also coming *forward*, and as long as the motion is forward, and fast, it hardly matters where the foot hits. Maybe it is a couple of cm's behind the other. So don't worry too much about where that foot should hit.

As the feet pass, you should continue to exert pressure on your forward-swinging leg, from the foot and on up. Your knee gets into the act, then the upper leg just above the knee; and then, with some

skiers, the hips contribute to the thrust.

The Hip Problem

Warning: Some skiers use a lot of hip motion, which is acceptable under certain conditions—if your tempo is low, for example. If perforce you are skiing slowly you can take time to twist the hips a bit, but with fast tempo there is hardly time to twist the hip forward, then untwist it.

A worse situation occurs when a skier initiates his forward leg-drive with the hip. By doing this he loses the opportunity to get that slingshot effect of swinging through with the leg, beginning with the foot, at maximum speed.

These hippers look powerful sometimes, but don't worry about them. They almost never score.

Finally, you can look at it this way. X-C racing is getting yourself around the track in the fastest manner. During the single stride this is accomplished by first powering one ski ahead down the track, then the other, and so on. Clearly, the fellow who gets his ski ahead the fastest is going to have an advantage. Suppose his every forward leg-swing takes just a fraction of a second less than his competitors'— well, there are a lot of strides in a race and these fractions add up.

So, as long as your forward leg-drive accelerates, at least until your legs pass one another, it can never come through too fast. Remember that. Of course momentum and glide are other considerations and these will be covered below.

The kick

There's no doubt that the kicking leg in each stride needs to have its ski somewhat anchored to the snow or track. This anchoring is done by setting the wax, which in turn usually is accomplished by a downward push through the ski onto the snow. This motion is often accompanied by a little hitch in the leg— really a slight flexing of the knee just before the final and more vigorous push down-and-back.

The key to the kicking phase of the stride is to get as much thrust along the track as possible, without slipping. Imagine how much kick, and therefore thrust along the track, you could get by pushing straight back. It would be similar to the thrust a swimmer gets when he turns and kicks off the wall at one end of the pool. Of course your kick is never this effective, but it's something to think about.

Snow conditions and the wax you are using have a lot to do with the kind of kick you utilize. As I've hinted, in klister-snow conditions only poor wax will prevent you from having all the kick you need: you can horse it here, kicking hard and even later than normal, and using maximum power. On packed pow-

der, on the other hand, you may find it necessary to kick down into the track a bit sooner, or to kick less vehemently. If you think about it, you'll find concentrating on the forward leg-drive will help here too.

If the kick is powerful the leg will straighten out behind. To many observers it will look as if the rear leg does not actually straighten out and this leads some coaches to tell their skiers they aren't kicking hard enough, etc. However, with the expert skiers it takes good photography actually to show the leg straightening out, it all happens so fast. The leg whips back and, like a rubber band, immediately recoils slightly. This immediate recoil is relaxing and a part of good technique.

If the kick is not powerful, the leg of course will not straighten out behind, and the skier will not go too fast. Beginner skiers have this fault occasionally, and it's usually because they have not developed the balance or the strength necessary to ski properly, with good power.

So now we have two things to think about. While one leg starts

52 (near strip) & 53 (frames far right). You might call these vertical sequences an international blueprint for the diagonal as you compare the skier at left with the one on the right. Although from different countries, these top racers show few, if any, differences in form.

swinging forward in a relaxed manner the other leg is tensed and making a real power stroke—the kick. Then, the roles are reversed and the kicking leg relaxes while the forward-swinging leg takes over and drives ahead. It sounds easy and it is, if you don't try and analyze it so much that it slows down your movements. Remember, these actions take place with lightning speed.

The arm-swing

I've seen lots of skiers get their stride mixed up by trying to do something special with their arms. For sure, if you can move your arms and legs naturally, as you do in walking, you won't have to worry much about co-ordinating the movements of all your limbs. But there are several elements of the arm-swing that seem so important to me that I want to discuss them here. I have had good success in approaching most technique problems by concentrating on slight changes in arm movements. So I will break the arm-swing down into two components, mainly for the sake of analysis. Don't get the idea that because I talk about the power stroke (or back-swing) and the forward arm-swing, these movements actually are separated in a herky-jerky manner. If you think about using the arms as you use your legs—that is, using both the forward leg-drive and the

kicking motion down and back to propel yourself along the track— you will be on your way to attaining proper technique.

In general, use your arms like the conductor of an orchestra, to help direct the motions of the rest of the body. Hold on, though!—whatever you do, don't wave your arms like a maestro; instead, use them to control your leg tempo and your body position.

And don't force anything with the arms. For instance, don't force your arm straight ahead and hold it there just because someone tells you to. Or don't swing the arm across in front of your body just because you see someone else doing it.

The Power Push

I'll define the power push as that part of the poling motion which occurs from the instant the pole basket hits the snow until the arm begins its forward swing again. Or look at it this way: as soon as the basket hits the snow you should begin to get a push from it. This push is initiated by a tensing of the hand, wrist and forearm and a downward motion of the forearm. Two of the most common errors in poling are (1) planting the pole too far ahead and having to ski by it before any downward pressure can be applied, and (2) pulling the forearm back slightly, parallel to the track, before beginning the downward push

128

or thrust. Neither of these bad habits will do.

As the strong, downward motion of the forearm continues, the rest of the poling arm and shoulder assists so greatly that, with a strong skier, the arm is almost flung to the rear.

This power stroke should continue to be vigorous until the arm passes the hip. It's fairly easy to check this by standing to the side of a skier and looking for daylight between the poling arm and the hip.

With a Flick of the Wrist

One new gimmick being used by a lot of U.S. racers is flicking the wrist before the arm's power push is completed, or just as the hand gets to the hip. The wrist flicks, the hand opens momentarily to let go of the pole, then the hand grasps the pole handle again for the forward arm-swing. These wrist-flickers end up with their wrist cocked at almost a right angle to their forearm. It's a means for relaxing the arm, I suppose.

This premature relaxing of the arm usually causes a related, more serious, flaw in technique: Often the flick triggers a relaxation of the whole body, and everything stops, particularly the forward leg-drive. For a moment such skiers look like statues. All I can say is that it's a very relaxing way to ski, but not a very fast way to race, because any skier will slow up and lose momen-

tum if the forward leg-drive stops too soon.

Still, if the wrist-flick does not in any way inhibit the forward leg- or knee-drive, then I would admit, begrudgingly, that there isn't much power lost in the stride—only that small amount that can be gained by using the arms properly.

In sum: For good (meaning efficient) technique, the wrist and hand should act as extensions of the forearm— the wrist is kept stiff, and in line with the forearm—until after the arm passes the body on its power push to the rear. Then, the hand opens, the fingers point down toward the track or toward the tail of the ski, the arm relaxes momentarily, and the hand grasps the pole again for the forward swing.

The Forward Arm-swing

I've been talking about the backswing of the arm being the power push, and that's true. This is a strength you can develop in your dry-land training. But the forward arm-swing is really a more subtle motion, and the differences evident in the use of this forward swing separate the good skiers from the also-rans.

In addition to dictating tempo, the forward swing of the arm should be used to keep your body in a proper position and to maintain momentum in your stride. The arm should swing forward in concert with the rest of the body in a way to help you get down the track as fast and as smoothly as possible.

Consider an arm-swing that is rather stiff, fast, and perhaps too early. The effect of it would be to set your butt back slightly, as if you were about to sit down. Alternatively, if the arm-swing is too late and your upper body is already well forward, the swing will be incomplete and will not help to generate maximum forward momentum—unless of course you really extend your arm, in which case you take a chance on tipping over forward.

There is no one speed and method for swinging the arm forward. It all depends on the condition of the track. For instance, on a very fast track, which allows a little more time in each stride because the glide is longer, the good skier will delay his arm-swing ever so slightly at the beginning—not by holding his arm in an extended position behind him, but by starting the forward motion more slowly than usual. Or, sometimes a skier will swing an arm forward at about the usual rate but actually cross it slightly in front of his body, just to take a little more time. (Hence my earlier warning about not mimicking others' idiosyncrasies: if a good skier crosses his arm in front he may do it only under these conditions.)

Actually, fast tracks that require a change in arm tempo are pleasant problems to be faced with, and you can learn a lot about your own skiing under these conditions. You may find your timing is off, or that you are working too hard for the speed you generate.

Momentum

The true technician will ski in such a way as to maintain his momentum no matter what comes along, especially on flat terrain; he can do change-ups, go into double-poling, ski around corners, or do anything else without losing his speed. The novice will show a noticeable decrease in speed in doing these things. If you have been watching skiers for a long time it's easy to focus on this aspect. Squint until the skier is just a blob on the landscape—pay no attention to arms, legs, body position, etc. Then ask the blob to go from a diagonal stride to a double-pole, or to ski using the diagonal around a slight corner. Check to see if the blob decelerates.

Deceleration

Deceleration is usually caused by faulty body position. The skier is not forward far enough to be able to ski off the ball of his foot, whether he's going into a double-pole, a change-up, or skiing a corner. One method of keeping forward is to use the arms properly, because

130

if your arms swoop forward at the right time you'll be all set.

Skiing Corners

A wonderful practice for learning to keep your momentum is to ski a large figure-eight on, say, a soccer field. Make the curves flat enough so you must ski, rather than *skate*, the turns. (Occasionally there will be one or two little skate turns in there, but that's O.K.) As you ski around, check your momentum to see if you can ski the left corners as well as the right ones.

There are two basic methods for skiing corners. Let's go around a left turn.

1. You can slide the right ski forward and stem it slightly to the left with each stride, and then bring the left ski alongside.

2. Or, you can pivot the left ski on its shovel when it is in its rearmost position. Just twist it slightly, aiming it more to the left, and scoot it forward with your next leg-drive; in this instance bring the right ski alongside.

The better skiers use a combination of both these methods. However, in general you should initiate your turn with the outside ski. Too many skiers begin with the inside ski.

54. Taking a left turn at full stride.

55. A U.S. Team drill in close formation to perfect individual timing and compare momentum. (Components of their one-step double-pole are discussed below.)

Checking for Momentum

You may not realize why you are losing momentum at certain times, and the best way to find out is to ski with a friend who is more powerful or better than you are. With his permission, jump in right behind him and follow him so closely that occasionally your ski tip clicks his ski tail.

Matching him stride for stride will give you an opportunity to compare lots of facets of technique. Do you appear to kick as hard?—to drive your leg forward as hard, as fast, and as far? Are your arm motions synchronized with his? Do you have any extra upper-body motions that impair your ability to keep up with him? Do you move as quickly, and do you relax as long—

and are you working as hard? Do you keep up with him when going from single-poling to the double-pole, then back to single-poling again?

Try to analyze your technique against his, and then see if you can make adjustments in your efficiency through practice and training.

CPTK 2: The ability to maintain momentum is one of the most valuable aspects of good technique.

Style Differences

There is always a danger in trying to copy someone, or in trying to determine proper technique by analyzing another person's skiing. Body builds vary, strengths vary, even the skis and waxes one uses dictate technique in part. If you pick out one

132

skier you know, one who happens to be a top racer, and compare him with other international stars, chances are you will find several dissimilarities. Don't worry. Assess his ability according to:

CPTK 3: Good technique means having good forward leg-drive; a good kick; using the arms to help get along the track and to help maintain momentum. And maintaining momentum, period.

If any skier has all these attributes, then he has good technique, no matter what quirks he may have in his style (such quirks as bobbing his head slightly or crossing one arm in front of his body, and so on).

The double-pole

First, I'll dispose of the two- or three-step double-poles. These are an old-fashioned technique in which skiers took two or three steps forward preparatory to using both poles simultaneously. Taking this many steps is both unnecessary and slow.

So we're left with the one-step double-pole and the no-step double-pole—both very valuable. There are many similarities between the diagonal technique and these two double-poles. I'll hit on them throughout.

The One-step

An excellent way for beginners to learn to ski is by swinging both arms forward along with one leg. Reaching forward with the arms seems natural to almost everyone, but driving that leg forward is not always so easy. But the same leg-drive I talk about in the diagonal is im-

---

Be Sure He's a Friend, Though

There is probably nothing in the world more infuriating to an x-c skier than having someone skiing behind him who's continually clicking on the heels of his skis. So always arrange to ski behind him first, and don't keep it up too long.

In competition it can be a really dirty trick. In the 1972 Olympic relays in Sapporo I was dismayed to see one skier come into the stadium and ski more than one-half a kilometer right on the heels of the man in front of him. He wasn't just clicking the leader's heels, either: he was riding on the man's skis by a foot or more—so much that it made difficult striding for the front-runner. I'm surprised that the lead skier didn't turn around and whale him one.

portant here in the one-step double-pole. The poles are planted in the snow at the proper angle and the skier leans down on them, pushes, and away he goes. It's kind of a thrill for a person who is on skis for the first time.

The practiced racer does the same thing, but is more vigorous and quick about it. He often swoops out with both arms and gets so far forward over his skis that only putting both poles into the snow keeps him from tipping over. The forward drive is helped along by one leg—either one—that drives ahead too. The practiced racer also kicks with his rear leg as part of this one-step double-pole. The kick to the rear by one leg and the forward movement of the other leg occurs simultaneously and it's almost like a scissors action—just as in the diagonal.

You should learn to lead with either leg. Often you will be in a situation where the track dictates that you must lead with a particular leg, as in approaching a corner. Or sometimes one ski will be a bit more slippery than the other and you might prefer to lead with that one

56. Stages in the one-step double-pole. Not all skiers use a hand-carry so high as his—but of course it's an individual matter (and with a champion skier like this, remember the old saying: "If it works, don't fix it").

134

continually, while kicking with the less slippery ski.

I'm not going to dwell too much on the details of the double-pole but I will make a few more general statements.

Summarizing the one-step double-pole, in a fast track it's possible to ski at optimum speed without putting full power into each stroke, as in the diagonal. In fact, you might help wear yourself out by extra-vigorous poling motions when they wouldn't be really contributing to your progress along the track. This is a situation where it helps if you know the optimum effort and speed that is called for in a particular situation.

If the poles are pushed 'way out behind, and even up into the air slightly, it is probably a mistake.

First, the last part of a real long backward thrust may not give you that much extra power.

More important, however, is that all this takes time. The tempo of the double-pole, as in the diagonal, is

Concentration as Part of Technique

Concentration? Concentrate, it's very important? Well, it's true—even though it doesn't sound very important or impressive, somehow. Yet most top racers come in after a race mentally exhausted. You may question this, but who knows the limits here? When do you go under mentally?

You see, there's a hidden element in an x-c race. Of course there's your conditioning and technique, your frame of mind, the wax, your position in the running order, the track (do you like it—how is the snow, etc.?), and all these matters are important. But you can throw any or all of them right out the window if you can't concentrate all the time, marshaling all the things you've learned for this race, and apply them.

Just forget about some weakness in your technique or forget to vary your techniques and approaches to the big hills in the course. Or forget the track. Or forget where the next food station is. Or, and this may sound silly, forget to breathe. Or to relax. Or don't pay attention to the subtleties in the track, the little dips and twists.

Forget any of these and there will probably be a lot of racers who score better than you, at least in the academics of the race.

CPTK 4: In tough competition you must get an A in Academics, which include Attention.

controlled by the arms. It might be faster, and easier, to pole less vigorously and more often. In this situation you should cut off the power push of the arms right beside your body.

·The No-step

With the new fiberglass skis the no-step double-pole has become increasingly important. These skis are so fast that it makes it a bit awkward to try even the one-step double-pole in most situations.

Almost everything I've said about poling in the one-step double-pole applies to the no-step double-pole. And be sure not to get hung up by using an extra long poling motion.

One of the key things here, as in the one-step, is to get your body weight into the poling motion. You've practiced this on roller skis and you should remember that technique. Pole and use your arms for some power until your hands are about level with your hips, then really lean on the poles with your upper body. You'll be surprised at some of the body positions that show up in a series of photos taken of double-poling, but these awk-ward-looking positions are usually a result of good technique, i.e., getting your weight into the poling motion.

Double-pole Tempo

One good way to test for the best tempo in any double-pole is to stage a few races with other skiers on parallel tracks. Or go behind one skier and use a different tempo from his and see if you can keep up with him. You will find often that the faster tempo, accompanied by a less vigorous push, will stand you in good stead.

When slower tempos are called for there is a little weight-shift you can use which is fun. At the end of the poling stroke, as you are straightening up again, raise your hands high, elbows bent, and rock your weight back slightly onto your heels. This should produce a slight planing effect and will help speed you up, or at least maintain your speed for a longer time. This shifting of the weight should be used as part of a thrust along the track and must follow soon after the poling. And you can't lean back too far or else you won't be in a good position to take another double-pole.

16. Technique for Uphill

Anyone who has raced knows that it's the uphill stretches that make or break you. Yet despite the agonies I've suffered racing up hills I must say that I still enjoy them more than the flats. I suppose that is partly due to the challenge of figuring out the best and fastest way to get up one of the things: there are so many choices and factors to consider that it becomes a fun problem to solve. On the flats it's usually simply a choice of using the diagonal or the double-pole, and just going, going, going; so, for me, the flats have always been tougher from a psychological point of view.

Since half of a racer's time is spent on the uphills every aspiring competitor should spend a great deal of time training for the hills. The training takes two forms: conditioning, and practicing techniques.

It's a bit too simplified to talk about one flat technique and one uphill technique. Excluding the double-pole, we might find some agreement for just one flat technique with slight modifications to fit snow conditions, but no experienced skier will ever admit to having only one uphill technique.

Before Choosing a Method

Before I explain some uphill techniques I will list the important variables to consider when attacking the hills during a race.

1. *Steepness.* Clearly, the slope of the hill is important. In some instances you might be forced to herringbone; in others you might be able to double-pole. There are all sorts of shades between these two extremes.

2. *Length.* If the hill is very short, with a good recovery section after it, you will want to get over the hill in the fastest possible manner, even to the point of thrashing a bit. On the other hand if the hill is long, you will need to pace yourself by using different techniques as well as by varying your speed.

3. *Your state of conditioning.* If you are in good shape and very strong, you will be able to use more of the different techniques than someone who is not so fortunate (i.e., out of shape).

4. *The wax.* Naturally, your wax will be a factor in the techniques you use. You might have no choice and be forced to herringbone every hill. Heaven forbid!

5. *The point in the race.* If you are near the end of a race you may want to take a chance on going under, because the extra time you might save by going as fast as possible is worth the risk. At any other point in the race you must be sure not to go under on a hill, no matter what technique you use.

For flat hills: the diagonal

On flat uphills most good skiers use the diagonal—the same technique that is used on the flats. This has already been covered and after a good season on the roller skis—the uphills, remember?—you will be better equipped for skiing a strong diagonal on the hills.

You should concentrate on getting some glide with each stride. If you can glide, then see if you can get about 6–8 cm more with each stride. It helps if you maintain a slightly lower body position and concentrate on the forward leg-drive with just a little hip thrust at the end of the forward leg-drive. Using the hips consciously this way is O.K., as long as you do it at the correct time. The danger is that some skiers use the hip to initiate a kicking action, forward or backward, and this is a mistake. The correct time for any hip action, again, is at the *end* of the stride. The foot penduls through, the knee drives ahead, the upper leg gets into the act with some thrust, and then the hip polishes it off.

57 (near frames) **& 58** (middle strip) **& 59** (frames far right). For these three vertical sequences I asked the skiers to start off on the right ski and use the diagonal to take this flat (gradual) uphill at moderate speed. No frame taken by my motor-drive camera has been omitted: to look for any differences in technique would be sheer nitpicking.

139

Generally, using the diagonal on flat uphills is a very businesslike procedure. You need a strong forward drive and a strong arm push; there's no time for change-ups, or you'll lose your momentum. You must concentrate on the track and be aware of any little bumps, ripples or kickholes made by preceding skiers. These kickholes offer you a platform to spring off from, and you have to take these as they come, in rhythm. In good competition, under certain snow conditions, the kickholes in the track are pronounced. Woe to the skier who cannot use them! If he doesn't, it's almost like the difference between climbing stairs in the normal way by stepping on the treads, and trying to go up by stepping on the risers.

Some skiers have trouble knowing when to shift over to another technique. The time varies with each skier of course, but if you are having a hard time maintaining the diagonal, or your glide has stopped, or you are getting stiff and tired, it's probably time to change. The key is usually that you are not getting any glide in each stride. Under these conditions most of your forward leg-drive is going to no avail.

The double-pole also can be used under fast conditions on flat uphills, and I won't say any more than this —it's very fast and a good technique to have in your repertory. It's not too tiring when done under the right conditions.

For Steeper Hills

Well, here we are. This is where it's at. The racer who wants to finish at the top of the result list must be strong on these uphills. There's no way around it. A lot of time is spent on these hills and this is where the separations are made.

I'll mention two different techniques for attacking the steeper hills. Both require a high degree of conditioning, both require that you keep your momentum, and both require skis waxed well.

Almost Running

First, imagine having snowshoes on, or short GLM skis, instead of the longer x-c skis. Thus equipped, how would you run up the hill? Actually I answered the question for you, since you would probably use motions very similar to those used in running on foot. The body would be fairly upright; you would land fairly hard on each foot or at least push off fairly hard on each foot. And you'd go just like that.

That's about the best way to describe this running technique, which is used by most of the top racers now. It's nothing beautiful to look at, it isn't too graceful. But it's pow-

60 (near strip) **& 61** (frames far right). Edi Hauser and Alfred Kaelin, at far right— Swiss skiers competing in the 1975 North American Championships—show differences in form as they attack a steep uphill early in the 15-km race.

140

erful, fast, and therefore effective. The ski is belted down into the track, thus setting the wax. The arms are used for some push but also as stabilizers to a degree. This is because the running motion is a bit rough and some skiers sway from side to side slightly in anchoring the ski or setting the wax. Thus the poles keep the skier from tipping too far to the side.

The new fiberglass skis have lent themselves to the utilization of this latest hill-climbing technique that I call running. Or maybe the skis, being so stiff, are causing the changes to take place in hill techniques. It takes a fair amount of force to flatten the ski under you until the wax is in contact with the snow and will therefore hold you from slipping so you can take your next step. This force is best gained by nearly slamming the ski into the snow, as I have mentioned.

In this connection there is another subtle use of the body which I spoke of in Chapter 6 (distance training), and I want to emphasize it again here.

Getting up the hills is the most important part of a race and you must marshal everything you can. If you ask yourself where your largest muscles are and how you can use them to get you up the hill, you can begin to see the importance of trying to use your upper-leg and butt muscles in climbing. If you can use these powerful muscles in any way,

even by a slight straightening at the waist with each step, you will be able to ski uphill more powerfully. I tell my skiers to try to twitch their butts, even to imagine using these muscles in skiing uphills. Trying to use a minimum amount of knee flexion seems to help here too. In other words, take each step or stride with the knee as stiff as is practical.

In a few years there will no doubt be many skiers and coaches using this very subtle technique, but for now I know of only a handful of skiers in the United States who can do it. It has not been practiced or studied to a great degree. It's new, for now, and difficult. But you should try it.

The whole technique is very vigorous. You almost have to get mad at the track. Call it bulling up the hill if you like. There it is.

Hill-bounding Again

The other method for climbing is very similar to the hill-bounding exercise prescribed for dry-land training. In hill-bounding, during each stride or bound you keep your momentum going and it carries you forward onto the lead ski. You set your wax and almost simultaneously bound to the next ski. This takes a great deal of finesse in keeping the ski flat (or placing it where it won't be so likely to slip—such as a section of track that is less steep than surrounding sections), and using a lot of forward ankle-bend, which in turn means having rubber-like knees and ankles that help you to use a lot of flexion, thus cushioning each bound.

You must think about coming off the ball of each foot with each step. Don't think about such things as getting the foot forward, or kicking back, or sneaking through the woods like an Indian, and so on: these ideas are likely to lead to faulty technique. Keep your weight forward, keep your feet so close to being under you that you don't have to struggle to get into the position where you set the wax and spring off with the next step.

One of the worst things you can do is slide or kick your foot forward and weight the heel of the ski, for then you have to overcome gravity in order to be able to get into the position where you can slide the other foot forward so you can weight your heel and then have to overcome gravity in order to—— I'm getting tired. How about you?

The length of the bound depends on the steepness of the hill and your own strength and build. On very steep hills where you can bound, the length is necessarily shortened. But if you are in good shape the bound will actually take you farther than sliding the ski forward would do. This extra distance comes from the spring and the forward-rolling motion of the body. In fact, some of the real brutes bound and have enough power to get a short glide,

even on some of the steep uphills.

Your arms of course are very useful, but you should not depend on them too much for power in this stride. If you do, you will slow up and get tired, both at the same time. Your legs are the tools to use in getting uphill. If you need a lot of help from the arms your wax probably isn't good enough, and you should switch techniques. However, it's fine to use the arms as an aid to balance, for a little extra push at the right time, and to prevent serious backsliding. Remember that the arms are not, and never will be, the primary propelling force for getting up any hill in the most economical manner.

The differences between this good bounding technique and bulling it are a matter of body motion. In hill-bounding there is more knee and ankle flexion, the tempo is a bit slower, each stride is longer since you attempt to bound forward more, and it's smoother-looking. In comparison the running technique might be illustrated this way $\mathcal{UUUU}$ and the hill-bounding technique this way $\frown\frown\frown$.

CPTK 5: In hill-climbing, above all get maximum use from your legs and butt.

The dogtrot

I dubbed this method in an earlier book and it's still a pretty good way for getting up steep hills. The dogtrot is not as fast as running or ski-bounding and therefore it's easier. It's a nice step to use when you're tired. (I don't really want to call it an old person's technique since I have been guilty of using it in races all my life.)

Dogtrotting is almost like ski-bounding, but with two vital differences. First, the length of each stride is shorter, hence my calling it a trot. Second, there is no emphasis on springing off the ball of the foot and straightening the leg underneath while moving forward and upward. Instead, you almost fall forward off the ball of the lead foot and save yourself from tipping over into the snow by getting the other foot ahead. These important differences make for a pretty relaxed technique.

The body position is the same as that in ski-bounding; also the same is the idea of keeping your feet under you and not being forced to overcome gravity by getting the lead foot too far ahead. The poling action in a dogtrot need not be quite so vigorous as in ski-bounding, and it's also easier to use a lot of change-ups.

The herringbone

I must confess that I never have been too swift at the herringbone, but I have seen a lot of skiers who find this method very relaxing. They'll break into a herringbone while others are still ski-bounding.

62. Dartmouth skiers doing dry-land herringbone practice on Oak Hill.

Herringboning

There's no question of the importance of the herringbone and it should be practiced on dry land every chance you get. Running up sandbanks or gravel pits offers possibilities for such practice.

The important point in the herringbone is again to use the legs and not to concentrate too much on the use of the poles and arms. In fact, sometimes you're likely to get all fouled up with your poles getting in the way; some skiers will just lift their poles and bull it up the hill with the herringbone.

Using the legs will require edging the skis enough to keep them from slipping, and this in turn requires a certain amount of flexibility. One of the most common errors is to take steps that are too long, or to lean too far forward. In this extreme forward position you are not pushing with your skis against the hill so much, but rather against the top layer of snow. In this case you're likely to slip since the snow on hills that require the herringbone is always beat-up and softer than in other sections of the track.

So stay as upright as you can, take shorter steps rather than longer ones, and then begin to work on your tempo. The difference in tempos is absolutely startling. Some

63. This sequence shows how a racer can use body-build, conditioning, good technique and concentration to best advantage.

145

Random Controversy

Coaches and students of x-c are continually studying various elements of the sport and during the past years a few of these people have focused on uphill skiing, and come up with an interesting theory. Allowing for certain average or natural strength differences, the argument goes on to invoke certain laws of physics and the like and concludes that a lighter person has certain mechanical advantages over a heavier person in climbing hills and therefore can go up faster. I'm not so sure about this and based on my own observations herewith offer Caldwell's Conjecture: Strength is an overriding factor in climbing hills and a strong, big person with good technique probably has an advantage over a strong, smaller person with good technique.

---

skiers look like human eggbeaters going up hills with the herringbone, and others (me?) look like old cows.

Getting it all together

Assuming you have all these techniques at your disposal, you still have to decide which ones to use. In a race on a long hill I would suggest that you begin conservatively, even using the dogtrot as a warm-up. (It's better to cool it at the bottom of a long hill and come off the top like a jet rather than really to fire in at the bottom and crump out at the top.) Then, after getting the feel of the situation, you might start a more aggressive diagonal, or some running or ski-bounding.

Vary your techniques with the terrain and according to how you feel. Be sure to exhale and inhale deeply all the time—use change-ups and different techniques as a method of relaxation. Keep the top of the hill in your mind, and then ski fast off the top—toward the next downhill.

17. Technique for Downhill

You don't spend much time on downhill sections of a race course (unless you fall down), and therefore good downhill technique has often been undervalued. It's true that with reasonable skiing ability and a bit of practice you can reach a point where you won't be losing much time on anyone. Still, there are several small points worth noting, points that champions will know about.

But First the Variables

There are several factors that help determine your speed down a hill and they are fairly easy to understand.

Because of their design, some skis are just plain faster than others. Often the skis with soft tips go faster, and this is because the tips bend easily to conform better with the small bumps or ripples in the track. Narrower skis are usually faster too.

The wax and the ski bottoms also make a difference.

But if all these factors are equal, have you ever noticed that another fellow can always beat you on a downhill? Even if you swear it's the skis and you switch with him, he beats you again. Well, he sure can ski downhill better than you, and that's all there is to it. He probably steers his skis ever so carefully, making sure the tips do not dig into the edge of the track. He probably rides back on his skis occasionally. If he is standing straight up he weights his heels, if he crouches he presents less wind resistance and again weights the tails of his skis. He probably unweights, or rides up over bumps, better than you. And so on.

The whole idea is to present as little friction as possible between the skis and the snow, and to present a minimum of wind resistance. The planing effect gained by leaning back is a help. Clearly, unweighting over bumps and not hitting the edge of the track with ski tips also helps. These are all fine distinctions, but they separate the skiers.

What to do

The most important thing you can do during a race is to relax on the downhills. If holding a crouch is going to tire you, forget it. Stand up and lean back, weighting the rear of your skis, and relax. Or lean over slightly

64. A rock-steady tuck is just about perfect form for straight downhill sections.

and rest your forearms on your legs, just above the knees. This will cut wind resistance a little and is very restful.

If you have the training—the technique plus the conditioning—then go ahead and try to ride a flat ski. Don't edge any more than necessary; lean back, crouch, and steer your turns holding that crouch, especially at slower speeds where straightening up would present a lot of wind resistance; and ride the bumps by unweighting or flexing the legs (knees). On good straight tracks you can even let your head drop for short sections until your nose is pointing down toward the track: this cuts wind resistance and is more restful than holding your head up to look at what is ahead.

On fast winding downhills, you must possess good Alpine ability and treat your skis just as you would Alpine skis. The newest fiberglass x-c skis, particularly those made by some of the world's leading Alpine ski manufacturers like Fischer, behave very much like Alpine skis and you can carve good fast turns with them. In rough terrain they follow the track very well too, if you either steer them or use the whole ski to make a turn.

It may seem paradoxical that I am stressing Alpine skiing right here instead of the step turn, the skate turn and even the Telemark turn—that most elegant maneuver unique to x-c. These turns are the hallmarks of touring technique, which in today's racing you just don't have time for. Alpine methods have superseded these classics in top-level racing.

No matter what else you do on downhills, breathe deeply. Exhale as much as you can—force everything out, then inhale slowly and deeply. In addition to getting more O_2 into your system this may also help relax you.

Grand Prix Stuff

In Sapporo during the 1972 Olympics many of the coaches checked their wax before every race on a section of track near the start. This section had a steep downhill followed by a long flat and we often went out there and took turns skiing down to see how far out on the flat we could coast: the farther we coasted, the better the wax.

A bunch of coaches from one country would usually go in succession. Each would coast to a stop, hop out of the track, make his mark, and wait to see where his countrymen would stop; invariably they would all stand around for a few minutes after their test and discuss the wax. At this point our staff would boom down. I happened to have a particularly fast pair of skis with good bottoms and soft tips. I always waxed that pair with the fastest wax I knew of for the particular snow condition that day and when I skied down the hill I rocked back on my heels so far and so hard that my toes were practically sticking up through the tops of my boots. I held my downhill tuck until my legs burned. In addition, the track had a little left skate turn at the bottom—and if there is one turn I can do (even in a tuck) this happens to be it—the skate turn to the left.

Weighing more than the average coach, I guess I had about all the advantages possible on a well-packed track, so it's no wonder that I invariably won the International Wax Race. Of course I made the best of it, coasting by the other coaches and shaking my head at them in disbelief, or chortling ever so slightly, or just acting as if this were the way it always was.

18. The Use of Tracks

We have swung around nearly full circle on the business of track-setting and I think that it's time for a slightly different approach.

When I began skiing x-c about 1942 we used to practice in loose snow until enough of us had produced a track with our skis. That track, at best, was pretty wobbly. On race days we looked forward to being able to ski in a better track, one prepared by the same method but with greater care.

It wasn't long before we all sensed a need for pole tracks, and so the organizers of the better races used to make four parallel tracks in the snow. We used the middle two tracks for our skis and the outside two for the poles. This was a big advance! At about the same time we all got the idea of having snowshoers, or skiers sidestepping the course, to pack the snow—and this was great. The only problem was to get the tracks in before the snow froze solid.

As late as 1966 the Norwegians, who were running the FIS champion-ships, employed their army to work on the courses. A few hundred soldiers were on the course every day, shoveling snow, sidestepping the courses, and putting in tracks "by hand." Meanwhile in this country we had already switched to mechanical snowpacking devices and track sleds.

From about 1966 on, our x-c skiers have come more and more to depend on good tracks for racing and for practice. Coaches continually exclaim that you can't practice ski-racing techniques and tempos unless you have a good, fast, hard-packed track, just like the ones you will be racing on. Well, that's mostly correct—but at the same time I think we have gone too far: our skiers are spoiled by too many good tracks and are losing out in several respects.

For one thing, I don't care where the race is, you don't always get a good track. Anyone who has been in competition long enough knows that. So there is an advantage in being something of a mudder. And you don't develop a mudder's ability by staying in good tracks all the time.

For another, many skiers are losing training opportunities because "the tracks aren't set" or "the snowmobile broke down." This is ridiculous, of course. If you are interested in being a good competitor you should get out to train under all conditions.

I was most impressed with Oddvar Braa and Magne Myrmo, two of Nor-way's leading skiers who visited me during their stay in the States in February of 1973. We had just been blessed with an eight-inch, wet-powder snowstorm. It was the Norwegians' last day in Putney and they wanted to practice before leaving at noon for a race that evening, but we didn't have time to set any tracks. However, some boys were working on one of our trails, getting it ready for an upcoming race, and they had gone out into the woods on a snowmobile for a couple of kilometers. The Norwegians put on some yellow klister, the only wax that would work that day, went out and skied back and forth on the snowmobile tracks for about 30 km, then came back in smiling and happy. Excellent workout, they said. I thought of the number of U.S. skiers who wouldn't have skied that day, either because there were no tracks, or because the waxing conditions were tough.

Further, by skiing in tracks that aren't perfect, having little quirks and bumps or soft spots, you will develop better balance and a kind of strength that isn't developed by skiing in those deep, hard, good, straight tracks.

Perhaps I can draw a parallel between weight-lifting and logging. You can lift weights, using all the proper techniques and safeguards, and develop all sorts of strength for lifting those weights. But this conditioning doesn't necessarily train you to stand on a sidehill with a chainsaw trying to limb a tree, or to stand with one foot perched up on a stump trying to throw four-foot chunks of wood over a windfall or a pile of brush you have just cut.

Still more: skiing in some loose snow, or on crust, can help develop good technique and strength. I've skied with people my own weight on light crust and watched them sink through because of the way they kicked—too hard and all at once. I've seen lots of skiers who couldn't set their wax even in the loose snow that sometimes accumulates in a good race track during a snowstorm. And by skiing through a little snow you can get marvelous strength and balance training for your stride.

And finally, skiing without tracks is a nice diversion. Usually it's one pack of fun. That's the way this x-c stuff started, after all.

Index

Index

Index

Index